Project Earth Science: Meteorology

Revised 2nd Edition

Project Earth Science: Meteorology

Revised 2nd Edition

by William R. Veal
and Robert A. Cohen

National Science Teachers Association

Arlington, Virginia

SCL
P9432m
2011

Claire Reinburg, Director
Jennifer Horak, Managing Editor
Andrew Cooke, Senior Editor
Judy Cusick, Senior Editor
Wendy Rubin, Associate Editor
Amy America, Book Acquisitions Coordinator

Printing and Production
Catherine Lorrain, Director

National Science Teachers Association
Francis Q. Eberle, PhD, Executive Director
David Beacom, Publisher

Art and Design
Will Thomas Jr., Director
Tracey Shipley, Cover Design
Front Cover Photo: NOAA Photo Library
Back Cover Photo: NOAA Photo Library
Banner Art © Gerry Boughan / Dreamstime.com

Revised 2nd Edition developed, designed, illustrated,
and produced by
Focus Strategic Communications Inc.
www.focussc.com

Library of Congress Cataloging-in-Publication Data

Veal, William R., 1965-
 Project earth science. Meteorology / by William R. Veal and Robert
Alan Cohen. -- Rev. 2nd ed.
     p. cm.
 Rev. ed. of: Project earth science. Meteorology / by P. Sean Smith and
Brent A. Ford. c1994.
 Includes index.
 ISBN 978-1-936959-03-7 (print) -- ISBN 978-1-936959-98-3 (e-book) 1.
Meteorology--Experiments. 2. Meteorology--Study and teaching (Middle
school) 3. Meteorology--Study and teaching (Secondary) I. Cohen,
Robert Alan, 1963- II. Smith, P. Sean. Project earth science.
Meteorology. III. National Science Teachers Association. IV. Title. V.
Title: Meteorology.
 QC869.3.S65 2011
 551.5078--dc23
                              2011020174

Featuring SciLinks—a new way of connecting text and the Internet. Up-to-the minute online content, classroom ideas, and other materials are just a click away. For more information go to www.scilinks.org/Faq.aspx.

Table of Contents

Readings

Acknowledgments

Several people contributed to the development of this new edition of *Project Earth Science: Meteorology*. The volume began as a collection of Activities and Readings from Project Earth Science (PES), a teacher enhancement project funded by the National Science Foundation. Principal investigators for this project were Iris R. Weiss, president of Horizon Research, Inc.; Diana Montgomery, research associate at Horizon Research, Inc.; Paul B. Hounshell, professor of education, University of North Carolina at Chapel Hill; and Paul Fullagar, professor of geosciences, University of North Carolina at Chapel Hill.

Project Earth Science provided inservice education for and by middle school Earth science teachers in North Carolina. Activities and Readings in this book underwent several revisions as a result of suggestions provided by PES teacher-leaders, principal investigators, and the project staff and consultants. PES leaders made this book possible through their creativity and commitment to the needs of students and classroom teachers. P. Sean Smith and Brent A. Ford were the authors of the first edition and were part of the PES team.

We thank the many people who contributed to this revised second edition.

One author (William Veal) thanks his graduate assistants, Bridget Downing and Loring Ward, who helped in the editing of the Activities and Readings. We also thank Adrianna Edwards and Ron Edwards of Focus Strategic Communications Inc., Oakville, Ontario, Canada, for their considerable efforts in preparing this volume for publication. We would also like to thank the rest of the Focus team for their efforts: Linda Aspen-Baxter, developmental editor; Nancy Szostak, designer and formatter; Sarah Waterfield, illustrator; Linda Szostak, copyeditor and proofreader. The authors appreciate the helpful suggestions made by reviewers Timothy Cooney and Paul D. Fullagar.

Project Earth Science: Meteorology, Revised 2nd Edition, is published by NSTA Press. We thank everyone at NSTA who helped with this volume, and we especially appreciate the efforts of the publisher, David Beacom. NSTA safety columnist, author, and consultant Ken Roy reviewed the entire manuscript for safety compliance. NSTA Press managing editor Jennifer Horak led NSTA's in-house team for the revised second edition.

Introduction

Project Earth Science: Meteorology is one of the four-volume Project Earth Science series. The other three volumes in the series are Astronomy, Geology, and Physical Oceanography. Each volume contains a collection of hands-on Activities developed for middle-level students plus a series of Readings intended primarily for teachers, but that could also be useful to interested students.

Additions and Changes to Revised 2nd Edition

The Activities and Readings sections have been rewritten to improve clarity and scientific currency, and to suggest additional teaching and learning strategies. The Resources section at the back of this book has been updated. At the beginning of each Activity, there is now a Planner to quickly provide information about that Activity. Sections within the Activities are more clearly delineated for students and teachers. There are new subsections for students within Activities entitled Safety Alerts!, What Can I Do? and Fast Fact. Additional new subsections included for teachers are How Do We Know This?, Safety Alerts!, Connections, Differentiated Learning, and Assessment.

Within each Activity, there now is a section for teachers titled Preconceptions. A preconception is an opinion or view that a student might have prior to studying a particular topic. These opinions may not be accurate because the student does not have the correct information, has interpreted his or her interaction with the environment differently, or does not understand that information. Each possible preconception that we list with each Activity actually is a misconception. Asking students about their preconceptions at the outset of a new instructional topic can provide useful information about what students already know and what misinformation needs to be corrected for them to have a good understanding of the topic. The preconceptions we list are, of course, only examples of incorrect ideas that some students might have. Most groups of students are imaginative enough to come up with many other preconceptions!

About Project Earth Science: Meteorology

This book is divided into three sections: Activities, Readings, and Resources. The Activities in this volume are organized under three broad concepts. First, students investigate the atmosphere, the gases and particulates contained in the atmosphere, and the impact of these gases on weather phenomena. Second, students perform Activities investigating the complex systems that lead to the development of wind and forms of precipitation. This section focuses on radiant energy, the hydrologic cycle, and forms of precipitation. In the third section, students study weather phenomena, such as fronts and hail, interpret weather maps and symbols, and chart the course of a hurricane.

A series of overview Readings supports the Activities. By elaborating on concepts presented in the Activities, the Readings are intended to enhance teacher preparation and serve as additional resources for students. The Readings also introduce supplemental topics so that you can link contemporary science to broader subjects and other disciplines.

The Resources provide supplemental materials that you can use in your classroom as part of the Activities or as separate information sources. The Resources section includes government agencies, organizations,

ix

books, and classroom materials, including posters, internet sites, and media. These are annotated and contain the necessary information for gaining access to them.

Creating Scientific Knowledge

Project Earth Science: Meteorology presents a variety of opportunities for you to discuss the creation and evolution of scientific knowledge. For example, students might consider

- how models help develop—yet sometimes restrict—our conceptions of nature
- how scientific knowledge changes over time
- how our choice of measurement scale affects our perceptions of nature and of change

Models and analogies are extremely effective tools in scientific investigation, especially when the subject under study proves to be too large, too small, or too inaccessible for direct study. Although meteorologists often use models, students must be reminded that models are not perfect representations of the object or phenomenon under study. It is essential that students learn to evaluate models for strengths and weaknesses, such as which phenomena are accurately represented and which are not. When using models, it is good to discuss both their advantages *and* their limitations.

As students learn science, it is easy for them to lose sight of the fact that scientific knowledge evolves. As scientists gather more data, test hypotheses, create new models, and develop more sophisticated means of investigation, their understanding of natural phenomena often changes.

With growing information from new technology and expanded understanding, scientific knowledge changes: what seemed impossible to many at the start of the 20th century is accepted in the 21st century.

You should emphasize this changing nature of science—it is what makes scientific inquiry special as a form of knowledge—and encourage students to investigate in more detail how scientific knowledge evolves.

Observing and the Problem of Variables and Predicting

Central to understanding how science evolves is appreciating the limits of our perceptions of change. We observe the world as it is, and we come to understand the world by limiting or controlling the variables that may change. We automatically limit and control the variables in any situation so that we may make sense of the surrounding environment. Meteorology tends to encompass a constellation of variables when interpreting and predicting the weather. When more variables that cannot be controlled are placed in an equation for interpretation, the prediction ability is limited.

To illustrate this point, ask students to consider what they will do next summer from June to August. They may want to make predictions based upon what they did the previous summers, but they may make predictions based upon certain information they currently know. For example, camps, family vacations, and work schedules may be variables that influence what students will be able to do in the summer. Other variables unknown to students at this time may add to the difficulty in making predictions about the summer.

Collecting data, working with variables, interpreting data, and making predictions are all process skills that scientists use on a daily basis. Meteorology involves the collection of many data types from wind speed to amount of precipitation. The combination of all of these data help meteorologists understand the current weather conditions and make forecasts. When working with variables, the goal is often to collect data on one variable while holding all other variables constant. In a dynamic system such as the atmosphere, this is relatively difficult to accomplish. However, if enough data can be collected over multiple areas and time frames, the accuracy of the data interpretation is enhanced.

The data collection and interpretation by meteorologists leads them to be able to predict the weather and infer the effects of weather on humans. Human pollution and impact on the environment have been shown to influence the weather regionally and globally. For example, the clearing of forests and the burning of fossil fuels are contributing to the faster-than-normal greenhouse effect and global warming. Understanding how these environmental effects influence the weather involves the use of many data points, models of how variables interact, and interpretation of the data. Ultimately, meteorologists use models that take into account these data to understand the human impact.

It is important for you to discuss the concepts of variables and predicting and how scientists use these to collect and interpret data. You should encourage students to raise questions about the different variables used in these Activities and how the data collected are used to make predictions and interpretations.

Getting Ready for Classroom Instruction

The Activities in this volume are designed to be hands-on. In developing them, we tried to use materials that are either readily available in the classroom or inexpensive to purchase. Note that many of the Activities also could be done as demonstrations.

Each Activity has two sections: a Student section and a Teachers' Guide. Each Student section begins with Background information

to explain briefly, in nontechnical terms, what the Activity is about. The Objective states what students will learn. Then there is Vocabulary, which includes important meteorological terms that students should know. This is followed by a list of the Materials needed, and an estimate of the amount of Time that the Activity will take. Following this introduction is a step-by-step Procedure outline, and a set of Questions and Conclusions to facilitate student understanding, encourage constructive thinking, and advance the drawing of scientific conclusions.

Each Student section concludes with additional activities for students in What Can I Do? and interesting information about the topic in Fast Fact. Safety Alerts! appear throughout to warn students about dangers in given Activities. Fast Facts, which also appear throughout, are tidbits of information to intrigue students or to provide particulars that will support the Activities. At the end of the Student sections, there are one or more reproducible BLMs (Black Line Masters) for students to fill out.

The Teachers' Guide contains a What Is Happening? section—a more thorough version of the background information given to students. The How Do We Know This? section explains techniques or research methods that meteorologists currently use to generate knowledge related to the Activity. This is followed by a section of possible student Preconceptions, which can be used to initiate classroom discussions. Next comes a summary of What Students Need to Understand, and Time Management discusses the estimated amount of time the Activity will take. The Objective section spells out what students do and learn, while Key Concepts ties the content of the Activity to categories of physical meteorologic content described on pages xii–xiii. Preparation and Procedure describes the setup for the Activity.

In some cases, we suggest other ways to do the Activity in a section titled Alternative Preparation. Some Activities could be done as a demonstration, for instance, although we advocate giving students the opportunity and responsibility for doing the Activities.

To challenge students to extend their study of each topic, a section on Extended Learning is provided. For relating the science in each Activity to other disciplines, such as language arts, history, and social sciences, there is a section on Interdisciplinary Study. Connections is a margin feature that links meteorology to a similar process or concept in astronomy, geology, or physical oceanography. The final portion of each Teachers' Guide includes possibilities for Differentiated Learning, Answers to Student Questions, and suggestions for Assessment.

Although the scientific method often is presented as a "cookbook" recipe—state the problem, gather information, form a hypothesis, perform experiments, record and analyze data, and state conclusions—students should be made aware that the scientific method provides an approach to understanding the world around us, an approach that is rarely so straightforward. For instance, many factors can influence experimental outcomes, measurement precision, and the reliability of results. Such variables must be taken into consideration throughout the course of an investigation.

As students work through the Activities in this volume, make them aware that experimental outcomes can vary and that repetition of trials is important for developing an accurate picture of concepts they are studying. By repeating experimental procedures, students can learn to distinguish between significant and insignificant variations in outcomes. Regardless of how carefully they conduct an experiment, they can never entirely eliminate error. As a matter of course, students should be encouraged to look for ways to eliminate sources of error. However, they also must be made aware of the inherent variation possible in all experimentation.

Finally, controlling variables is important in maintaining the integrity of an experiment. Misleading results and incorrect conclusions often can be traced to experimentation where important variables were not rigorously controlled. You should encourage students to identify experimental controls and consider the relationships between the variables under study and the factors held under control.

Key Concepts

The Activities are organized around three key concepts: the origin and composition of Earth's atmosphere; factors that contribute to weather; and the interaction of air masses.

Key Concept I: The origin and composition of Earth's atmosphere

Earth is surrounded by a thin band of gases called the atmosphere. The atmosphere originated billions of years ago and has evolved to its present state. The atmosphere originated as outgassing, and its present composition supports life. The depth of the atmosphere and the air molecules help determine the air pressure and where weather occurs. Human activity has a profound effect on the atmosphere, which in turn influences the climate.

Key Concept II: Factors that contribute to weather

There are many factors that contribute to the weather. These factors include a myriad of data that are collected from weather stations across the globe. For example, temperature,

wind speed and direction, humidity, and atmospheric pressure are data that meteorologists use to predict and describe the weather. The forecast will change depending upon how each variable changes and interacts with the other. The Sun is a major source of radiant energy that influences the weather. Differences in radiant energy striking Earth's surface result in different surface and air temperatures. Differences in air temperature and Earth's rotation affect air circulation and wind. Water is critical for life on Earth and is found in three different phases: solid, liquid, and gas. The amount of water on Earth is conserved, and the large amounts of heat absorbed and released with changes in phase influence cloud formation and storm circulation.

Key Concept III: Interaction of air masses

Large bodies of air with similar properties of temperature and humidity are called air masses. These air masses have similar properties in most horizontal directions at any given altitude. Weather forecasting involves determining the characteristics of moving air masses. Air masses move across regions as an entity that maintains similar properties. Many times air masses with different properties will interact along a front. The difference in properties of the two air masses leads to weather phenomena such as thunderstorms, tornadoes, hail, sleet, and lightning.

Project Earth Science: Meteorology and the National Science Education Standards

An organizational matrix for the Activities in *Project Earth Science: Meteorology, Revised 2nd Edition*, appears on pages xvi–xvii.

The categories listed along the *x*-axis of the matrix, listed below, correspond to the categories of performing and understanding scientific activity identified as appropriate by the National Research Council's 1996 *National Science Education Standards*.

Subject and Content: Specifies the topic covered by an Activity.

Scientific Inquiry: Identifies the "process of science" (i.e., scientific reasoning, critical thinking, conducting investigations, formulating hypotheses) employed by an Activity.

Unifying Concepts and Processes: Links an Activity's specific subject topic with "the big picture" of scientific ideas (i.e., how data collection techniques inform interpretation and analysis).

Technology: Establishes a connection between the natural and designed worlds.

Personal/Social Perspectives: Locates the specific meteorology topic covered by an Activity within a framework that relates directly to students' lives.

Historical Context: Portrays scientific endeavor as an ongoing human enterprise by linking an Activity's topic with the evolution of its underlying principle.

Project Earth Science: Meteorology hopes to address the need for making science—in this case, meteorology—something students do, not something that is done to students. The Standards Organizational Matrix on pages xvi–xvii provides a tool to assist you in realizing this goal. These standards are currently being updated, and this edition has used the new framework for the updated standards as its guiding document.

xiii

Safety in the Classroom Practices

The teaching and learning of science today through hands-on, process, and inquiry-based activities make classroom and laboratory experiences effective. Addressing potential safety issues is critical to securing this success. Although total safety cannot be guaranteed, teachers can make science safer by adopting, implementing, and enforcing legal standards and best professional practices in the science classroom and laboratory. Safety in the Classroom Practices includes both basic safety practices and resources. It is designed to help teachers and students become aware of relevant standards and practices that will help make activities safer.

1. When working with glassware, wires, projectiles, or other solid hazards, students should use appropriate personal protective equipment, including safety glasses or goggles, gloves, and aprons.

2. Use caution when working with glassware (e.g., beakers, thermometers, etc.) in that they are fragile and can break, potentially cutting skin.

3. Glassware subjected to large temperature changes can suffer thermal shock and break. Handle with care.

4. Use caution when working with glass thermometers and stirring rods. They can break easily and cut/puncture skin.

5. Use caution when working with hot water—it can burn skin.

6. Wipe up any spilled water immediately off the floor—it is a slip and fall hazard.

7. Lighted bulbs can get hot and burn skin. Handle with care.

8. Be careful when working with lamps, metal lamp covers, etc.—skin can be burned. Notify your teacher immediately if you or your lab partner is burned.

9. When working with lamps, keep away from water or other liquids—electrical shock hazard.

10. Never use flames or sparks (e.g., lighting or lit matches) near aerosol cans. Many cans contain flammable fluids and can explode or form a hazardous flame.

11. Use caution when working with scissors, wire, or other sharp objects such as aluminum can edges or tabs or straight pins as they can cut or puncture skin.

12. Never consume food or drink that has been either brought into or used in the laboratory.

13. Teachers should always model appropriate techniques before requiring students to cut, puncture, or dissect, and so on.

14. Markers can have volatile organic compounds (VOCs) that can irritate the eyes, nose, and throat. Use in well-ventilated areas, or use only low-VOC markers.

15. Clear the area of falling or tripping hazards such as desks, other furniture, or equipment before activities requiring open floor space.

For additional safety regulations and best professional practices, go to
NSTA: Safety in the Science Classroom: *www.nsta.org/pdfs SafetyInTheScience Classroom.pdf*

NSTA Safety Portal: *www.nsta.org/portals/ safety.aspx*

Standards Organizational Matrix

Activity	Subject and Content	Scientific Inquiry	Unifying Concepts and Processes
Activity 1 **Weather Watch**	Local weather observation and connection to larger weather patterns	Develop descriptions, predictions, and models using evidence	Systems, order, and organization; evidence, models, and explanation; constancy, change, and measurement
Activity 2 **Making Gas**	Origins of Earth's atmosphere	Conduct an investigation; systematic observation; interpreting data	Scale and quantity: proportional relationship between different quantities; cause and effect
Activity 3 **The Pressure's On**	Existence and effects of air pressure	Develop explanations using evidence; think critically and logically to make the relationships between evidence and explanations	Cause and effect: mechanism; system and system models: defining
Activity 4 **The Percentage of Oxygen in the Atmosphere**	Atmospheric gases	Collecting, analyzing, and interpreting data	Cause and effect: mechanism and prediction (causal relationships)
Activity 5 **It's in the Air**	Particulate matter	Recording observations; creating conclusions based on evidence	Patterns; models
Activity 6 **Why Is It Hotter at the Equator Than at the Poles?**	Sunlight hits Earth's surface at different angles causing different amounts of light energy to be absorbed.	Collecting, analyzing, and interpreting data	Energy and matter: flows, cycles, and conservation
Activity 7 **Which Gets Hotter: Light or Dark Surfaces?**	Energy transfer	Devising a testable hypothesis	Energy and matter: flows, cycles, and conservation
Activity 8 **Up, Up, and Away!**	Density and temperature	Applying and using scientific knowledge	Cause and effect: mechanism and prediction; energy and matter: flows; stability and change (conditions and factors)
Activity 9 **Why Winds Whirl Worldwide**	Air molecules, air pressure, and wind	Modeling; asking questions	Cause and effect: mechanism and prediction; system and system models
Activity 10 **Recycled Water: The Hydrologic Cycle**	Hydrologic cycle	Modeling; asking questions	Patterns; cause and effect: mechanism
Activity 11 **Rainy Day Tales**	Hydrologic cycle, or water cycle	Communicating; applying and using scientific knowledge	Systems and system models
Activity 12 **A Cloud in a Jar**	Cloud formation	Modeling; asking questions	Cause and effect: mechanism; system and system models
Activity 13 **Just Dew It!**	Dew point	Collecting, analyzing, and interpreting data; asking questions	Cause and effect: mechanism; energy and matter: flows
Activity 14 **Let's Make Frost**	Water vapor and frost	Collecting, analyzing, and interpreting data; asking questions	Cause and effect: mechanism; energy and matter: flows
Activity 15 **It's All Relative!**	Relative humidity	Asking questions; collecting, analyzing, and interpreting data	Cause and effect: mechanism
Activity 16 **Moving Masses**	Interactions between air masses	Modeling; applying and using scientific knowledge	Patterns: organization; system models
Activity 17 **Interpreting Weather Maps**	Interpreting weather maps	Modeling; applying and using scientific knowledge	Patterns; system and system models; stability and change
Activity 18 **Water Can Be Supercool!**	Phases of water	Collecting, analyzing, and interpreting data; asking questions	Cause and effect: mechanism
Activity 19 **Riding the Wave of a Hurricane**	Components and path of a hurricane	Asking questions; modeling; collecting data	Patterns and similarity (organization); system models

National Science Teachers Association

Technology	Personal/Social Perspectives	Historical Context	Key Concept
Research and information fluency	Science and technology in society; natural hazards	Science as a human endeavour; nature of science; history of science	II III
Creativity and innovation	Scientific perspective of nature	Evidence supporting a theory	I
Creativity and innovation	Scientific perspective of nature	Changing knowledge of science	II
Communication and collaboration	Populations, resources, and environments	Science as a human endeavor	I
Critical thinking, problem solving, and decision making	Personal health; populations, resources, and environments; risks and benefits; science and technology in society	Evidence supporting conclusions	I II
Creativity and innovation; critical thinking, problem solving, and decision making	Populations, resources, and environments	Evidence supporting a theory	II
Creativity and innovation	Populations, resources, and environments	Evolving theories	II
Creativity and innovation	Scientific perspective of data	Evidence supporting a theory	II
Communication and collaboration	Science and technology in society	Changing knowledge of facts	II
Research tools: simulations; communication and collaboration	Populations, resources, and environments	Changing understanding of water	II
Research tools: simulations	Science and technology in society	Evidence supporting a theory	II
Critical thinking, problem solving, and decision making	Populations, resources, and environments	Evidence of supporting a theory	II
Critical thinking, problem solving, and decision making	Scientific perspective of nature	Changing understanding of science	II
Critical thinking, problem solving, and decision making	Scientific perspective of nature	Changing understanding of science	II
Critical thinking, problem solving, and decision making	Science and technology in society	Evidence supporting conclusions	II
Research and information fluency	Scientific perspective of variables	Changing knowledge of observations	III
Digital citizenship; research and information fluency	Teamwork; natural hazards	Historical methods of science	III
Digital citizenship	Scientific perspective of nature	Changing understanding of science	II
Digital citizenship; research and information fluency	Populations, resources, and environments; natural hazards	Changing understanding of observations	III

Activities at a Glance Matrix

Activity	Pages	Subject and Content	Objective	Materials
Activity 1 Weather Watch	1–13	Local weather observation and connection to larger weather patterns	Identify patterns in the weather by carefully observing local and national weather for several days. Test the utility of the patterns by using those patterns to make short-term weather forecasts.	Each student will need: national weather map every day for two weeks (the teacher will display these); pencil and colored pencils or crayons; two weeks (10 days) of data sheets (5 BLM 1.1 and 10 BLM 1.2) per student. If weekend observations are asked for, then more data sheets and maps will be needed.
Activity 2 Making Gas	15–27	Origins of Earth's atmosphere	Recognize that small changes, when continued over very long time periods, can result in big changes and, based on this, describe how volcanic outgassing can be used to explain the origins of Earth's atmosphere.	Each group of students will need: 12 effervescent antacid tablets, airtight jar plus lid—about 0.5 L (a canning jar works well), cold water, five clear plastic cups, small plastic bag, spoon and plastic knife, paper towels or other absorbent material for spills, safety goggles
Activity 3 The Pressure's On	29–37	Existence and effects of air pressure	Demonstrate how air exerts forces on things.	Each group of students will need: sturdy paper cup, index card, straight pin, water, sink or catch basin
Activity 4 The Percentage of Oxygen in the Atmosphere	39–47	Atmospheric gases	Determine the percentage of oxygen in the atmosphere.	Each group of students will need: two test tubes, one 600 ml beaker, several grams of iron filings, ring stand, two utility clamps, 100 ml graduated cylinder, glass-marking pencil
Activity 5 It's in the Air	49–57	Particulate matter	Investigate the amount and types of particulate matter in the air.	Each student (or group) will need: two white coffee filters; strainer or funnel; magnifying glass; shallow pot, pan, bucket, or cookie sheet with sides (something that will offer a large surface area of water); white dinner plate (disposable paper plates work well); tap water; microscope (if available)

Time	Vocabulary	Key Concepts	Margin Features
• One class period for the introduction to the Activity • 10 minutes each day for a period of two weeks to record required information on data sheets • One class period to analyze and discuss the data at the end of the Activity	Temperature, Precipitation, Atmospheric pressure, Front, Meteorologist	II III	What Can I Do?, Fast Fact, Connections, Resources
• 30 minutes to prepare for the investigation on the first day • 50–60 minutes on the second day to observe and record what happens when the lid is released, complete the investigation in which the variables are changed, and respond to Student Questions	Outgassing, Effervescent	I	Safety Alert!, What Can I Do?, Fast Fact
30 minutes	Air pressure	II	What Can I Do?, Fast Fact, Connections, Resources
• 15–20 minutes to set up the Activity • 5–10 minutes each day for several days • 20–30 minutes for the final data collection, calculations, and data analysis	Chemical reaction, Control	I	What Can I Do?, Fast Fact, Connections
• Day 1: 50–60 minutes to set up the Activity • Day 2: 15 minutes to examine and record data • Day 3: 15 minutes to strain water and spread the filter out to dry • Day 4: 30 minutes to examine the filter, record observations, and answer questions	Particulate matter	I II	What Can I Do?, Fast Fact, Connections, Resources

Activity	Pages	Subject and Content	Objective	Materials
Activity 6 Why Is It Hotter at the Equator Than at the Poles?	59–71	Sunlight hitting Earth's surface at different angles, causing different amounts of light energy to be absorbed	Investigate how the angle of sunlight affects the heating of a surface.	Each group of students will need: three identical Celsius thermometers (glass or metal backed), reflector lamp with clamp and 60-watt incandescent bulb, ring stand with iron ring, utility clamp, one sheet of black construction paper, stapler or tape, several books or blocks to prop thermometers, meter stick, scissors
Activity 7 Which Gets Hotter: Light or Dark Surfaces?	73–81	Energy transfer	Investigate how surface color affects heat flow when exposed to light.	Each group of students will need: heat lamp or reflector lamp with 100-watt incandescent bulb; one black metal can or cup (can be painted or covered with paper); one white metal can or cup (can be painted or covered with paper); two lids/covers with slits, one for each of the cans or cups, insulated if possible; two thermometers; ruler or meter stick
Activity 8 Up, Up, and Away!	83–91	Density and temperature	Investigate the effect of temperature on air density.	Each group of students will need: balloon, empty 475 ml or 600 ml glass bottle with a small opening, bucket of ice water, bucket of hot water, safety goggles for everyone
Activity 9 Why Winds Whirl Worldwide	93–101	Air molecules, air pressure, and wind	Investigate how pressure differences create wind.	Each group of students will need: balloon (long balloons work better than round ones), string or fishing line (5 m), drinking straw (full length), clear tape, two chairs (optional)
Activity 10 Recycled Water: The Hydrologic Cycle	103–113	Hydrologic cycle	Use the properties of water and water vapor to describe the parts of the hydrologic cycle.	Each group of students will need: clear plastic shoe box with lid, small plastic cup, sealed plastic bag filled with sand or soil, water, ice, heat lamp or reflector lamp with 100-watt incandescent bulb
Activity 11 Rainy Day Tales	115–125	Hydrologic cycle, or water cycle	Explore the ways water moves through Earth's hydrologic cycle.	Each student will need: notebook paper, blank white paper (for illustration)
Activity 12 A Cloud in a Jar	127–135	Cloud formation	Investigate the conditions that must be present for clouds to form.	Each group of students will need: 1 L (or larger) clear glass jar with lid (large-mouth jars work best), ice cubes or crushed ice, hot water (very warm water will do), matches, can of aerosol spray (air freshener is suggested), black construction paper, safety goggles, flashlight (optional)

Time	Vocabulary	Key Concepts	Margin Features
50–60 minutes	Season, Angle of sunlight	II	Safety Alert!, What Can I Do?, Fast Fact, Connections, Resources
30–40 minutes		II	Safety Alert!, What Can I Do?, Fast Fact, Connections, Resources
30 minutes	Air density	II	Safety Alert!, What Can I Do?, Fast Fact, Connections
15–20 minutes	Wind	II	What Can I Do?, Fast Fact, Connections, Resources
50–60 minutes	Evaporation, Water vapor, Condensation, Hydrologic cycle	II	Safety Alert!, What Can I Do?, Fast Fact, Resources
Three class periods of 50–60 minutes	Molecule, Transpiration, Hydrologic cycle	II	What Can I Do?, Fast Fact, Connections, Resources
50–60 minutes	Cloud	II	Safety Alert!, What Can I Do?, Fast Fact, Connections, Resources

Activity	Pages	Subject and Content	Objective	Materials
Activity 13 Just Dew It!	137–147	Dew point	Determine the dew point of the air.	Each group of students will need: Celsius thermometer (alcohol), shiny can with top removed (aluminum cans work well), glass stirring rod or wooden stirrer, water at room temperature, ice (crushed or cubes work best)
Activity 14 Let's Make Frost	149–159	Water vapor and frost	Relate the formation of crystals to the phase change from vapor to solid.	Each group of students will need: aluminum or tin can (8 oz.) with the top removed (black cans work the best), 10 g table salt, 4 oz. crushed ice
Activity 15 It's All Relative!	161–173	Relative humidity	Use evaporative cooling to determine relative humidity.	Each group of students will need: 6 cm × 6 cm piece of gauze, clear plastic tape, two indoor/outdoor alcohol thermometers, water, two sturdy paper plates or pieces of cardboard
Activity 16 Moving Masses	175–183	Interactions between air masses	Learn what types of clouds form when a cold front moves into an area of warm air.	Each student will need: scissors, blue crayon, tape or glue, paper or thin cardboard (letter-size)
Activity 17 Interpreting Weather Maps	185–195	Interpreting weather maps	Interpret a basic weather map and understand weather station symbols.	Each student will need: colored pencils, pencil
Activity 18 Water Can Be Supercool!	197–205	Phases of water	Investigate the properties of water below the freezing point.	Each group of students will need: crushed ice, large test tube, 400–600 ml beaker or similar size jar, salt, water, thermometer, stirring rod
Activity 19 Riding the Wave of a Hurricane	207–220	Components and path of a hurricane	Track the position of Hurricane Ike and distinguish between a hurricane watch and a hurricane warning issued by the National Weather Service.	Each student will need: pencil and eraser, ruler

Time	Vocabulary	Key Concepts	Margin Features
50–60 minutes	Humidity, Saturation, Dew point	II	Safety Alert!, What Can I Do?, Fast Fact, Connections, Resources
30 minutes	Frost, Snow, Deposition	II	Safety Alert!, What Can I Do?, Fast Fact, Connections, Resources
50–60 minutes	Relative humidity	II	Safety Alert!, What Can I Do?, Fast Fact, Connections, Resources
30–40 minutes	Air mass, Front	III	Safety Alert!, What Can I Do?, Fast Fact, Connections, Resources
50 minutes	Weather forecast, Station model	III	What Can I Do?, Fast Fact, Connections, Resources
50 minutes	Supercooled, Hail	II	Safety Alert!, What Can I Do?, Fast Fact, Connections, Resources
50 minutes	Hurricane, Storm surge	III	What Can I Do?, Fast Fact, Connections, Resources

Activity 1 Planner

Activity 1 Summary

Students observe and record data about local and national weather for two weeks and then use this data to identify patterns in the weather that can be used to predict future weather at their location.

Activity	Subject and Content	Objective	Materials
Weather Watch	Local weather observation and connection to larger weather patterns	Identify patterns in the weather by carefully observing local and national weather for several days. Test the utility of the patterns by using those patterns to make short-term weather forecasts.	Each student will need: national weather map every day for two weeks (the teacher will display these); pencil and colored pencils or crayons; two weeks (10 days) of data sheets (5 BLM 1.1 and 10 BLM 1.2) per student. If weekend observations are asked for, then more data sheets and maps will be needed.

Time	Vocabulary	Key Concepts	Margin Features
One class period for the introduction to the Activity 10 minutes each day for a period of two weeks to record required information on data sheets One class period to analyze and discuss the data at the end of the Activity	Temperature, Precipitation, Atmospheric pressure, Front, Meteorologist	II: Factors that contribute to weather III: The interaction of air masses	Fast Fact, What Can I Do?, Connections, Resources

Scientific Inquiry	Unifying Concepts and Processes	Technology	Personal/Social Perspectives	Historical Context
Develop descriptions, predictions, and models using evidence	Systems, order, and organization; evidence, models, and explanation; constancy, change, and measurement	Research and information fluency	Science and technology in society; natural hazards	Science as a human endeavour; nature of science; history of science

National Science Teachers Association

Weather Watch

Background

Without looking out the window, do you know what the weather is like right now? Do you remember what the weather was like when you woke up today? Were there any clouds in the sky this morning? If so, what did they look like? If you have trouble answering these questions, you are not alone. Most people do not pay very much attention to the weather until it interferes with something they plan to do. Rain can cause a baseball game to be canceled. Snow can cause the cancellation of school. When these things happen we notice the weather, but much of the time we ignore it.

By not paying more attention to the weather, we not only miss many of the interesting things that go on in the atmosphere; we also might miss the fact that the weather is not random. There are patterns to the weather, and we can use those patterns to make short-term weather forecasts. To identify these patterns, we must first observe the weather. There are two methods of observation that we can use. One method is to look at the weather occurring at a single location and see how it changes from day to day. What kind of pattern might we notice? For example, is it possible to predict short-term weather changes by looking at the clouds? The other method is to see how the weather differs from place to place at a particular time. What kind of pattern might we notice? For example, is it possible to predict weather changes by looking at the weather in nearby locations?

Fast Fact

In 1743, Benjamin Franklin recognized that storms tend to move from southwest to northeast along the eastern United States.

In 1771, Johann H. Lambert (the same person whose projection map is used for most wall maps) proposed making weather observations at different places at the same time throughout the world.

Objectives

Identify patterns in the weather by carefully observing local and national weather for several days.

Test the utility of the patterns by using those patterns to make short-term weather forecasts.

SCILINKS
THE WORLD'S A CLICK AWAY

Topic: weather maps
Go to: *www.scilinks.org*
Code: PSCM 001

Activity 1

In practice, **meteorologists** (scientists who study the atmosphere) use both methods of observation. You will explore how the weather changes from day to day where you live. Using maps that your teacher will provide, you will explore how the weather differs from place to place. As you make your observations outside and from the maps, think about how the **precipitation** where you live may be related to weather changes both at your location and at locations around you.

Procedure

1. Obtain a weather watch data sheet (**BLM 1.1**) and a weather map template of the United States (**BLM 1.2**) for each day you will collect data.

2. Each day, copy, draw, color, or outline the information from the national weather map for that day onto **BLM 1.2**. This may include the following, depending on the national weather map used:

    (a) Areas of precipitation

    (b) Locations of high and low **atmospheric pressure** (indicated by Hs and Ls)

    (c) **Fronts** (the key on **BLM 1.2** will help you identify the type of fronts according to the symbols on the national weather map)

3. Each day, record the daily weather conditions at your location on **BLM 1.1**. This includes the following:

    (a) Clouds — Describe the amount of the sky that is covered by clouds. Use "clear" if there are very few clouds or no clouds. Use "overcast" if the entire sky is covered. Otherwise, use "partly cloudy" or "mostly cloudy." Also, describe what the clouds look like. Use words like *fluffy*, *flat*, *wispy*, *large*, *small*, and so on. If you happen to know the scientific names for the various cloud types, use them (e.g., *stratus*, *cumulus*, *cirrus*). If the clouds change during the day, make a note of how the clouds changed and the general times that the changes occurred.

    (b) Precipitation — Record the type (rain, snow, hail, etc.), amount, and duration (steady or intermittent) of any precipitation that occurred during the day. Also, record the general times it occurred. If there is a rain gauge at your school or if you can obtain the precipitation amount from the weather report on television, radio, or in the next day's newspaper, record that information as well.

    (c) Other — Describe any other weather (e.g., cold, warm, or windy). If you are able to obtain any other measurements, like the high and low **temperatures** for the day or the atmospheric pressure, record those as well.

4. Repeat steps 1 to 3 for two weeks using a new set of data sheets for each day. (If your teacher wants you to make observations over the weekend, be sure to take home extra copies of the data sheets.)

5. At the end of two weeks, arrange your weather watch data sheets (**BLM 1.1**) and weather maps (**BLM 1.2**) chronologically, with the oldest first and the newest last.

Questions and Conclusions

1. Examine your weather watch data sheets (**BLM 1.1**). On which days did you observe precipitation at your location?

2. For each day that you observed precipitation at your location, examine **BLM 1.1** for the day just prior to it. Is there anything common on those days? For example, were the cloud patterns the same prior to each day that precipitation was observed? If you observed atmospheric pressure at your location, did the atmospheric pressure rise (or fall) in the days leading up to when precipitation was observed? If you observed temperature, did the temperature rise (or fall) in the days leading up to when precipitation was observed?

3. For each day that you observed precipitation, look at the national weather map (**BLM 1.2**) for that day. Is there anything common on those days? For example, if you recorded the locations of fronts on your maps, was there a front near you at that time? If so, what kind? If you recorded high and low atmospheric pressure locations, was there a high (or low) area near you at that time?

4. For each day that you observed precipitation, look at **BLM 1.2** for the day just before it. Is there anything common on those days? For example, was there an area of precipitation nearby? If so, was the area of precipitation generally to a particular side, like west of you or east of you? Was there a front nearby or a high (or low) area nearby? If so, were they generally to a particular side, like west of you or east of you?

5. Look at your first national weather map (**BLM 1.2**). Can you find a front or large area of precipitation in the western part of the nation? If not, look through the rest of the weather maps until you find one.

   (a) Now look at the national weather maps (**BLM 1.2**) following the one with the front or precipitation. Has the front or precipitation moved? If so, in which direction did it move? As it moves, does it change shape? If so, how?

   (b) Find other fronts or patterns of precipitation and see if they moved in the same direction. Did they? If not, describe the direction in which they moved. Do they also change shape? If so, how?

6. From your answers to question 5, would you say there is a general direction of weather movement over North America? If so, what is that direction?

Materials

Each student will need:

- national weather map every day for two weeks (the teacher will display these)
- pencil and colored pencils or crayons
- two weeks (10 days) of data sheets (5 BLM 1.1 and 10 BLM 1.2) per student. If weekend observations are asked for, then more data sheets and maps will be needed.

Time

- One class period for the introduction to the Activity
- 10 minutes each day for a period of two weeks to record required information on data sheets
- One class period to analyze and discuss the data at the end of the Activity

Activity 1

7. Look at the last data sheet (**BLM 1.1**) that you completed. Based on your answers to questions 2 to 6, what is your prediction for tomorrow's weather in your location?

8. Based on your answers to questions 2 to 6, which is more useful when making a forecast—the observations made at your location or the weather maps? Why?

9. Are there any areas of the country that you think might be easier to forecast than others? Why?

10. The method you are using to make a forecast is also the method used by meteorologists to make a forecast. However, they only use this method when making a short-term prediction—a couple of hours or a day at most. Why might they find this method lacking when predicting more than a day in advance?

Weather Watch Data Sheet

Date:	Time of Observation:

Cloud Observation:

Precipitation:

Other (weather, temperature, pressure, etc.):

Weather Watch Data Sheet

Date:	Time of Observation:

Cloud Observation:

Precipitation:

Other (weather, temperature, pressure, etc.):

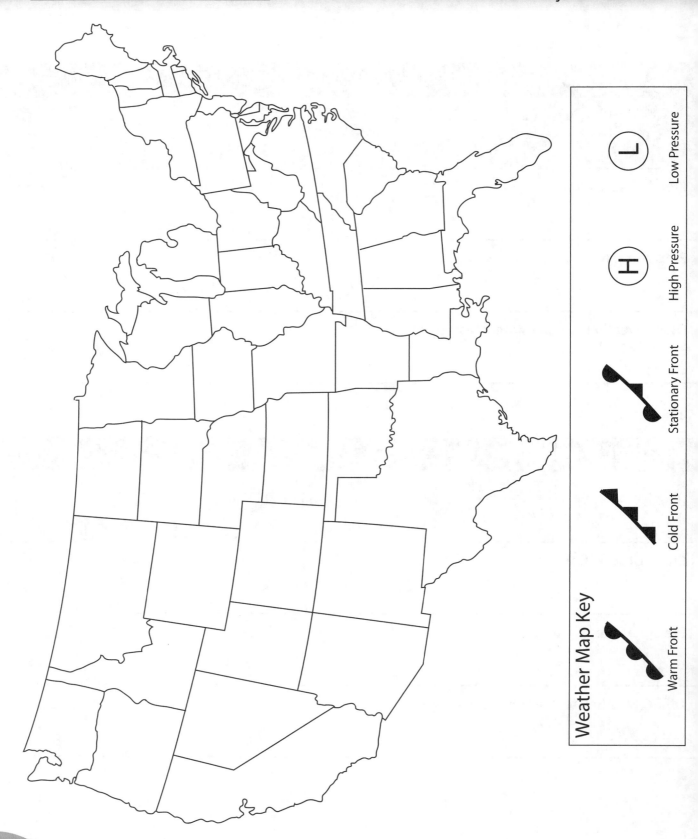

Weather Map Key

Warm Front   Cold Front   Stationary Front   High Pressure   Low Pressure

H   L

Weather Watch

What Is Happening?

People usually pay little attention to the weather, which can be considered the aspects of the atmosphere that impact our activities (as opposed to climate, which is the statistical average weather for a specified interval of time). We rely on the media to tell us what weather to expect in the near future. With modern technology, we can access information about the weather with very little effort. This has not always been the case. Long before there were weather satellites, radar, and television, people predicted the weather by carefully observing atmospheric conditions around them over a long period of time.

This Activity will encourage students to be more aware of local and national weather. They will also learn that by being very observant, they can predict short-term weather changes. The idea that weather is not random allows us to make predictions about the weather, but only if we can first identify how the weather changes. For the most part, precipitation in the middle latitudes (from 30° to 50° north and south of the equator) moves from west to east. At the same time, precipitation systems evolve and change.

How Do We Know This?

How are weather systems tracked on maps?

Before 1960, most meteorologists used their hands to plot data and construct weather maps. For short-term forecasts of six hours, the predictions were fairly accurate, but these mostly depended on the experience of the local meteorologist. Graphs were used to plot the data, and forecasts were extended beyond a day by extrapolating the data to the next day. Modern computers analyze large amounts of weather data and use specific models to interpret the data. Atmospheric models are mathematical equations that use atmospheric temperature, pressure, winds, and moisture at different levels of the atmosphere.

Satellites assist with weather prediction by observing the weather using both visible light and infrared light. The advantage of infrared light is that it can be observed at night, not just during the day. All objects emit infrared light, with warmer objects emitting more. In this way, satellite pictures can distinguish between the colder clouds and the warmer surface of Earth. In addition, infrared light emitted by Earth is absorbed by moisture in the atmosphere, so satellites can produce maps of moisture as well.

Objectives

Identify patterns in the weather by carefully observing local and national weather for several days.

Test the utility of the patterns by using those patterns to make short-term weather forecasts.

Key Concepts

II. Factors that contribute to weather
III. The interaction of air masses

Materials

Each student will need:

- national weather map every day for two weeks (the teacher will display these)
- pencil and colored pencils or crayons
- two weeks (10 days) of data sheets (5 BLM 1.1 and 10 BLM 1.2) per student. If weekend observations are asked for, then more data sheets and maps will be needed.

Time

- One class period for the introduction to the Activity
- 10 minutes each day for a period of two weeks to record required information on data sheets
- One class period to analyze and discuss the data at the end of the Activity

Tracking the movement of systems only works to make predictions about the weather if the systems do not change shape, structure, or intensity significantly.

Except for very short-term forecasts (like over a couple of hours), meteorologists do not typically use the methods discussed in this Activity. Instead, they use computer models that apply ideas of physics to the atmosphere to simulate how the atmosphere will evolve over time. The results of these simulations are available online. Although interested students should be encouraged to make use of these simulations, such use does not develop the scientific inquiry skills of identifying and testing relationships that are being addressed by this Activity.

Preconceptions

Ask students, "How are weather forecasts made? What information do weather forecasters use? How accurate are weather forecasts?" Students may have the following preconceptions:

- A weather forecast is an accurate account of future weather patterns and conditions.
- A weather prediction is based on one observation and temperature reading, not many data points and models.

What Students Need to Understand

- Through careful observation of local weather conditions, short-term weather changes can be predicted.
- Weather conditions in other relatively nearby areas can be used to predict local weather.
- The general pattern of atmospheric movement in the United States is from west to east.
- To identify patterns, start by making observations. After patterns have been identified, the scientific approach is to test those patterns to see if they can be used to make predictions.

Time Management

This Activity will take about 10 minutes each day for a period of two weeks. Ten minutes should be enough time for students to record all the required information on their data sheets. At least one class period should be set aside to introduce the Activity, and another to analyze and discuss the data and answer the questions at the end.

Preparation and Procedure

Before the Activity begins, use a K-W-L chart as a strategy to determine what students already know and any preconceptions they have. Discuss what students know about weather prediction. Record their ideas and background knowledge in the What We **K**now column of the K-W-L chart. Then, ask students what they want to know about weather prediction. Record their questions in the What We **W**ant to Know column of the K-W-L chart. Return to this chart after completing this Activity to record what students learned in the What We Learned column.

Make arrangements in advance to have national weather maps on hand for a period of two weeks. (An archive of U.S. Analysis/Radar Composite maps is available at *www.hpc.ncep.noaa.gov/html/sfc_archive.shtml*; other sources of the current map include *www.intellicast.com/National/Surface/Mixed.aspx* and *www.usatoday.com/weather/fronts/latest-fronts-systems.htm*.) Rather than give each student a copy of the weather map, make a transparency and use it with an overhead projector, or project a national weather map from an online source on a Smart Board or with a multimedia projector. If a weather map is not available, it may be possible to record the televised national weather report and show it to the class.

Each student will need two weeks (10 days) of data sheets (**BLM 1.1** and **BLM 1.2**). (If weekend data gathering is desired, then additional sets of data sheets should be distributed. Note: The Activity will be much more meaningful if weekend data collection is done.)

The most difficult aspect of this Activity is finding a two-week period certain to have noticeable weather changes. The National Weather Service gives extended forecasts that include general weather predictions as much as seven days in advance. By noting these, it is easier to find a time when students will have a chance to see significant weather changes. Late fall through early spring is best in terms of the number of active frontal systems.

When first showing the surface map in class, ask students to point out what characteristics they see and what questions they might have. Some of the items they may notice (or you may encourage them to notice) include the following:

- There are Ls and Hs on the map. Ask what they represent. (They represent regions of lower or higher atmospheric pressure, which is investigated in Activity 3.)
- There are regions of green or blue. (These represent regions where it is raining or snowing.)
- There are lines representing the state and country boundaries.
- There may be lines labeled with numbers around 1,000. (These indicate the atmospheric pressure.)
- There may be fronts (blue, red, and/or purple lines) that indicate temperature differences.
- There may be dashed lines that indicate "troughs" (other boundaries in the atmosphere that are not characterized by temperature differences).

- The time indicated on the map will likely be given in 24-hour time (so that 3:00 p.m. is indicated as 1500). You might ask students whether the time is the same at every location. (It is not.) The time indicated on the map represents the time in Greenwich, England (along the prime meridian) and is usually indicated with a "Z," "UTC," or "GMT" next to the time (e.g., "2100Z").

Alternative Preparation

If your class does not have two weeks to observe the weather each day, substitute the daily observations with a two-week sequence of weather maps, which can be provided all at once from an online weather map archive (e.g., *www.hpc.ncep.noaa.gov/html/sfc_archive.shtml*; use U.S. Analysis/Radar Composite).

Extended Learning

- Arrange a field trip to the closest National Weather Service office (generally at airports or universities), a nearby television station, or a university meteorology department to give students an opportunity to talk with meteorologists. Local meteorologists might be willing to visit your class.
- Have students research how weather maps are constructed. These maps contain hundreds of pieces of information collected from all over the nation. Activity 17 has more information on this topic.
- Meteorologists in the eastern parts of the United States can predict weather by watching weather systems move across the continent. In other areas, meteorologists do not have this advantage. Encourage students to find out where forecasters in the western part of the continent look for approaching weather.

Interdisciplinary Study

Making predictions based on what we know is a part of all areas of study. When we read, we make predictions about what is going to happen in a story or a book based on what we know or what we have learned about the characters, situation, or setting. When we design investigations in science, we make predictions about what we think will happen based on what we know.

There are many books that students could read detailing stories where characters are surprised by the weather, such as *The Perfect Storm* by Sebastian Junger (1997, W.W. Norton & Company, Inc.).

Differentiated Learning

- For ESL students or students who have difficulty recording the data onto **BLM 1.1** and copying the information from the National Weather Map onto

BLM 1.2 each day, have them work with a partner who can model the steps and help them make the correct entries.

- For students who have difficulty finding the patterns and making conclusions in response to the questions on the Student Activity pages, you may wish to work through the questions, one at a time, as a group. First, help students sequence their weather watch data sheets and maps in the correct order from oldest to newest. Then, read each question and identify what it is asking them to do. Guide these students to locate the appropriate weather watch data sheets and weather maps, and identify the patterns.

- For students who complete this Activity early, challenge them to research how people predicted the weather before meteorologists predicted the weather with forecasts. How did people whose livelihoods depended on the weather (e.g., farmers, sailors, fishers, loggers) predict the weather?

Answers to Student Questions

Note: Answers to questions 1 to 3 will vary with students and will also depend on whether they refer to a shower/thunderstorm (a relatively brief period of precipitation) or steady rain/snow. Be sure that students understand the difference between the two. A set of possible answers is provided for each alternative.

1. This response depends on location. If precipitation was observed every day, or on no days, students should skip question 2 and answer the remaining questions with another location in mind.

2. Typically, the cloud cover progresses from clear to more and more cloudy to overcast. However, this sequence might happen too quickly to see that progression (particularly for periodic afternoon thunderstorms common in the summer).

   In terms of cloud types, atmospheric pressure, and temperature, it may be difficult to find a pattern with only two weeks worth of data, as the sequence of events may depend on the type of weather that is observed (e.g., steady rain or snow versus a quick shower or thunderstorm). It may also be difficult to find a pattern if the weather is only observed once a day as the evolution of weather events may occur too quickly to reliably identify a pattern. It also depends greatly on the geographic area. The key here is not to get the "correct" relationship, but rather just to identify some plausible relationships that can be tested. The following are some general guidelines:

   - In terms of cloud types, if steady rain or snow is observed, then the previous day high, wispy clouds (cirrus) and then certainly lower, more overcast (stratus) clouds would be observed. For showers/thundershowers, it may be that clear skies and then some small or large puffy clouds (cumulus and cumulonimbus) would be observed, in that order. Answers, however,

Connections

The process of identifying and testing patterns is a very powerful scientific skill. For example, if you get a rash at seemingly unpredictable times, a doctor might suggest that you record everything you eat each day to see if you have an allergy to a particular food. The doctor can then look at the days when you get a rash and see if there is something common about what you ate on those days. Once some possible food allergy candidates are identified, they are removed from your diet as a test to see if the symptoms go away. In this sense, it is similar to recording the weather each day — seeing if some aspect of the weather is related to when precipitation was observed, and then testing the relationship by making additional forecasts.

can be more complex. In some places (parts of Texas and California, for example), lower-level clouds (stratus) arrive before the high wispy clouds (cirrus), which can block the view of "expected" cloud sequences. With thunderstorms, there are times when the high wispy clouds (cirrus) from the thunderstorm "anvil" move in first, and the clouds get lower and darker just before the thunderstorm arrives.

- In terms of atmospheric pressure, the atmospheric pressure typically drops as the rain/snow approaches and rises afterward. For showers/thundershowers, this drop and rise may occur relatively rapidly.

- In terms of temperature, during the winter and in the eastern half of the United States, the temperature typically warms prior to precipitation and cools afterward, with clear skies associated with colder temperatures. However, in other parts of the country, the reverse may be true.

3. As with question 2, it may be difficult to find a pattern with only two weeks worth of data. Not only does the pattern depend on the type of weather that is observed; the relationship may be complex. Again, the key here is not to get the "correct" relationship but rather to identify some plausible relationships that can be tested. The following are some general guidelines:

- For steady rain/snow, there is probably a warm front close by, whereas for showers/thundershowers, there is probably a cold front close by. Stationary fronts can also give steady rain/snow. Over the western mountains, thunderstorms often form even without the presence of a front.

- If the locations of high and low pressures are computer generated, they may appear in many different places, and it can be hard for students to identify a pattern. Most often, low atmospheric pressure is associated with precipitation, although the center of the low pressure may not be coincident with the location of the precipitation.

4. In many areas, particularly in the eastern half of the United States, we expect fronts and precipitation to move to the east or northeast. Consequently, students should find that fronts and precipitation are to the west or southwest of their location the day before they observe precipitation.

5. In many areas, particularly in the eastern half of the United States, we expect fronts and precipitation to move to the east or northeast. However, they also tend to change, with the precipitation getting more or less intense, and/or more or less organized, and the fronts changing their orientation. This can be difficult to see if they move quickly, especially if only one map is used each day. You might find it useful to also show students maps for intermediate times.

6. Yes, weather generally moves to the east or northeast.

7. If students find that the movement of precipitation is the best indicator of how the weather evolves, students should predict that they will experience the weather that is to the *west* of their location. Otherwise, they can use some other pattern that they identified.

8. In general, it is more useful to look at weather maps, but that depends on geographic area. The key is to get students to realize that the two approaches (time sequence versus weather map) have different characteristics.

9. Some students may think that the east coast is easier to forecast since east coast weather progresses from the west. Others may think that west coast or desert southwest is easier to forecast since it tends not to change as much from day to day.

10. Using only day-to-day observations and weather maps, it is difficult to make a forecast more than a couple of hours (or a day at most) into the future because the intensity, structure, and direction of weather systems change from day to day.

Assessment

- Prior to beginning the Activity, you can use the K-W-L chart to assess students' background knowledge about weather and its causes, weather fronts and how they move, and weather predictions.
- During the Activity, observe students daily as they record their data on **BLM 1.1** and copy the national weather map onto **BLM 1.2**. Monitor the accuracy of the data they record and the care and attention they show as they copy the national weather map onto a map of the United States.
- At the end of the Activity, ask students what they learned about weather, weather fronts and how they move, and weather predictions. Record their responses on the K-W-L chart and take note of what they learned and how their responses have changed.
- At the end of the Activity, you can assess the answers to student questions.

Resources

www.hpc.ncep.noaa.gov/html/sfc_archive.shtml

www.intellicast.com/National/Surface/Mixed.aspx

www.usatoday.com/weather/fronts/latest-fronts-systems.htm

Activity 2 Planner

Activity 2 Summary

Students learn about the origins of Earth's atmosphere and investigate the concept of outgassing when they dissolve effervescent tablets in water.

Activity	Subject and Content	Objective	Materials
Making Gas	Origins of Earth's atmosphere	Recognize that small changes, when continued over very long time periods, can result in big changes and, based on this, describe how volcanic outgassing can be used to explain the origins of Earth's atmosphere.	Each group of students will need: 12 effervescent antacid tablets, airtight jar plus lid—about 0.5 L (a canning jar works well), cold water, five clear plastic cups, small plastic bag, spoon and plastic knife, paper towels or other absorbent material for spills, safety goggles

Time	Vocabulary	Key Concept	Margin Features
30 minutes to prepare for the investigation on the first day 50–60 minutes on the second day to observe and record what happens when the lid is released, complete the investigation in which the variables are changed, and respond to Student Questions	Outgassing, Effervescent	I: The origin and composition of Earth's atmosphere	Safety Alert!, Fast Fact, What Can I Do?

Scientific Inquiry	Unifying Concepts and Processes	Technology	Personal/Social Perspectives	Historical Context
Conduct an investigation; systematic observation; interpreting data	Scale and quantity: proportional relationship between different quantities; cause and effect	Creativity and innovation	Scientific perspective of nature	Evidence supporting a theory

Making Gas

Activity **2**

Background

The original atmosphere of Earth was not like its atmosphere today. The original atmosphere was composed mainly of hydrogen and helium gases. Our current atmosphere contains very little of those gases. Instead, it contains mostly nitrogen and oxygen, with a small amount of water vapor and other gases. Why did the atmosphere change? Where did the hydrogen and helium go, and from where did the nitrogen and oxygen come? One possible source is volcanoes. Volcanoes? What comes out of volcanoes is molten rock. However, that rock contains dissolved gases, much like soda pop contains dissolved gases. In this Activity, you will explore how gases can be dissolved in a liquid or solid, what influences how those gases are released from the liquid or solid into the atmosphere, and how that process can be used to explain why there is as much oxygen in the atmosphere as there is.

Vocabulary

Outgassing: The release of gases to the atmosphere from hot, molten rock during volcanic activity.

Objective

Recognize that small changes, when continued over very long time periods, can result in big changes and, based on this, describe how volcanic **outgassing** can be used to explain the origins of Earth's atmosphere.

THE WORLD'S A CLICK AWAY

Topic: composition of the atmosphere

Go to: *www.scilinks.org*

Code: PSCM 002

Activity 2

Vocabulary
Effervescent: To emit small bubbles of gas.

Materials
Each group of students will need:

- 12 effervescent antacid tablets
- airtight jar plus lid—about 0.5 L (a canning jar works well)
- cold water
- five clear plastic cups
- small plastic bag
- spoon and plastic knife
- paper towels or other absorbent material for spills
- safety goggles

Time
- 30 minutes to prepare for the investigation on the first day
- 50–60 minutes on the second day to observe and record what happens when the lid is released, complete the investigation in which the variables are changed, and respond to Student Questions

Figure 2.1
Place the sealed glass jar on paper towels and put on safety goggles before you open the jar.

SAFETY ALERT
Wear safety goggles when the lid is released on the glass jar.

Procedure

1. Fill the jar three-fourths full with cold water—the colder the better. Drop two **effervescent** tablets in the water and immediately seal the jar. Record what you observe on your making gas data sheet (**BLM 2.1**).

2. Allow the water to warm to room temperature overnight.

3. The next day, observe the contents of the jar closely but do not loosen or ope the jar. Record on **BLM 2.1** what you observe.

4. With your group members, discuss what might happen when you open the ja Record your prediction on **BLM 2.1**.

5. Place the jar on paper towels on a desk or table. Put on your safety goggles and open the jar. (See **Figure 2.1**.) Record on **BLM 2.1** what you observe.

6. What will happen to the results if you change the effervescent tablets and/or the temperature of the water? Arrange the five clear plastic cups in a row and label them, or label a piece of paper in front of them, with the following:

- A: two whole effervescent tablets added to hot water
- B: two effervescent tablets cut in half and added to hot water
- C: two effervescent tablets crushed into powder and added to hot water
- D: two effervescent tablets cut in half and added to cold water
- E: two effervescent tablets crushed into powder and added to cold water

7. Add hot water to the first three cups (A, B, and C) until they are each half full. Add cold water to the last two cups (D and E) until they are each half full.

8. Use the plastic knife to cut four effervescent tablets in half (two will be added to hot water (B) and two will be added to cold water (D) in step 11).

9. Place four effervescent tablets in the plastic bag and crush the tablets with the spoon (half of the crushed tablets will be added to hot water (C) and half will be added to cold water (E) in step 11).

10. Make predictions on **BLM 2.2** about what will happen when you add the whole, halved, and powdered effervescent tablets to the different cups of hot and cold water.

11. Add the whole, halved, and powdered effervescent tablets to the correct cups of hot or cold water and record what you observe. Compare your results and observations with your predictions.

Questions and Conclusions

1. When the main ingredients in the effervescent tablets mix with water, they react and create carbon dioxide gas. What evidence is there that such a reaction was happening when you added the tablets to the water?

2. When you observed the contents of the sealed jar on the second day, was the reaction still going on (that is, was carbon dioxide still being produced)? How do you know?

3. What evidence is there that some carbon dioxide was dissolved in the water prior to you opening the lid?

4. In what way is this similar to soda pop?

5. In what way is this similar to volcanic outgassing (where gases dissolved in magma are released during an eruption)? (See **Figure 2.2**.)

6. Although there is a lot of outgassing during a volcanic eruption, it is still very small compared to the size of the atmosphere. Why might scientists say that it would take a few billion years for this process to produce the atmosphere we have today?

7. When you used different water temperatures for the effervescent tablets, what pattern was created based on your results?

8. When you used whole, halved, and powdered effervescent tablets, what pattern was created based on your results?

Fast Facts

- The main ingredients in an effervescent antacid tablet are similar to the main ingredients in baking powder. The main ingredients in baking powder also react during baking to produce carbon dioxide, with the bubbles of carbon dioxide helping batter to "rise."

- Unlike the reaction you observed in this Activity, only about 10 to 20% of the released gas in volcanic outgassing is carbon dioxide. Most of the volcanic outgassing is water vapor, which condenses eventually into water. The reason our atmosphere is not mostly carbon dioxide is thought to be due to the formation of photosynthetic algae and plants, which absorb carbon dioxide and produce oxygen. This is the main reason why oxygen makes up a significant portion of our current atmosphere.

- One of the largest volcanic eruptions on record was in Indonesia in 1815. A cloud of dust and sulfuric acid was released into the stratosphere causing a "Year without a Summer." In the year after the eruption, volcanic ash in Earth's atmosphere shielded Earth from the Sun's radiation, resulting in less than normal warming at Earth's surface.

Activity 2

What Can I Do?

Research what happens when bread is baked. Why does bread rise? What causes the bubbles in a loaf of bread? How does this relate to the idea that gases evolve out of solids or liquids?

Figure 2.2
Before a volcano erupts, gases are dissolved in its magma. As the magma comes closer to the surface, the pressure on it decreases. The gases can no longer remain dissolved and are released into the atmosphere in a process called outgassing.

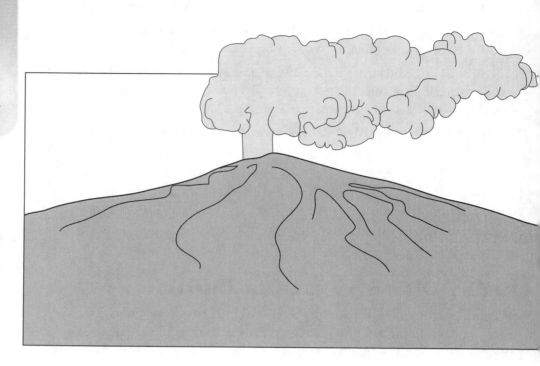

Making Gas Data Sheet

Record what you observe when you add two antacid tablets to cold water in the glass and seal it.

Record what you observe in the jar after the water has warmed to room temperature.

Predict what will happen when you open the jar.

Record what you observe when you open the jar.

Conditions	Prediction	Observations
A: Whole effervescent tablets and hot water		
B: Halved effervescent tablets and hot water		
C: Powdered effervescent tablets and hot water		
D: Halved effervescent tablets and cold water		
E: Powdered effervescent tablets and cold water		

Making Gas

What Is Happening?

Earth's atmosphere today barely resembles the original atmosphere. The keys to understanding the evolution of Earth's atmosphere are found in geologic and biological activities. Current scientific evidence suggests that as Earth formed (from accumulating gas, dust, and larger particles), it grew warmer, finally becoming a sphere with a molten core and an atmosphere consisting primarily of hydrogen and helium (much like the Sun). Over the course of four billion years, the hydrogen and helium, being very light, escaped to outer space. Those gases were replaced by oxygen and nitrogen, for the most part. The source of the oxygen and nitrogen is thought to be volcanic outgassing (contributions from comet impacts might also have been significant).

Gases are dissolved in magma much like carbon dioxide is dissolved in soda pop. This is modeled by the water in the Activity. As the magma comes closer to the surface, the pressure on it decreases. As the pressure decreases, the gases can no longer remain dissolved and are released into the atmosphere

How Do We Know This?

How do we know that the percentage of atmospheric oxygen has changed over time?

The content of carbon dioxide and oxygen in the atmosphere is inferred from fossils (ice core data only goes back 1 million years or so). For example, primitive bacteria are anaerobic, meaning that they do not use oxygen (they currently can be found in low-oxygen environments, like swamps). The fossil record also shows that oxidized iron is not found prior to about 1 to 2 billion years ago and, thus, there must not have been much oxygen in the atmosphere before then.

Scientists use ice core samples to determine the concentration of oxygen and other gases in the atmosphere for more recent records (centuries and millennia, as compared to billions of years). Scientists drill into ice sheets and glaciers to collect cylindrical samples of ice. Over the centuries and millennia, oxygen, carbon dioxide, and other gases have dissolved in rain and ice. An analysis of the dissolved gases in the ice at different levels makes it possible to determine the percentage of atmospheric gases during a specific time period in history. For example, air bubbles trapped in ice cores taken from Greenland and Antarctica reveal that carbon dioxide levels were about 30% lower during cold glacial periods than during warmer periods.

Objective

Recognize that small changes, when continued over very long time periods, can result in big changes and, based on this, describe how volcanic outgassing can be used to explain the origins of Earth's atmosphere.

Key Concept

I. The origin and composition of Earth's atmosphere

Materials

Each group of students will need:

- 12 effervescent antacid tablets
- airtight jar plus lid—about 0.5 L (a canning jar works well)
- cold water
- five clear plastic cups
- small plastic bag
- spoon and plastic knife
- paper towels or other absorbent material for spills
- safety goggles

Time

- 30 minutes to prepare for the investigation on the first day
- 50–60 minutes on the second day to observe and record what happens when the lid is released, complete the investigation in which the variables are changed, and respond to Student Questions

(a process called outgassing). In the same way, the carbon dioxide is released when the lid is removed in the Activity, or the top of a soda pop bottle is removed. The temperature is also a factor. The increased temperature helps the gases release into the atmosphere.

Unlike the Activity in which the released gas was carbon dioxide, the gases released in volcanic eruptions are mostly water vapor (80–90%), with carbon dioxide making up most of the rest. This raises the question of why the current atmosphere is not mostly water vapor and carbon dioxide. The reason why the water vapor is not a large part of the atmosphere is because there is a limit to how much water vapor can exist without condensing—most of the water vapor condenses (forming the lakes and oceans).

The amount of carbon dioxide decreased when algae and plants evolved because they consumed carbon dioxide by photosynthesis. (See **Figure 2.3**.) Carbon dioxide was absorbed and oxygen was produced (plants also use respiration, which follows the reverse process, but in not as great an amount). This, along with the breaking down of water vapor by intense solar radiation into hydrogen and oxygen (a process thought to be responsible for 1–2% of current levels), led to an increase in oxygen levels. (See **Figure 2.4**.)

Figure 2.3
During photosynthesis, plants absorb carbon dioxide and release oxygen into the atmosphere.

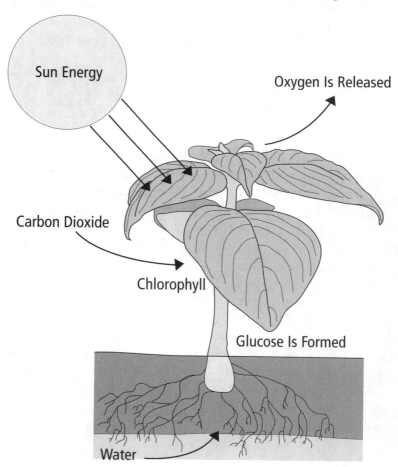

Sun Energy

Oxygen Is Released

Carbon Dioxide

Chlorophyll

Glucose Is Formed

Water

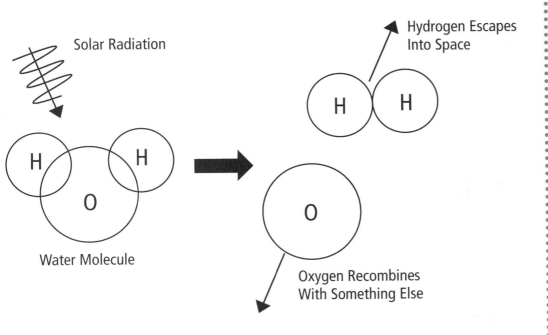

Solar Radiation

Hydrogen Escapes Into Space

H H

H H
O

Water Molecule

O

Oxygen Recombines With Something Else

Figure 2.4
Solar radiation breaks down water into hydrogen and oxygen.

This illustrates how small changes over long periods can produce large changes, as currently carbon dioxide accounts for only a tiny fraction of the atmosphere. You can also extend this discussion to investigate how the amount of carbon dioxide is slowly increasing due to the burning of fossil fuels, which is essentially returning to the atmosphere some of the carbon dioxide that was removed over the past 2 billion years. Even though the carbon dioxide output of a single car or individual may be small, the continual use of fossil fuels over time has led to measurable changes.

One aspect of the atmospheric makeup that is not addressed by this Activity is the issue of why nitrogen makes up most of the current atmosphere. One reason is that nitrogen is not reactive and has relatively low solubility in water; therefore, even though volcanic emissions do not include much nitrogen, it is allowed to build up in the atmosphere over time. Impact by comets may also have contributed nitrogen to the atmosphere.

Preconceptions

Ask students, "Have you ever opened a soda pop can that has been in the refrigerator? Did it make a sound? What sound?" And, "Have you ever opened a warm soda pop can? Was the sound it made different than the cold soda pop can?" Students may have the following preconceptions:

- Gases cannot dissolve in a solid or a liquid.
- Gases come from outer space.
- Air and oxygen are the same thing.
- The early atmosphere came from angels blowing air on Earth.

What Students Need to Understand

- Earth's atmosphere has evolved over time and continues to evolve today.
- Earth's atmosphere was outgassed from its interior.
- Gas dissolved in magma within Earth is released to the atmosphere when the magma rises to the surface due to decreases in pressure.

Time Management

Finding out what students know about the evolution of Earth's atmosphere and where its gases come from, explaining the process of outgassing and the origin of Earth's atmosphere, and setting up the materials for the Activity will take approximately 30 minutes on the first day. It will take a class period on the second day to observe and record what happens when the lid on the glass jar is released, complete the investigation in which the variables are changed, and respond to Student Questions.

Preparation and Procedure

Before setting up the materials for the Activity, assess students' background knowledge by asking them questions such as the following:

- How did Earth's atmosphere form?
- Where did the gases that make up Earth's atmosphere come from?
- Can Earth's atmosphere change or has it always been as it is today?

Then, build your explanation of how Earth's atmosphere evolved from what students know. Use the Background information and diagrams in **Figures 2.1, 2.2, 2.3,** and **2.4** to explain the process of outgassing and how oxygen is added to the atmosphere. Explain to students that the Activity will model what happens during the process of outgassing.

The tablets you use in this Activity need to be effervescent. Many antacid tablets are not effervescent. Antacid tablets tend to consist of a base such as calcium carbonate, which reacts with the acid in your stomach to produce carbon dioxide and water. Although tap water is slightly acidic, it is not acidic enough to produce much of a reaction with something like calcium carbonate. Effervescent tablets, on the other hand, consist of both an acid and a base. The two are in a dry form, so they do not react with each other until they are placed in water. Baking powder is an example of such a combination (and likely could be used instead of effervescent tablets), where the base is sodium bicarbonate (baking soda) and the acid is something like cream of tartar. When the acid and base are combined with water, the reaction takes place, producing carbon dioxide.

The water used for this Activity initially should be cold. This may require refrigerating the water for some time before the tablets are added to it. The tablets should be added to the cold water at least two hours before students release the lid on the jar (preferably the day before). Cold water is preferred because the rate of reaction is proportional to temperature; thus, using cold water will slow down the reaction so that only a little of the carbon dioxide will be produced by the time the lid is placed on the jar. Once the lid is placed on the jar, no carbon dioxide can escape, and so it is no longer a problem if the water warms up at that point. In fact, warmer water is preferable at the end because the solubility of carbon dioxide in water decreases with temperature. Consequently, more carbon dioxide will be released if the water is warm. Make sure the lids are airtight so that carbon dioxide does not leak out.

Opening the jar can produce the same results as opening a warm can of soda pop. *Teacher and students should wear safety goggles.* Ensure that students do not hold the jar near their clothes when they release the lid. Instruct them to set the jar on a flat surface on paper towels to catch or absorb any water that may spill.

SAFETY ALERT
Wear safety goggles when the lid is released from the glass jar.

Alternative Preparation

If jars with lids or effervescent tablets are not available, or if you do not have two consecutive days available for this Activity, it may be sufficient to use soda (or perhaps baking powder and water) to illustrate the effect of carbon dioxide coming out of solution.

You may wish to conduct this Activity as a teacher-led demonstration instead.

Extended Learning

Students could investigate gases coming from specific volcanoes, and find out what effects, if any, these gases have had on people nearby (e.g., health, economic resources).

Interdisciplinary Study

The idea of small changes building up over long periods of time can be applied to savings, as for retirement. Students can investigate how much money they will have if they save $1 every day until they are 65.

Differentiated Learning

- For students who have difficulty understanding how the Activity illustrates the process of outgassing, you may wish to illustrate what happens when gases are released from magma when they reach Earth's surface in diagrams that correspond with the stages of the Activity. For example, adding the tablets to cold water, sealing the glass jar, and waiting for the water to reach room temperature corresponds with gases being dissolved in magma below Earth's surface. When the lid is released, the pressure inside the jar decreases just as the pressure decreases when magma reaches Earth's surface. Each step of the process should contain arrows that reflect pressure and movement of gases.
- For students who finish this Activity early, challenge them with one of the following options:
  - Search online for the main ingredients in the effervescent tablets that produce the carbon dioxide.
  - Compare Earth's atmospheric makeup with those of other planets and think of reasons why the makeup is different.
  - Develop different variables students might use to test the ability of the effervescent tablets to release gas. For example, they could use a different liquid (milk, soda, or mud) or use different kinds of tablets to see if they produce the same results.

Answers to Student Questions

1. There were bubbles coming off the tablets.
2. No, there were no more bubbles coming off the tablets (or no tablets were observed).
3. The foaming of the water due to bubbles forming within the water implied that some carbon dioxide was dissolved in the water prior to opening the lid.
4. In soda pop, as with this Activity, bubbles are formed within the liquid.
5. As the magma "depressurizes," the gases are released.
6. For a relatively small process, like volcanic emissions, to be responsible for a big change, such as the change from hydrogen/helium to oxygen/nitrogen in the atmosphere, it must have taken place over a very long time period.

7. The hot water allowed the reaction to proceed faster than the cold water.

8. The powdered tablets had more surface area, which allowed the reaction to proceed faster. The halved tablets should have reacted slightly faster due to the increased surface area.

Assessment

- Before beginning work on the Activity, assess prior student knowledge by asking students what they know about the formation of Earth's atmosphere.
- During this Activity, observe students as they record their observations on **BLM 2.1**, make predictions and record their observations on **BLM 2.2**, and discuss their responses to the Questions and Conclusions.
- After this Activity, ask students what they learned about outgassing and the origins of Earth's atmosphere. Take note of what they learned and how their responses have changed from the beginning of the Activity.
- After this Activity, you can assess the answers to student questions.

Activity 3 Summary

Students discover that air exerts pressure and that this pressure can hold water in an inverted paper cup.

Activity	Subject and Content	Objective	Materials
The Pressure's On	Existence and effects of air pressure	Demonstrate how air exerts forces on things.	Each group of students will need: sturdy paper cup, index card, straight pin, water, sink or catch basin

Time	Vocabulary	Key Concept	Margin Features
30 minutes	Air pressure	II: Factors that contribute to weather	What Can I Do?, Fast Fact, Connections, Resources

Scientific Inquiry	Unifying Concepts and Processes	Technology	Personal/Social Perspectives	Historical Context
Develop explanations using evidence; think critically and logically to make the relationships between evidence and explanations	Cause and effect: mechanism; system and system models: defining	Creativity and innovation	Scientific perspective of nature	Changing knowledge of science

The Pressure's On

Background

There must be air around us, or otherwise we wouldn't be able to breathe. Is there any other evidence that there must be air around us?

Although we usually cannot feel the air, there are times when the force of the air is obvious. The wind associated with tornadoes and hurricanes can do great damage, for example. Such extremes are not necessary, however, to demonstrate the force of the air. We can observe how air can exert forces on things just by standing outside during a windy day or by holding a hand out a car window while riding along the street.

The force of the air has to do with differences in **air pressure**. In fact, some people are sensitive to small changes in air pressure, which can cause pain in their ears or joints (due to old injuries or arthritis). The phenomenon of ears "popping" when changing altitude is due to a change in air pressure as well (as the body equalizes the air pressure inside the ears with movement of air through the eustachian tubes). Differences in air pressure influence the wind as well as cloud formation, and air pressure observations can help meteorologists predict weather patterns. This Activity will give you an opportunity to see how air pressure can produce some unexpected results.

> ### Vocabulary
> **Air pressure:** A measure of how much the air pushes on things.

Topic: composition of the atmosphere
Go to: www.scilinks.org
Code: PSCM 002

Objective
Demonstrate how air exerts forces on things.

Activity 3

Materials

Each group of students will need:

- sturdy paper cup
- index card
- straight pin
- water
- sink or catch basin

Time

30 minutes

What Can I Do?

- Next time you are in an airplane, check to see if your ears pop during takeoff or landing. If they do, what might be going on?
- Poke a straw through the side of a plastic bag (if the plastic is thick, it may be necessary to make a small hole for the straw with a pen or pencil). Seal the opening of the bag, with tape if necessary. Also, as best you can, seal any openings between the straw and bag with tape. Place a textbook on top of the bag and ask a classmate to lift the textbook using only her or his "breath."

Figure 3.1
How to hold the cup around the rim at the bottom so the cup does not bend during Trial 2

Procedure

Trial 1

1. Working over a sink or a catch basin, fill a cup with water until it is at the point of overflowing or it overflows (after the water has overflowed, it should be at the point of overflowing). Cover the top of the cup with an index card. Make sure that the cup is filled to the point of overflowing when you cover it with the index card, as it is important that no air remains inside the cup (only water). Once the index card is on the cup, make sure it is touching the entire rim.

2. In the box labeled Trial 1 Prediction on **BLM 3.1**, predict what will happen to the water if you turn the cup over, with the index card covering it, and then let go of the index card (but not the cup). Explain why you think the water will do that.

3. While holding the index card on top of the cup, carefully turn the cup over. Hold the cup firmly around the rim at the bottom so that the cup is held securely but not so firmly that the cup deforms (bends). Remove the hand holding the card. What happens? Record your observation in the box labeled Trial 1 Observation on **BLM 3.1**.

Trial 2

1. Repeat the Trial 1 procedure, but this time slowly turn the cup sideways (not completely upside down), holding the edge of the card to keep it in place. (See **Figure 3.1**.) Remove the hand holding the card. Record your observations in the box marked Trial 2 Observation on **BLM 3.1**.

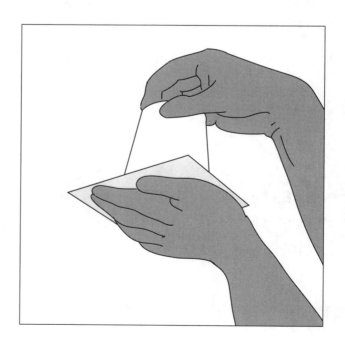

Trial 3

1. Repeat the Trial 1 procedure, but this time after turning the cup upside down, use a straight pin to carefully make a hole in the bottom of the cup. Remove the pin. Record your observations in the box labeled Trial 3 Observation on **BLM 3.1**.

Trial 4

1. Repeat the Trial 1 procedure, but hold a finger securely over the hole in the bottom of the cup when you turn it over (so that no air can get into the cup through the hole). Record your observations in the box marked Trial 4 Observation on **BLM 3.1**.

Questions and Conclusions

1. Why does the water stay in the cup for Trials 1, 2, and 4, but not for Trial 3?

2. Based on your observations, in which direction(s) is air pressure being exerted on the water and index card? In other words, in which trial(s) was air pushing upward on the water/card, in which trial(s) was air pushing sideways on the water/card, and in which trial(s) was air pushing down on the water/card?

3. Try to explain why we usually do not feel the pressure of the atmosphere around us. When do we feel air pressure?

Fast Facts

- The barometer, an instrument that measures atmospheric pressure, was invented in the 1600s.

- Some domed athletic stadiums use air pressure to support the cloth roofs. Even though the inside pressure is only about 0.1% greater than the outside air pressure, that difference is large enough to hold up roofs weighing 35 tons. When fans leave these stadiums, they may experience 30–40 mph winds when leaving the exit doors because of the air pressure difference inside and outside the domed stadium.

Trial 1 Prediction

Trial 1 Observation

Trial 2 Observation

Trial 3 Observation

Trial 4 Observation

The Pressure's On

What Is Happening?

Air pressure is a difficult concept for students to understand. We usually do not *feel* air pressure, not only because we live constantly exposed to it and our body's structure counteracts its effects, but also because the air pressure is exerted on us from all directions, thus leading to no net force on us. Only when there are rapid changes in pressure—when the airplane we are in changes altitude rapidly or when we drive quickly down a mountain road—will there be different pressures exerted on us (e.g., inside and outside our ear). In a similar way, life forms brought up from the bottom of the ocean need to be kept in pressurized containers to keep the pressures equal inside and outside their bodies, or else their bodies literally can explode. In the vacuum of space, astronauts need to wear pressurized suits to keep the pressures equal inside and outside their bodies. The Activity presented here gives students the opportunity to study the effects of air pressure and, specifically, to experience the fact that air pressure is exerted in all directions.

Objective
Demonstrate how air exerts forces on things.

Key Concept
II. Factors that contribute to weather

Materials
Each group of students will need:

- sturdy paper cup
- index card
- straight pin
- water
- sink or catch basin

Time
30 minutes

How Do We Know This?

How do we know that air exerts pressure?

Air is made up of many gas molecules. All of these air molecules piled on top of each other create weight or pressure on everything below them. The force of all of these air molecules on top of an area is related to the air pressure. Scientists use instruments called barometers to measure pressure. This instrument measures bars, which is a unit of pressure that describes the force over a given area. Evangelista Torricelli, an Italian student of Galileo, invented the barometer in 1644. One of the current units of barometric pressure is named after Torricelli and is called a torr (760 torr = 760 mm Hg). The Torricelli barometer uses an inverted tube of heavy liquid mercury. How much mercury is kept in the tube depends on the outside air pressure. The column is marked in inches or millimeters, thus giving a measurement of air pressure. The air pressure changes when a storm approaches. Generally, a storm is associated with lower air pressure, so a drop in air pressure usually signifies an approaching storm, while a rise in air pressure usually signifies fairer weather approaching. Instead of taking a mercury-filled barometer, you can use a sealed container without a liquid in it (an aneroid barometer), and measure how much the diaphragm on the aneroid barometer moves up or down due to the pressure of air on it.

Pressure is measured in terms of weight (or force) per unit area. In the simplest case, the air pressure exerted upon a surface—say, a tabletop—is equal to the weight (per area) of the column of air over that surface extending to the top of the atmosphere. Unlike weight, pressure is exerted on a body from all directions, not simply from overhead (just as water pressure is exerted on a fish from all sides). This is because molecules in air move randomly and thus are equally likely to travel in all directions.

Air pressure at Earth's surface is roughly equal to the pressure on the ground by an average-sized person standing on the balls of one foot. In this Activity, students are asked to place an index card over a paper cup and invert the cup. Amazingly (if no air is initially inside the cup and no air is allowed to get into the cup), the water does not fall out of the cup. The *weight* of the water in the cup (the gravitational force exerted on the water) is much less than the force exerted upward by the *air* below the cup. As a result, the card is held in place. Carefully turning the cup sideways (keeping the seal) has no effect; remember, pressure is exerted from all sides equally. The force exerted by the air is still greater than the weight of the water in the cup. (See **Figure 3.2**.)

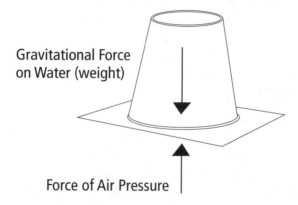

Gravitational Force on Water (weight)

Force of Air Pressure

Figure 3.2
The force exerted by the air is greater than the weight of the water in the cup.

However, when students make a hole in the bottom of the inverted cup, the water falls out of the cup freely because the hole allows the air to act downward on the contents of the cup, neutralizing the upward force exerted by the air from below. Thus, the weight of the water in the cup creates a net downward force. Hence, the water falls out of the cup.

The mechanism is similar when using a straw to drink. We lower the pressure at the top of the straw, leading to a difference in air pressure between inside and outside the straw. The outside pressure, being greater, pushes the liquid up the straw.

Preconceptions

Ask students, "Do you feel any air pressure on you right now?" And, "How do you know that there is oxygen and other gases in the air?" A typical response might be

• Air does not weigh anything because you cannot feel it.

What Students Need to Understand

- Air has weight and exerts pressure on everything with which it comes in contact.
- The force exerted on a surface by air is equal to the weight of a column of air above the surface extending to the top of the atmosphere.
- Air pressure is exerted equally in all directions.

Time Management

This Activity requires less than 15 minutes for students to complete. However, students should be given the opportunity to fully investigate this phenomenon and experiment with variations on the procedure, which might take an additional 20 minutes. This Activity works well as a station with other simple activities dealing with air pressure.

Preparation and Procedure

No special preparations are required for this Activity. You may need to assist students who have trouble getting the Activity to work. It is important that students work carefully and slowly. A break in the seal between the cup and card allows air into the cup, causing the water to fall. (Note: If students have trouble getting a seal between the cup and the index card, have them fill the cup completely with water and moisten the card slightly before placing it on the cup.) You might have students use a new index card for each trial, just so it does not get too soggy.

Give students the time to experiment with this phenomenon, trying a number of variations on the procedure to investigate the effects of air pressure. Encourage students to experiment with making the pinhole in other parts of the cup and comparing results. It is also illuminating to have students experiment with making a pinhole in the *index card* prior to putting it on the cup. They might be surprised to find that the water still stays in the cup. They can experiment with numbers and sizes of holes. Through this extension, they can learn why the water comes out of the cup when no index card is used.

If you have access to a screen mesh, cut out little squares and have students use the squares instead of the index cards. This is a little harder to get to work, but it is amazing when it does.

Alternative Preparation

To show how *differences* in air pressure result in forces, you can use the small plastic syringes (no needle) that are available at pharmacies. Have students pull the plunger almost all the way out and then place their finger on the tip. Keeping the finger on the tip (to prevent air from leaking out), have them close the plunger. They will find it is hard to close the plunger because of the air inside the plunger. This helps to illustrate that air can exert forces even though we cannot see the air.

Follow this up by asking students if the air around also exerts pressure. Ask them to release their finger and push the plunger all the way in. Then have students place their finger on the tip (to prevent air from getting in), pull the plunger out about halfway, and then release it. They will find the plunger is pushed back in. They will be tempted to say the air inside pulls the plunger in, but remind them that there is no air inside the syringe. It must be the air outside the syringe that is pushing the plunger in. We do not notice this force because it is usually balanced by air on the other side. That is why the plunger does not go back in if the finger at the end is removed.

Extended Learning

- Have students calculate the weight of the water in the cup and the air pressure on the index card. (Hint: Students will have to calculate the area of the cup's opening.) Challenge them to calculate the maximum height of a water column that could be held up by the index card. (Regardless of the size of the cup, air pressure will support a column of water 10 m high.)

- Have students investigate the limitations of early water wells and how technological advances have been used to overcome these limitations. As mentioned above, air pressure can support a column of water only about 10 m high. Early water wells depended only on air pressure to force water from below ground level to the surface. As such, the wells could be no more than about 10 m deep.

- If students do not realize it on their own, point out to them that air pressure is applied to them as well as to the card and cup. Challenge them to find out how their bodies can withstand such pressure without being crushed. Ask them what they think would happen to their bodies if they were in a place with no atmosphere (e.g., outer space). All students are probably familiar with the phenomenon of "ear popping" that may occur when there is a difference between air pressure and pressure in the middle ear. This is common when taking off and landing in an airplane.

- Advanced students can investigate why surface weather maps use the estimated sea-level pressure, not the measured surface pressure.

Interdisciplinary Study

- Consider the literary use of the phrase "under pressure." What does this phrase mean? Is this phrase used in a way that is consistent with what we have found in this Activity?

- In this Activity, we found that we only notice the air pressure when there is a different air pressure on two sides of an object. What other situations are there where we notice differences more than the property itself? For example, do we notice heights or differences in heights?

- Process skills, such as making observations, are important for collecting accurate data, both for scientists and other people. For example, many of the same skills that scientists use are also used by cooks, tailors, truck drivers, assembly line workers, teachers, and athletes. Have students select a profession and determine the observations they would make, what data they might collect, the skills they use in collecting the data, and how they use the data. Have students share the results with each other.

Differentiated Learning

- Some students will have difficulty holding the inverted cup and may get frustrated if the water does not stay in. For those students, the Activity with the syringes may be easier, both physically and conceptually.
- For students who finish the Activity early, challenge them to determine the limit for the size of the cup so that the phenomenon of unequal air pressure they investigated in this Activity will still work. They can repeat the steps in the procedure using different cup sizes that contain different amounts of water and have different diameter openings.
- Those students who want to explore the use of air pressure can go online and use the latest versions of Google Earth to overlay maps of weather data over a geographical area. This program can be used with the Warning Decision Support System—Integrated Information supplied by the National Oceanic and Atmospheric Administration (NOAA). Students can see if they can plot or overlay air pressure data with other weather data.

Answers to Student Questions

1. In Trial 3, the hole in the bottom of the inverted cup allowed air to enter the cup and exert a downward force on the top of the water; this, along with the weight of the water itself, was greater than the force exerted by the air upward on the bottom of the index card alone.

2. Air pressure is equal in all directions. It was pushing upward in Trial 1, sideways in Trial 2, upward and downward in Trial 3, and upward in Trial 4.

3. The pressure is the same all around us. We only sense a force when there is a difference in pressure on two sides of an object.

Assessment

- During the Activity, observe students as they record their predictions and observations on **BLM 3.1**. Also, observe them as they experiment with changes to the procedure.
- After the Activity, you can assess the Answers to Student Questions.

Connections

The Smithsonian Institute has a display and explanation of how air pressure integrates with flight and aircraft design. The website demonstrates and explains how airplanes fly and what keeps them aloft. Students can learn how to design a plane that flies faster or higher by changing certain variables. Go to *www.nasm.si.edu/exhibitions/gal109/htf/activities/forcesofflight/web/index.html*.

Resources

www.nasm.si.edu/exhibitions/gal109/htf/activities/forcesofflight/web/index.html

Activity 4 Planner

Activity 4 Summary

Students will create and observe a chemical reaction between iron and water that consumes oxygen to help them calculate how much oxygen is in the atmosphere.

Activity	Subject and Content	Objective	Materials
The Percentage of Oxygen in the Atmosphere	Atmospheric gases	Determine the percentage of oxygen in the atmosphere.	Each group of students will need: two test tubes, 600 ml beaker, several grams of iron filings, ring stand, two utility clamps, 100 ml graduated cylinder, glass-marking pencil

Time	Vocabulary	Key Concept	Margin Features
15–20 minutes to set up the Activity 5–10 minutes each day for several days 20–30 minutes for the final data collection, calculations, and data analysis	Chemical reaction, Control	I: The origin and composition of Earth's atmosphere	Fast Fact, What Can I Do?, Connections

Scientific Inquiry	Unifying Concepts and Processes	Technology	Personal/ Social Perspectives	Historical Context
Collecting, analyzing, and interpreting data	Cause and effect: mechanism and prediction (causal relationships)	Communication and collaboration	Populations, resources, and environments	Science as a human endeavor

The Percentage of Oxygen in the Atmosphere

Background

The atmosphere is made up of several different gases. Two of these gases, nitrogen (N_2) and oxygen (O_2), account for almost all of the atmosphere. The rest consists of very small amounts of the gases argon (Ar) and water vapor (H_2O), and even tinier amounts of other gases including carbon dioxide (CO_2). Each of these gases is important, but we are probably most aware of the importance of oxygen.

How do we know how much of each gas is in the atmosphere? We cannot see the individual atoms that make up the air and, even if we could, we would not be able to count all of the atoms to see which type of atom is most common. There are several ways to determine the percentage of oxygen in the atmosphere. In this Activity, you will take advantage of a **chemical reaction**—between iron and oxygen that forms rust—to find out just how much oxygen there is in the air. More specifically, you use the rusting of iron to *remove* the oxygen from the air. You will then see how much air is left after the oxygen has been removed.

> **Vocabulary**
> **Chemical reaction:**
> A change in which two substances combine to form a new substance with different properties.

Topic: composition of the atmosphere
Go to: *www.scilinks.org*
Code: PSCM 002

> **Objective**
> Determine the percentage of oxygen in the atmosphere.

Activity 4

Materials

Each group of students will need:

- two test tubes
- 600 ml beaker
- several grams of iron filings
- ring stand
- two utility clamps
- 100 ml graduated cylinder
- glass-marking pencil

Time

- 15–20 minutes to set up the Activity
- 5–10 minutes each day for several days
- 20–30 minutes for the final data collection, calculations, and data analysis

Vocabulary

Control: A duplicate setup that is not exposed to the treatment being investigated. The purpose of the control is to compare it with the setup that is exposed to the treatment so that the impact of the treatment can be identified.

Figure 4.1

Make sure the two test tubes—the control test tube and the test tube with iron filings in it—are both just below the surface of the water.

Procedure

1. Predict what percentage of the atmosphere you think is oxygen, and record this on **BLM 4.1** under the column labeled "Predicted Percentage of Oxygen in the Atmosphere."

2. Fill one test tube with water, and then empty the water so that the inside of the test tube is damp.

3. Take a small quantity of iron filings and sprinkle them in the bottom of the damp test tube. Do not worry if some of the filings get stuck to the side of the test tube.

4. Fill the beaker about two-thirds full of water and place it next to the ring stand.

5. Assemble the test tubes, beaker, and ring stand as shown in **Figure 4.1**. The second test tube is a **control** that will allow you to compare what happens when no iron filings are present.

6. Over a piece of paper, carefully turn the test tube containing the iron filings upside down. Do not be concerned if some of the filings fall on the paper. (The purpose of the paper is to catch the filings and avoid making a mess—carefully discard any iron filings on the paper as instructed by your teacher.) With both test tubes inverted (upside down), lower them into the water until the mouths of the test tubes are just below the level of the water, as shown in **Figure 4.1**. After the test tubes are mounted as shown, on the outside of each, mark the initial water level in both test tubes with the glass-marking pencil.

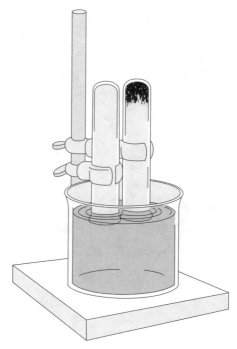

7. Allow the apparatus to sit for 24 hours. After this time, mark the water level in the test tube containing iron filings with the glass-marking pencil. Make sure you do not disturb or move the test tube. Also, observe the appearance

of the iron filings and record this in the chart at the bottom of **BLM 4.1** under the column "Observations." In addition, record the water level in the control test tube.

8. Continue marking the water level and recording observations about the iron filings test tube and the control test tube every 24 hours until the water level in the test tube with filings does not change for two days in a row.

9. To find out how much of the air was removed from the test tube with the iron filings, you first need to measure the volume of air that is left in that test tube and compare it to how much air is in the empty control test tube.

    (a) Remove the empty control test tube from the beaker and clamp. Fill the test tube with water to the level corresponding to how much air was in the test tube. Then pour that amount of water into the empty graduated cylinder. Read the volume and record it in the chart at the top of **BLM 4.1** under the column "Initial Volume of Air in Test Tube." After recording the volume, empty the graduated cylinder.

    (b) Remove the test tube containing iron filings from the beaker and clamp, and rinse the iron filings out of it.

    (c) Fill that test tube with water to the level of the last line that you marked with the glass-marking pencil. Pour this water into the empty graduated cylinder. Record this volume in the chart at the top of **BLM 4.1** under the column "Final Volume of Air in the Test Tube."

10. Subtract the final volume of air in the test tube from the initial volume of air that you recorded in the second column of the chart at the top of **BLM 4.1**. Record this difference in the column labeled "Volume of Oxygen."

11. Calculate the percentage of oxygen in the atmosphere by using the following equation. Record your answer in the chart at the top of **BLM 4.1** under the column "Percentage of Oxygen in the Atmosphere."

$$\text{Percentage of oxygen in air} = \frac{\text{Volume of oxygen}}{\text{Initial volume of air in the test tube}} \times 100\%$$

Questions and Conclusions

1. Explain your prediction for the percentage of oxygen in the atmosphere.

2. How did the percentage of oxygen that you predicted in the atmosphere compare with the percentage of oxygen determined from your experiment?

3. What happened to the iron filings in the test tube over the course of the experiment? What caused this change to happen?

4. What happened to the level of water in the test tube over the course of the Activity? Why do you think this happened? (Hint: Why does the level of water in a straw rise when you suck on the straw?)

5. According to your calculations, which gas makes up most of the atmosphere: oxygen or nitrogen? Are you surprised by this result?

Fast Fact

The percentage of carbon dioxide in the air has increased from about 0.03% to 0.04% in the last 60 years or so. Although this is a large increase for carbon dioxide, carbon dioxide is still a very small portion of the atmosphere.

The atmosphere is made up of four layers: the troposphere, stratosphere, mesosphere, and thermosphere.

What Can I Do?

Where did the oxygen go that was in the air? To find out, weigh the iron filings before and after they rust. Should they weigh the same? You may need to weigh the iron filings *along with* the test tube. Include any iron filings that may have fallen on the piece of paper.

Predicted Percentage of Oxygen in the Atmosphere	Initial Volume of Air in Test Tube (ml)	Final Volume of Air in Test Tube (ml)	Volume of Oxygen	Percentage of Oxygen in the Atmosphere

Day	Observations
1	
2	
3	
4	

The Percentage of Oxygen in the Atmosphere

What Is Happening?

Earth's atmosphere consists of several gases, but nearly all of it is made up of just two gases: nitrogen (N_2) and oxygen (O_2). Students often think that the atmosphere is all oxygen or mostly oxygen simply because they have heard the most about it, and they know they need to breathe oxygen in order to live. However, only about one-fifth of the atmosphere is oxygen. (For more information, see Reading 1: Earth's Atmosphere.)

A simple chemical reaction can be used to demonstrate this fact to students. The oxygen in the atmosphere reacts with many things in the environment in a process known as oxidation. The process actually creates a new substance with different properties. We are most familiar with the oxidation of metals;

How Do We Know This?

How do we know what percentage of the atmosphere is oxygen?

The relative proportion of oxygen to nitrogen in the atmosphere has been determined using various techniques since the 1700s, some of which are similar to this Activity. The results are fairly uniform, not only over time (since the 1700s), but also over various locations on Earth (the main reason for any variation is the variation in water vapor), and also altitudes (up to about 100 km above Earth's surface).

Scientists use high-altitude weather balloons in some cases to gather data at different altitudes. Airplanes and satellites provide other useful data. In terms of the atmosphere and the types of gases, gas samples from the weather balloons and airplanes are analyzed in a laboratory using gas chromatographs. For example, some balloons, each over 30 m in diameter, are dropped through the atmosphere from airplanes. Measurements are taken on temperature and moisture profiles, as well as of carbon dioxide.

Scientists are currently developing new computer systems and measurement instruments and techniques. The new data and results will help meteorologists expand their knowledge of atmospheric dynamics, chemistry, radiation, and their interactions.

Objective

Determine the percentage of oxygen in the atmosphere.

Key Concept

I. The origin and composition of Earth's atmosphere

Materials

Each group of students will need:

- two test tubes
- 600 ml beaker
- several grams of iron filings
- ring stand
- two utility clamps
- 100 ml graduated cylinder
- glass-marking pencil

Time

- 15–20 minutes to set up the Activity
- 5–10 minutes each day for several days
- 20–30 minutes for the final data collection, calculations, and data analysis

it commonly is called corrosion or rust. Living things are oxidized, too. Apples and lettuce leaves that have been cut turn brown when exposed to the air. This is a result of oxidation.

The specific reaction being observed in this Activity is the oxidation of iron. Iron, water, and oxygen combine to produce rust (iron hydroxide). Here, iron filings are used to consume all the oxygen in a sample of air. Students can determine the percentage of oxygen in the atmosphere by measuring the volume of the air before and after it reacts with the iron filings.

This reaction produces a little heat. To properly compare the volumes in the two test tubes, you should wait until the reaction has completely finished and there has been enough time for the temperature to return to room temperature.

Preconceptions

Ask students, "Have you gone outside lately and seen any metal objects that have rust on them? Does anyone know how the rust got there?" Also, "Have you seen a professional athlete breathe oxygen during a competition and wondered why?" Students may have the following preconception:

- The atmosphere contains mostly oxygen that we breathe.

What Students Need to Understand

- Earth's atmosphere is composed of several gases, not just oxygen.
- Oxygen comprises about one-fifth of Earth's atmosphere.
- Oxygen is a chemically active gas.
- Chemical reactions do not destroy or create matter—they just rearrange the matter.

Time Management

Allow 15–20 minutes to set up this Activity. Daily observations (about 5–10 minutes) are required for several days. The final data collection, calculations, and analysis of the results will take 20–30 minutes.

Preparation and Procedure

Be sure to have all the materials required for this Activity either centrally located or already distributed to the groups. Since the Activity takes more than one class period to complete, it may be difficult to have more than one class of students doing the Activity at once. If more than one class does the Activity at once, mark all the beakers clearly so that they do not become disorganized. Alternatively, you may do this Activity as a demonstration for all the classes.

Students do not need to worry if some filings get stuck to the side of the test tube. Actually, this is preferable so that the filings are more spread out.

Make sure students measure the amounts of water accurately for the Activity. Take time to show students how to set up the apparatus correctly. Students will be able to recreate the setup of the apparatus better if you provide a model. Make sure the test tubes are below the level of the water.

Percentages may be a difficult topic for younger students. Some preliminary class work with percentages will make this Activity more meaningful for younger students.

Alternative Preparation

This reaction can also be created using steel wool instead of iron filings. Students will need to soak the steel wool with vinegar (50:50 with water) for a minute or so to remove any oil from it. Remove the steel wool from the vinegar solution and shake it above a sink to remove the vinegar solution.

If glass-marking pencils are not available, a strip of masking tape can be placed along the length of the test tube. This will make it easier to make marks with a permanent marker.

If ring stands are not available, the test tubes could be placed directly on the bottom of the beaker. This just makes it difficult to mark the level to which the water has risen.

The control test tube is desirable but not crucial. Instead, students can initially measure the volume of the air by just measuring the volume of the test tube (filling it with water).

Extended Learning

- Students can explore whether 100% oxygen helps athletes recover more quickly from strenuous exercise.
- Students can research what would happen if the percentage of oxygen in the atmosphere were to change significantly.
- Students can weigh the iron filings before and after the experiment to show that the oxygen combined with the iron (i.e., it did not just disappear).
- Students can investigate if there is any oxygen in the air that they exhale by redoing the experiment using a test tube full of what they exhale. The easiest way to do this is with the steel wool. After it has been prepared, insert the steel wool in the test tube (steel wool works well because it will stay inside the test tube when the tube is inverted). Place the test tube in the water and fill it entirely with water. Invert the test tube and insert a section of rubber tubing into it. Blow into the rubber tubing to force out the water in the test tube. Remove the rubber tubing and leave the test tube inverted in the beaker.

Interdisciplinary Study

• Have students develop a scenario about what would happen to all green plants in their neighborhood if all of the carbon dioxide in the atmosphere were to slowly deplete.

Differentiated Learning

• Have one or more groups add six drops of lemon juice to a third test tube with iron filings. This can be used as an alternative variable. The lemon juice acts as a catalyst and speeds up the reaction. Students should make observations about the time and speed at which the oxygen is consumed compared to the control and regular iron filing test tubes.

• Use labeled diagrams to illustrate what happens in the test tube with the iron filings to enhance ESL students' understanding.

Answers to Student Questions

1. Answers will vary with students but should be based on the fact that the introduction to the Activity specifically states that nitrogen and oxygen make up almost all the atmosphere. Consequently, students' prediction should be less than 100%. How much less depends on whether they think oxygen or nitrogen is more prevalent, and to what extent.

2. This answer will depend on students' calculation of the percentage of oxygen in the atmosphere.

3. The iron filings rusted. The iron reacted with the water and the oxygen in the air.

4. The level of water rose in the test tube. Originally, the air pressure outside the test tube was the same as the air pressure inside. During the reaction, oxygen was removed from the air in the test tube as it formed rust on the iron filings. As this happened, air pressure inside the test tube decreased, and the water was forced up into the test tube by the air pressure outside the test tube. This process is similar to what was investigated in Activity 3.

5. This answer will depend on students' calculation of the percentage of oxygen in the atmosphere. Many students assume that oxygen is more prevalent than nitrogen and are surprised to find that the opposite is true.

Assessment

- During the Activity, informally assess how accurately students are marking the level of the water in the test tube, making their data entries, and recording their observations on **BLM 4.1**.
- At the end of the Activity, you can assess students' data entries, calculations, and observations on **BLM 4.1** and the Answers to Student Questions.

Activity 5 Planner

Activity 5 Summary

Students will use filtration to determine the amount and type of particulates in the air.

Activity	Subject and Content	Objective	Materials
It's in the Air	Particulate matter	Investigate the amount and types of particulate matter in the air.	Each student or group will need: two white coffee filters; strainer or funnel; magnifying glass; shallow pot, pan, bucket, or cookie sheet with sides (something that will offer a large surface area of water); white dinner plate (disposable paper plates work well); tap water; microscope (if available)

Time	Vocabulary	Key Concepts	Margin Features
• Day 1: 50–60 minutes to set up the Activity • Day 2: 15 minutes to examine and record data • Day 3: 15 minutes to strain water and spread the filter out to dry • Day 4: 30 minutes to examine the filter, record observations, and answer questions	Particulate matter	I: The origin and composition of Earth's atmosphere II: Factors that contribute to weather	What Can I Do?, Fast Fact, Connections, Resources

Scientific Inquiry	Unifying Concepts and Processes	Technology	Personal/Social Perspectives	Historical Context
Recording observations; creating conclusions based on evidence	Patterns; models	Critical thinking, problem solving, and decision making	Personal health; populations, resources, and environments; risks and benefits; science and technology in society	Evidence supporting conclusions

48

It's in the Air

Background

The atmosphere is mostly made up of gases such as nitrogen (N_2) and oxygen (O_2). These gases are made up of extremely small molecules, much too small for us to see with our eyes. Despite their small size, they can act together to exert large forces on objects, as seen in Activity 3.

Such gas molecules, however, are not the only thing present in the atmosphere. Have you ever flown in an airplane and seen a layer of yellow-brown on the horizon? Such smog or haze is not caused by gases like nitrogen (N_2) and oxygen (O_2). Instead, they are due to airborne particles. Most of these particles, though huge compared to the gas molecules, are still too small to see with our eyes. Yet, in large concentrations, certain types can be a health hazard and produce smog. On the other hand, many of these particles play an important natural role in the formation of clouds, snow, and rain.

At first, you may think the particles are the result of pollution. While much of the **particulate matter** in the atmosphere is the result of humans polluting the air, there are also natural sources of particles. Wind-blown dust and pollen are examples, but there are many other natural sources. In this Activity, you will use a technique for examining the presence of such particles in the air.

> **Vocabulary**
> **Particulate matter:** A mixture of small particles and liquid droplets that are suspended in the air.

Topic: composition of the atmosphere
Go to: www.scilinks.org
Code: PSCM 002

Objective
Investigate the amount and types of particulate matter in the air.

Activity 5

Materials

Each group will need:

- two white coffee filters
- strainer or funnel
- magnifying glass
- shallow pot, pan, bucket, or cookie sheet with sides (something that will offer a large surface area of water)
- white dinner plate (disposable paper plates work well)
- tap water
- microscope (if available)

Time

- Day 1: 50–60 minutes to set up the Activity, examine the filter paper, make observations, and collect data
- Day 2: 15 minutes to examine and record what is observed on the dry control filter paper
- Day 3: 15 minutes to strain the water that has been exposed to the air through the experimental filter and spread it out to dry
- Day 4: 30 minutes to examine and record what is observed on the dry experimental filter and answer questions

Procedure

1. Use a magnifying glass (or microscope, if you have one) to observe one of the filter papers carefully. Draw and record what you observe in the space labeled "Unused Filter" on **BLM 5.1**.

2. Label one of the coffee filters to identify your group (perhaps with everyone's first initial), and also with a "C" to designate this as the control filter paper. Place this filter paper in the strainer or funnel, or if you have an automatic drip coffee maker, use its filter paper holder instead of the strainer or funnel.

3. Fill a pot or pan half full with water, and then immediately strain this water through the filter paper. This trial serves as your control experiment to determine what, if any, particles are present in your water. With this information, you can more accurately determine how many particles come from the air when you get the results of the second part of this experiment.

4. Carefully remove the filter paper and spread it out on the plate.

5. Allow the plate to sit undisturbed until the filter paper is completely dry. Do not place the plate near an air vent or an open window where a breeze could blow stray particles onto your filter paper or blow any particles on your filter paper away. (Either would ruin your control.)

6. For the second part of this experiment, fill the pot or pan again with the same amount of water as you used for the control experiment above.

7. Do not strain this water yet. Set this water outside in a place where it will not be disturbed. Leave the pot in this place for at least one day, or for two days if possible. (If you cannot go outside, place your pan near an air vent or an open window.)

8. When your first filter paper—your control filter—is completely dry, use a magnifying glass (or microscope, if you have one) to examine the filter paper carefully. (Without the magnifying glass, you may miss many of the particles.)

9. Draw and record what you observe in the box labeled "Control Filter" on **BLM 5.1**.

10. When you are ready to strain the pot of water that has been exposed to air for a day or two, label the second coffee filter with your group members' initials, and also with an "E" to designate this as the experimental filter. Place this filter paper in the strainer or funnel.

11. Take the filter paper and strainer outside to the pot, and carefully pour the water through the filter paper.

12. After the water filters through the strainer, take the filter paper and pot inside. Rinse the sides of the pot with a small amount of water and pour this through the filter paper as well.

13. Carefully remove the filter paper and spread it out on the plate to dry. As with the first filter paper, allow the plate to sit undisturbed until the filter paper is completely dry. Be sure that there is no breeze near the filter paper while it dries because a breeze could blow stray particles onto your filter paper or blow any particles on your filter paper away.

14. When the experimental filter is completely dry, use your magnifying glass (or microscope) to examine the filter paper carefully. (See **Figure 5.1**.)

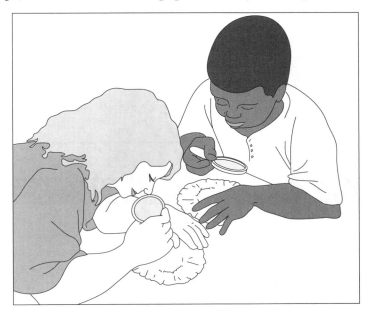

What Can I Do?

Determine what you can do about pollution in your area or city. Search for your local Pollution Prevention (p2) site at *www.epa.gov/p2/pubs/local.htm*.

Figure 5.1
Use a magnifying glass to examine the particulate matter on the experimental filter.

15. Draw and record what you observe in the box labeled "Experimental Filter" on **BLM 5.1**. Compare what you see on this second filter paper with what you saw on the control filter.

Questions and Conclusions

1. When you examined the second coffee filter (labeled "E"), were there more (or fewer) particles than you expected? How would you describe the colors and sizes of the particles? Can you identify any of the particles on the second coffee filter?

2. Where do you think the different kinds of particles came from?

3. What are some harmful effects that these particles can have?

4. What time of year did you do this Activity? When might you have found more particles and when might you have found fewer particles? Why?

5. What weather conditions would increase the amount of particles in the atmosphere? What weather conditions could decrease the amount of particles in the atmosphere?

6. Where might there be areas of your city or town where the particles could be worse or more concentrated than where you did the Activity? Why do you think this?

Fast Fact

The first known air pollution law was enacted in England in 1306. At that time, people became aware of the ill effects on the environment of burning high-sulfur coal.

Draw and record what you observe for each filter. Compare your results at your location to the results from other groups and their locations.

Unused Filter

Control Filter

Experimental Filter

Teachers' Guide to Activity 5

It's in the Air

What Is Happening?

In addition to the gases in the atmosphere, there is also a significant amount of particulate matter. Among other sources, these particles come from volcanoes, wind erosion of soil, forest fires and burning in general, and from both industry and agriculture. These particles have both beneficial and harmful effects. They provide the surfaces on which cloud droplets, raindrops, hailstones, and snowflakes form. Activity 12 and Activity 18 discuss this aspect of the atmosphere in more detail.

The length of time a particle remains suspended in the atmosphere depends on the balance between two processes. Gravity pulls the particles toward Earth's surface, but the particles can move in the opposite direction with atmospheric turbulence. Under normal conditions, only particles with diameters less than 10 micrometers (μm) remain in the atmosphere long enough to be considered atmospheric particulates.

The weather influences the amount of particles in the air. Since cloud droplets form on particles, any type of precipitation will carry particulate matter out of the air to the ground, which cleans the air in a sense. Very windy conditions will do just the opposite and carry large amounts of particulate matter into the air. This can cause respiratory and visibility problems.

How Do We Know This?

How do we know the atmosphere contains particulate matter?

Scientists use satellite data from NASA's Multi-angle Imaging Spectro-Radiometer (MISR) that orbits aboard NASA's *Terra* satellite. This satellite uses nine viewing angles to measure the brightness, color, and contrast of reflected light. One result from the data collected is the regional and global impact of different types of particulate matter and clouds on climate. They also use the Moderate Resolution Imaging Spectroradiometer (MODIS) instrument that orbits aboard both NASA's *Aqua* and *Terra* satellites. Researchers also use output from a chemical transport model called GEOS-Chem to create images. The outputs from this instrument help scientists understand issues related to atmospheric composition such as particulate matter.

Objective

Investigate the amount and types of particulate matter in the air.

Key Concepts

I. The origin and composition of Earth's atmosphere
II. Factors that contribute to weather

Materials

Each group will need:

- two white coffee filters
- strainer or funnel
- magnifying glass
- shallow pot, pan, bucket, or cookie sheet with sides (something that will offer a large surface area of water)
- white dinner plate (disposable paper plates work well)
- tap water
- microscope (if available)

Time

- Day 1: 50–60 minutes to set up the Activity, examine the filter paper, make observations, and collect data
- Day 2: 15 minutes to examine and record what is observed on the dry control filter paper
- Day 3: 15 minutes to strain the water that has been exposed to the air through the experimental filter and spread it out to dry
- Day 4: 30 minutes to examine and record what is observed on the dry experimental filter and answer questions

It may be difficult to convince students of the presence of particulate matter in the atmosphere because they cannot readily see it. In this Activity, students will use simple filtration to investigate the amount and kinds of particulate matter in the atmosphere.

Preconceptions

Ask students, "Can you see the air?" "Do you know if there is anything in the air?" Students may have the following preconceptions:

- Wind is not made up of anything; it just moves air.
- Solid particles cannot be suspended in the air.

What Students Need to Understand

- Although their small size prevents us from seeing them, significant numbers of particles are present in the atmosphere.

Time Management

This Activity will take class time over four days (three days if you decide to leave the sample of tap water exposed to the air for one day instead of two). On the first day, it will take students 50–60 minutes to set up the Activity (examine the unused control filter and record what is observed, strain tap water through the control filter, spread the control filter out to dry, and set the tap water outside in a location where it will not be disturbed). On the second day, provide students with 15 minutes to examine and record what is observed on the dry control filter. On the third day, provide students with 15 minutes to strain water that has been exposed to the air through the experimental filter and spread it out to dry. On the final day, students will need approximately 30 minutes to examine and record what is observed on the dry experimental filter and answer questions.

Preparation and Procedure

Little preparation is required for this Activity. Some tap water has a significant quantity of particulates in it. If this is encountered, it would be best to use distilled or prefiltered water. Depending on the region of the continent, there may be times of the year when the odds of detecting large quantities of particles are greater than usual. For example, in the southeast, spring is a good time to do the Activity because of the pollen in the air.

If a microscope is available, it is useful in examining particles on the coffee filters. As an alternative to using coffee filters, the water may just be observed in the pot. Some particles may be even more visible in this way.

Alternative Preparation

Students can do this Activity at home as long as the instructions are made clear. The materials for the Activity (with the exception of the magnifying glass or microscope) are likely to be found at home. If students do this Activity at home, the results from different locations (near a factory, near a highway, in farmland, etc.) can be compared. Students should bring their control and experimental coffee filters to school for examination and comparison. Wrapping each coffee filter separately with plastic food wrap and placing the coffee filter in a plastic bag are two ways to make the filters easily transportable.

Extended Learning

- Repeat the experiment, but in a more quantitative fashion. Draw a grid on the filter paper, then count the particles in some of the squares and calculate the average. Then, by finding the area of the filter paper, students can calculate the number of particles in the water sample. Particle counts such as these are included regularly in weather reports. Students can monitor these particle counts in conjunction with this Activity.

- Students can investigate why some areas have more particulate matter in the air than others, and discuss ways to reduce amounts of particulate matter. Encourage students to consider the ways in which they contribute particulate matter to the atmosphere.

- Scientists are developing more modern and precise ground-based and satellite-based instruments. Students should search for new instruments that can detect different types of particulate matter. For example, the MODIS will deliver news about the latest information on images generated from the satellite. Go to *http://modis.gsfc.nasa.gov*.

- Students can also go to the GEOS-Chem website at *http://acmg.seas.harvard.edu/ geos/geos_people.html* and learn what scientists are researching, and how they are using the satellite data.

- Students can learn more about the MISR at *http://www-misr.jpl.nasa.gov*. This website provides a quiz archive of aerial images, world maps and animations, and a multimedia gallery for students.

Interdisciplinary Study

- Much has been written about air pollution, particulate matter, and smog. For a concise overview of air pollution, see Reading 4: Air Pollution and Environmental Equity.

- Reading 6: Global Warming and the Greenhouse Effect explains what gases are responsible for the greenhouse effect and the environmental effects.

Teachers' Guide 5

Connections

Mathematical modeling with computers: For policy makers to regulate emissions effectively, there needs to be a strong understanding of the relationships between emissions and resultant air pollutant concentrations. One of the primary tools employed for this purpose is atmospheric pollutant modeling.

• The human body's respiratory system has effective filtering mechanisms to prevent some particulate matter from entering the lungs. This Activity provides an opportunity to talk about the respiratory system and the effects of particulate matter on the human body.

Differentiated Learning

• To help ESL students understand the steps in the procedure, pair them with students who are proficient English language users. Model how students can read each step aloud and run their finger along under the text before completing the action required by each step so that ESL students can associate the oral sound of words with their written forms. Reading each step aloud and then performing the required task will enhance ESL students' understanding.

• The hands-on, visual nature of this Activity will help ESL students understand the concepts. Label what they observe on the experimental coffee filter with the term *particulate matter* so they understand the vocabulary.

Answers to Student Questions

1. This answer depends on the location. Students should be encouraged to give very detailed descriptions of the particles.

2. There are no "wrong" answers, although some are more reasonable than others.

3. Harmful effects of these particles include problems with breathing, allergies, and visibility.

4. Answers will vary with students. Spring and fall are times when many particles are in the air due to pollen, but this depends on the location. In western and southwestern states, winter and summer are better.

5. Windy or dry conditions will increase the amount of particulate matter in the air. Any type of precipitation will decrease the amount.

6. Answers will vary with students. Areas that might have more particulate matter are those near roads, in heavily populated parts of the city or town, or downwind from factory smokestacks.

Assessment

- At the beginning of the Activity, determine students' understanding of what particles might be in the air that they cannot see and where these particles might come from.
- During the Activity, monitor the care with which students draw and record what they observe on the control and experimental filters.
- At the end of the Activity, you can assess the answers to student questions.

Resources

www.epa.gov/p2/pubs/local.htm

http://modis.gsfc.nasa.gov

http://acmg.seas.harvard.edu/geos/geos_people.html

www-misr.jpl.nasa.gov

Activity 6 Planner

Activity 6 Summary

Students will examine how the temperature of an object depends upon its orientation relative to the radiation source in order to better understand why the Sun heats Earth differently at the equator than at the poles.

Activity	Subject and Content	Objective	Materials
Why Is It Hotter at the Equator Than at the Poles?	Sunlight hits Earth's surface at different angles causing different amounts of light energy to be absorbed.	Investigate how the angle of sunlight affects the heating of a surface.	For each group of students: three identical Celsius thermometers (glass or metal backed), reflector lamp with clamp and 60-watt incandescent bulb, ring stand with iron ring, utility clamp, one sheet of black construction paper, stapler or tape, several books or blocks to prop thermometers, meter stick, scissors

Time	Vocabulary	Key Concept	Margin Features
50–60 minutes	Season, Angle of sunlight	II: Factors that contribute to weather	Safety Alert!, What Can I Do?, Fast Fact, Connections, Resources

Scientific Inquiry	Unifying Concepts and Processes	Technology	Personal/Social Perspectives	Historical Context
Collecting, analyzing, and interpreting data	Energy and matter: flows, cycles, and conservation	Creativity and innovation; critical thinking, problem solving, and decision making	Populations, resources, and environments	Evidence supporting a theory

Why Is It Hotter at the Equator Than at the Poles?

Background

You are probably familiar with how the temperature is warmer during the day and cooler at night. Furthermore, you probably realize that it is warmest in the middle of the day, when the Sun is high in the sky, than in the morning or evening, when the Sun is low in the sky.

How high the Sun gets during the day depends on where you happen to be on Earth and the **season**. For locations close to the equator, the Sun can get close to directly overhead. For locations close to the poles, the Sun never gets far above the horizon. For some days of the year, the Sun never gets above the horizon at all.

So, why is there a difference in how high the Sun gets? And, how does the temperature depend on how high the Sun gets? You will explore these relationships in this Activity.

Vocabulary

Season: Specific time of the year associated with characteristic patterns of temperature and weather due to Earth's revolution around the Sun.

Angle of sunlight: How high the Sun is above the horizon and, therefore, the angle at which the Sun is shining on Earth's surface.

Topic: weather and energy
Go to: *www.scilinks.org*
Code: PSCM 003

Objective

Investigate how the **angle of sunlight** affects the heating of a surface.

Activity 6

Materials

For each group of students:

- three identical Celsius thermometers (glass or metal backed)
- reflector lamp with clamp and 60-watt incandescent bulb
- ring stand with iron ring
- utility clamp
- one sheet of black construction paper
- stapler or tape
- several books or blocks to prop thermometers
- meter stick
- scissors

Time

50–60 minutes

Figure 6.1
Cover the bulbs of the three thermometers with black construction paper.

SAFETY ALERT

1. Be careful when handling the reflector lamp. The bulb and cover may become hot.

2. Be careful when handling the glass thermometers; they may break.

Procedure

1. Use black construction paper to make a cover for the bulb of each thermometer, as shown in **Figure 6.1**. Cut a strip of black construction paper 5 cm × 10 cm. Fold the paper and staple four times. Insert the thermometer. Make three covers.

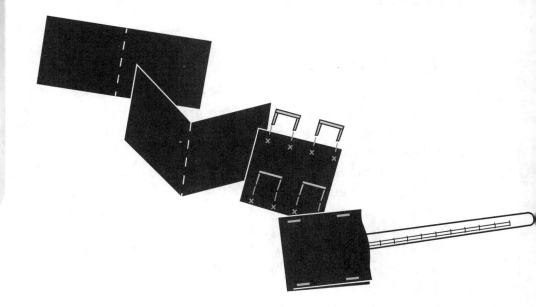

2. Prop the thermometers as shown in **Figure 6.2**. One thermometer should be vertical (A), one slanted at about a 45° angle (B), and one horizontal (C). Make sure you can easily read the scales without touching them during the experiment.

3. Attach the lamp to a ring stand and ensure that it will not move during your experiment. Adjust the lamp on the stand so that its bulb is centered 40 cm above the bulbs of the thermometers.

4. Before turning on the lamp, record the temperature for each thermometer under the column labeled "0 Minutes" on **BLM 6.1**. Predict what will happen to each thermometer over time. Record this on **BLM 6.1**.

5. Turn on the lamp and record temperatures for each thermometer every minute for 15 minutes. Do not move the thermometers when reading the temperatures. Also, do not block the light going from the lamp to the thermometers. Record all temperatures on **BLM 6.1**.

6. Use **BLM 6.2** to make a graph of *temperature versus time* for each thermometer. To make comparison easier, plot the results for all three on the same graph paper with different lines (solid, dashed, dotted) or different colors to show the results from each thermometer.

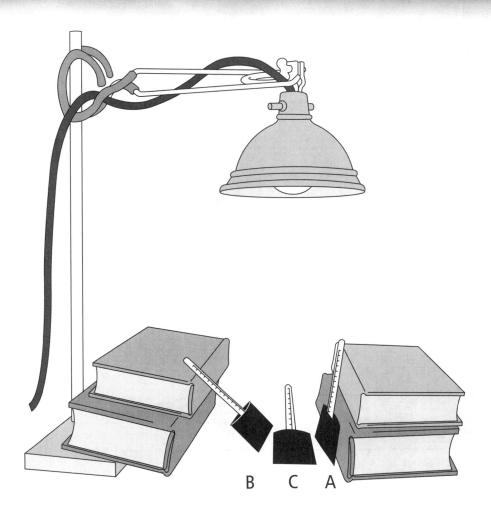

B   C   A

Figure 6.2
The position of each
of these thermometers
represents the way
sunlight strikes different
locations on Earth.

Questions and Conclusions

1. Which thermometer showed the greatest temperature increase? Why?

2. Which thermometer(s) best represents the way sunlight strikes the equator? The poles? What parts of the globe would the third thermometer represent?

3. Using what you learned in this Activity and the illustration in **Figure 6.3**, how can you explain the fact that the equator is hotter than the poles?

4. If you were given a data table that listed the average yearly temperatures for cities as you go away from the equator, do you think you would see a trend in the temperatures? If so, what would this trend be and why would it exist?

What Can I Do?

Is the temperature during the day highest when the Sun is highest? Record the temperature every hour or obtain the hourly temperature data for your location. What might be the reason for your results?

Activity 6

Figure 6.3
The amount of radiation energy absorbed at a particular location on Earth depends on the number of daylight hours and on the incoming angle of the solar rays. Compare the angle of the rays that strike near the equator with the angle of those that strike near the poles.

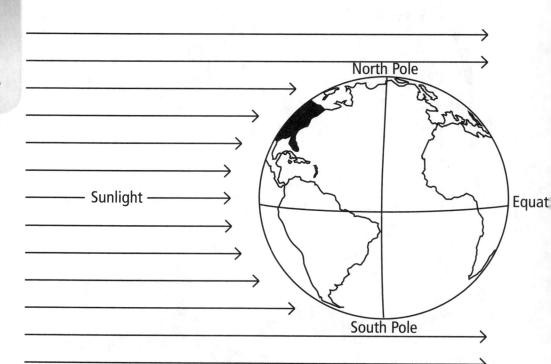

BLM 6.1: Recording and Predicting Temperature

Date_____   Activity 6: Why Is It Hotter at the Equator Than at the Poles?

Prediction: What will happen to each thermometer over time?																	
Thermometer A:																	
Thermometer B:																	
Thermometer C:																	
Time (min.)	0	1	2	3	4	5	6	7	8	9	10	11	12	13	14	15	Total change in temperature
Thermometer A:																	
Thermometer B:																	
Thermometer C:																	

BLM 6.2: Graph Grid

Date_____   Activity 6: Why Is It Hotter at the Equator Than at the Poles?

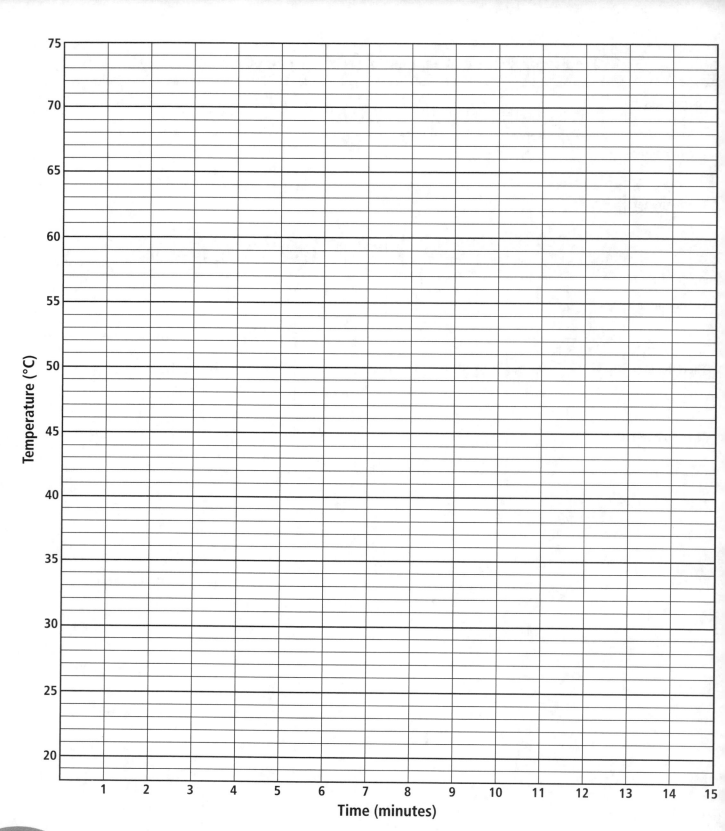

Why Is It Hotter at the Equator Than at the Poles?

What Is Happening?

Earth's shape determines how its atmosphere and surface are heated. Equatorial regions receive the maximum amount of solar radiation; polar regions receive the minimum amount. (Note: Earth's axis is tilted at about

How Do We Know This?

How do we know how the angle of sunlight affects the heating of Earth's surface?

Indigenous cultures all over the world have long known about seasons. Some of these cultures even built observational platforms from which they could observe the location of the Sun and stars over many years and decades. The knowledge gained from these data allowed them to plant certain crops for maximum yield, prepare for weather changes, and determine migration times.

The differential heating of Earth's surface has been determined by collecting temperature data at different points away from the equator on Earth's surface and comparing them. Analysis of the data indicates that, in general, the further away the data points are from the equator, the cooler the temperature in both summer and winter.

Since the Earth is a sphere, more solar energy arrives for a given surface area in the tropics than at higher latitudes, where sunlight strikes the atmosphere at a lower angle. Scientists use some of the same tools that the indigenous cultures used; observation and data collection over time. Today, scientists use electronic instruments to help them collect data. For example, satellites are equipped with infrared cameras, which can detect infrared radiation emitted by Earth's surface. Another satellite, GOES-R (Geostationary Operational Environmental Satellite "R"), uses different detectors to measure atmospheric data. One detector, Space Environmental In-Situ Suite (SEISS), is a collection of electron, proton, and heavy ion detecting sensors, and records solar radiation. The Extreme UV/X-ray Irradiance Sensor (EXIS) detects solar radiation and solar flares.

Objective

Investigate how the angle of sunlight affects the heating of a surface.

Key Concepts

II. Factors that contribute to weather

Materials

For each group of students:

- three identical Celsius thermometers (glass or metal backed)
- reflector lamp with clamp and 60-watt incandescent bulb
- ring stand with iron ring
- utility clamp
- black construction paper (one sheet per student or group of students)
- stapler or tape
- several books to prop thermometers
- meter stick
- scissors

Time

50–60 minutes

23.5° relative to its orbital plane, so the exact locations for maximum and minimum radiation vary throughout the year.) This experiment demonstrates the principle involved.

Due to the shape of Earth, sunlight strikes the surface at different angles in different places. In the experiment with the three thermometers positioned at different angles, the thermometer with its flat surface parallel to the light received the least amount of light energy. The thermometer with its flat surface perpendicular to, or facing, the light received the most amount of light energy. When a piece of paper is parallel to a light source (as is thermometer A), the light rays strike the paper at a very low angle, and less light strikes the paper. When the paper is tilted away from parallel (thermometer B), the light rays strike the paper at a greater angle and more light strikes the paper. The more perpendicular the paper is to the incoming light, the more energy it will receive and the quicker it will heat. The paper covering thermometer C will heat the quickest.

Note: It is common to refer to *direct* rays as those rays striking the surface of an object at a 90° angle (i.e., perpendicular), with *indirect* rays being those rays striking the surface with an angle less than 90°. Those terms have been avoided in this Activity to focus attention on the mechanism involved rather than on the meaning of *direct* and *indirect*.

The mechanism responsible for causing the equator to be warmer than the poles is the same mechanism responsible for winter being colder than summer. Earth's axis is tilted and, depending on which side of the Sun Earth happens to be on, the northern hemisphere could be tilted toward the Sun or away from the Sun. When the northern hemisphere is tilted toward the Sun, the Sun gets higher in the sky and the temperature is warmer (summer). When the northern hemisphere is tilted away from the Sun, the Sun does not get as high in the sky and the temperature is cooler (winter). When the northern hemisphere is tilted toward the Sun, the southern hemisphere is tilted away from the Sun. When the northern hemisphere is tilted away from the Sun, the southern hemisphere is tilted toward the Sun. This means that the seasons in the southern hemisphere are opposite to the seasons in the northern hemisphere. When it is summer in the northern hemisphere, it is winter in the southern hemisphere.

It is important to point out that the angle of the Sun is only one factor that contributes to the temperature. Another is the length of daylight. During summer, for example, areas away from the equator receive more hours of daylight than during winter, and this also contributes to summer being warmer. How warm it gets, though, depends on how warm it was prior to summer. At the start of summer, the poles actually receive more sunlight than the equator gets at the start of spring and fall. However, the poles start off quite a bit colder, after having no radiation at the start of winter. This dependence on previous temperatures also explains why the maximum temperature during the day tends to be in the early afternoon rather than exactly at noon, even though more sunlight is received at noon than is received later in the afternoon.

If Earth were not rotating, this differential heating would set up one global circulation cell with warm air at the equator rising and traveling toward the poles and cold air at the poles sinking and moving toward the equator. Earth's rotation makes for a much more complex global circulation pattern that involves several convection cells (see Reading 5: Weather and the Redistribution of Thermal Energy).

Preconceptions

Many people feel that the reason for the equator being warmer than the poles is because the equator is closer to the Sun than the poles. While this is true, the difference is not significant (only 0.004% closer). That is like moving the black paper strips 17 microns closer to the lamp in this Activity (a human hair is about 100 microns thick).

Many people also feel this is the reason for the seasons, with the Earth being closer to the Sun in the summer and farther away in the winter. This common belief is held by people of all ages, including teachers. If this were the case, both hemispheres would experience summer during the same months (actually, the northern hemisphere experiences its summer when Earth is *farther* from the Sun).

What Students Need to Understand

• Light at a low angle does not heat objects as quickly as light at a high angle.
• Since Earth is nearly round, the equator receives light at a greater angle than the poles receive, with a gradation in between.
• Due to the difference in the angle of sunlight (along with other factors), the equator is warmer than the poles.

Time Management

This Activity will take 50–60 minutes to conduct. Preparing the materials takes as much time as actually conducting the Activity. Therefore, the Activity can be done in less time if materials are prepared in advance.

Preparation and Procedure

Ensure that all materials are either centrally located or distributed to student groups. Do as much or as little preparation of materials (setting up lamps, covering thermometers) as desired. The more preparation ahead of time, the less time will be required for the Activity; however, the need for students to learn to use and set up laboratory equipment should be considered. Use alcohol-filled thermometers for this Activity, and *urge students to use caution* to avoid breaking the fragile thermometers and burning themselves on the lamp.

SAFETY ALERT
1. Be careful when handling the reflector lamp. The bulb and cover may become hot.
2. Be careful when handling the glass thermometers; they may break.

If you are using a light source other than a 60-watt incandescent bulb, it is important that you try this Activity first to determine which distances from the light give the best results. A compact fluorescent bulb, for example, will not produce as much heat as an incandescent bulb.

You may wish to use a globe and a flashlight as a light source to illustrate how the light from the flashlight strikes the surface of the globe at different angles, with the light being perpendicular at the equator and at decreasing angles toward the poles.

Alternative Preparation

The dependence of how much light is intercepted based on its incoming angle can be demonstrated by holding an index card in front of a beam of light and observing the size of the shadow on the wall. The larger the shadow, the greater the amount of energy that was intercepted by the card, and the warmer it will get.

Alternatively, you can use a flashlight and a piece of graph paper. (See **Figure 6.4**.) Holding the flashlight fairly close (10–15 cm) and perpendicular to the graph paper, trace the outlines of the beam striking the surface. Slowly tilt the paper (trying to keep the flashlight in the same place), occasionally tracing the new area covered by the beam. As the surface area covered by the light increases, the radiant energy from the flashlight beam disperses over a greater area. As a result, the heating effect of the incoming light diminishes.

Figure 6.4
When the flashlight rays are perpendicular to the paper, the energy is concentrated into a small area. When the flashlight rays strike the tilted paper, the same amount of light energy is dispersed over a greater surface area. The more energy received per area, the greater the temperature.

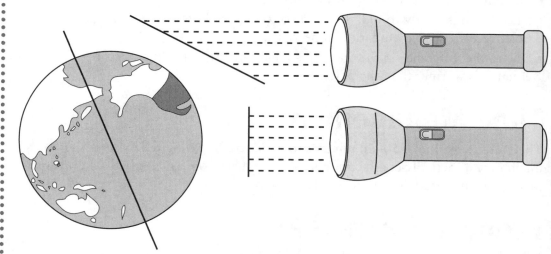

Extended Learning

- Ask students why black construction paper was used. Also ask them why the same color was used on each thermometer. Why not use different colors? The fact that different colored surfaces heat at different rates is another important factor in weather (see Activity 7).

- Have students search for temperatures of cities in the world located at different latitudes. The overall trend in these temperatures will show the amount of heat received at that location relative to the city's position from the equator. Abnormalities in the trends may lead them to investigate other factors that affect temperature (e.g., elevation and proximity to oceans).
- Encourage students to investigate the long days during the summer months and the long nights during the winter months at the poles. This should lead them to discover the tilt in Earth's axis of rotation and its relationship to seasons. This Activity leads naturally into a discussion of seasons and the preconceptions that surround the topic of seasons.
- Depending on the level of students, they may be able to reason that the atmosphere is heated differentially just as is the surface of Earth. It is this differential heating of the atmosphere, together with the rotation of Earth, that sets up the global circulation patterns of the atmosphere. Encourage students to make predictions and hypotheses about global circulation patterns, and then do research to find out if their hypotheses are reasonable.
- Have students tape a small alcohol thermometer to the northern hemisphere and one to the southern hemisphere of a globe. Shine a heat lamp on the globe, which is tilted 23.5°, and collect data over 10 minutes. Have students compare the temperature of each thermometer.

Connections

Some people may have heard about *perihelion* and *aphelion*. These terms refer to characteristics of the elliptical orbit of Earth about the Sun, perihelion being the point in the orbit at which Earth and the Sun are closest together, and aphelion being the point at which they are farthest apart. It is the axial tilt of Earth that causes seasons, rather than the fact that our distance to the Sun varies during a year (e.g., perihelion and aphelion). Go to *www.newton. dep.anl.gov/askasci/ast99/ ast99578.htm*.

Interdisciplinary Study

- Seasons in the northern and southern hemispheres are reversed. This Activity may provide a launching point for investigating cultural activities at the present time in the other hemisphere.
- Investigating how people live under conditions where the pattern of day and night is radically different from that at your latitude provides another launching point for investigating other cultures. Exploring how other groups adapt to seasonal changes in heating patterns (or to having little seasonal change, as near the equator) offers similar opportunities.
- Encourage students to investigate the people who live near the poles. In these locations, people experience days with close to 24 hours of sunlight in the summer months. In the winter months, people live in almost constant darkness. Have students learn about peoples' way of life and activities during the extreme summer and winter months. Students can read books about the Inuit culture and how they adapted their lives to the climate and amount of sunlight.

Differentiated Learning

- To help ESL students understand the steps in the procedure, pair them with students who are proficient English language users. Model how students can read each step aloud and run their finger along under the text before completing the action required by each step so that ESL students can associate the oral sound of words with their written forms. Reading each step aloud and then performing the required task will enhance ESL students' understanding.

- The hands-on, visual nature of this Activity will help ESL students understand the concepts. When discussing the concepts involved in this Activity, sketch and label diagrams to enhance understanding.

- For students who experience difficulty with graphing three sets of data on one graph, create an overhead transparency of **BLM 6.2**, and demonstrate how to plot the temperatures and create a different line type or color for each thermometer.

- For students who finish early, encourage them to explore why the atmosphere heats up differently than Earth's surface. When they find out how the atmosphere heats up, ask students to determine the relationship of the atmosphere and the rotation of Earth. This will lead them to discover global circulation patterns.

Answers to Student Questions

1. The horizontal thermometer (C) showed the greatest temperature increase because it intercepted the most light.

2. The horizontal thermometer (C) represents the equator; the vertical thermometer (A) represents the poles; the slanted thermometer represents about 45° latitude (approximately the latitude of Tasmania and southern Argentina in the southern hemisphere, or South Dakota and Romania in the northern hemisphere).

3. Land at the equator is oriented closer to perpendicular to the sunlight direction, whereas land at the poles is oriented closer to parallel. As this experiment shows, when the light is perpendicular to the surface, the surface warms more quickly than when the light is not as perpendicular. Therefore, all other things being equal, the equator is hotter than the poles.

4. Answers will depend on students, but they should see a trend. That trend should be one of general decrease in average yearly temperature as latitude increases toward the poles. Moving away from the equator, the elevation of the Sun becomes less and less. If students look at actual data, the trend may be less clear in areas close to major geographic features (e.g., large lakes, oceans, or mountains). These geographic elements also affect temperature.

Assessment

- At the beginning of the Activity, determine students' understanding of why Earth's surface temperatures decrease as you move away from the equator.
- During the Activity, observe students to ensure that they set up the apparatus and materials correctly, record the temperatures of the three thermometers accurately and without disturbing the thermometers, and graph the temperatures from the three thermometers correctly on one graph.
- At the end of the Activity, you can assess the Answers to Student Questions.

Resources

www.newton.dep.anl.gov/askasci/ast99/ast99578.htm

Activity 7 Planner

Activity 7 Summary

Students investigate how surface color affects heat flow when exposed to light.

Activity	Subject and Content	Objective	Materials
Which Gets Hotter: Light or Dark Surfaces?	Energy transfer	Investigate how surface color affects heat flow when exposed to light.	Each group of students will need: heat lamp or reflector lamp with 100-watt incandescent bulb; one black metal can or cup (can be painted or covered with paper); one white metal can or cup (can be painted or covered with paper); two lids/covers with slits, one for each of the cans or cups, insulated if possible; two thermometers; ruler or meter stick

Time	Key Concept	Margin Features
30–40 minutes	II: Factors that contribute to weather	Safety Alert!, Fast Fact, What Can I Do?, Connections, Resources

Scientific Inquiry	Unifying Concepts and Processes	Technology	Personal/Social Perspectives	Historical Context
Devising a testable hypothesis	Energy and matter: flows, cycles, and conservation	Creativity and innovation	Populations, resources, and environments	Evolving theories

Which Gets Hotter: Light or Dark Surfaces?

Background

Do you ever walk barefoot on warm, sunny summer days? If so, are there surfaces that you avoid so you will not burn your feet? On sunny summer days, is it better to wear light- or dark-colored clothing if you are trying to keep cool? Which type of clothing is best to wear on cold, sunny winter days if you want to get warm quickly? You probably have answered some of these questions before. In this Activity, you will learn the reason behind those answers.

Objective

Investigate how surface color affects heat flow when exposed to light.

Procedure

1. Slide a thermometer through the slit in each of the insulated lids so that the bulb of each thermometer will be about halfway down in the can (or cup), as shown in **Figure 7.1**. *Caution: Do not force the thermometers into the slits.* If they will not go in, make the slits slightly larger.

2. Place the lids on the cans (or cups).

3. Place the cans (or cups) side by side so that each is about 10 cm from the lamp, as shown in **Figure 7.1**. Keep the lamp turned off for now.

4. Record the initial temperature of each cup under the "0 Minutes" column on **BLM 7.1**.

Materials

Each group of students will need:

- heat lamp or reflector lamp with 100-watt incandescent bulb
- one black metal can or cup (can be painted or covered with paper)
- one white metal can or cup (can be painted or covered with paper)
- two lids/covers with slits, one for each of the cans or cups, insulated if possible
- two thermometers
- ruler or meter stick

Time

30–40 minutes

SAFETY ALERT

1. Do not force the thermometers through the slits. The glass bulbs may break.

2. The reflector lamp may become hot to the touch.

Activity 7

Topic: weather and energy
Go to: *www.scilinks.org*
Code: PSCM 003

Figure 7.1
The black metal can (or cup) and the white metal can (or cup) should not touch each other. They must be the same distance from the lamp.

 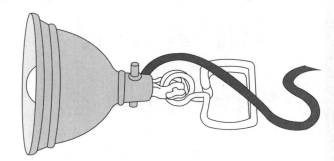

Fast Fact

Warmer air is less dense, which reduces the amount of lifting force that an aircraft's wings produce. This means that airplanes need longer runways for takeoffs and landings in hot weather.

What Can I Do?

Collect two pictures of the landscape with differing surface types and colors. Tape a thermometer to the back of each picture with the bulb directly behind the colored surface you are investigating. Record the temperature changes on the thermometers when the reflector lamp is placed above the pictures.

5. Predict what will happen to the temperature in each can (or cup) when the lamp is turned on. Record your prediction on **BLM 7.1** and explain your prediction. Will there be any differences in the temperature recorded in the cans (or cups)?

6. Turn on the lamp and record the temperature on each thermometer every minute for five minutes on **BLM 7.1**. While the light is on, do not touch, move, or disturb the cans (or cups) in any way.

7. Turn off the lamp and graph the temperatures you recorded for the black and white cans (or cups) on **BLM 7.2**.

Questions and Conclusions

1. What did you notice about the temperatures of the two cans (or cups)? How did this compare with what you predicted in step 5?

2. Which color (black or white) do you think reflects most of the light that is hitting it? What observation can you make that supports that?

3. Light that is not reflected off an object will be absorbed by that object. Based on your answer to question 2, which color (black or white) do you think absorbs most of the light that is hitting it?

4. Based on your answer to question 3, which color (black or white) should warm up quicker? Is your answer consistent with your observations in this Activity? Explain.

5. On a hot, sunny summer day, which would you rather wear outdoors—a white shirt or a black shirt? (Assume they are made of the same material.) Why?

6. What color roof would you want in a cold climate? What color roof would you want in a hot climate? Why?

7. Suppose red light is shining on two cups—one red and one green. The green cup appears black, but the red cup appears red. Which cup do you think will get warmer? Why? (Think about what color an object appears when it absorbs all of the light hitting it.)

Prediction

What will happen to the temperatures in the black can (or cup) and the white can (or cup) when the lamp is turned on? Will there be any difference in the temperature of the cans (or cups)? Explain your prediction.

_____

_____

_____

_____

Temperature Data Table

Time (min.)	Temperature (°C) White Can (or Cup)	Temperature (°C) Black Can (or Cup)
0		
1		
2		
3		
4		
5		

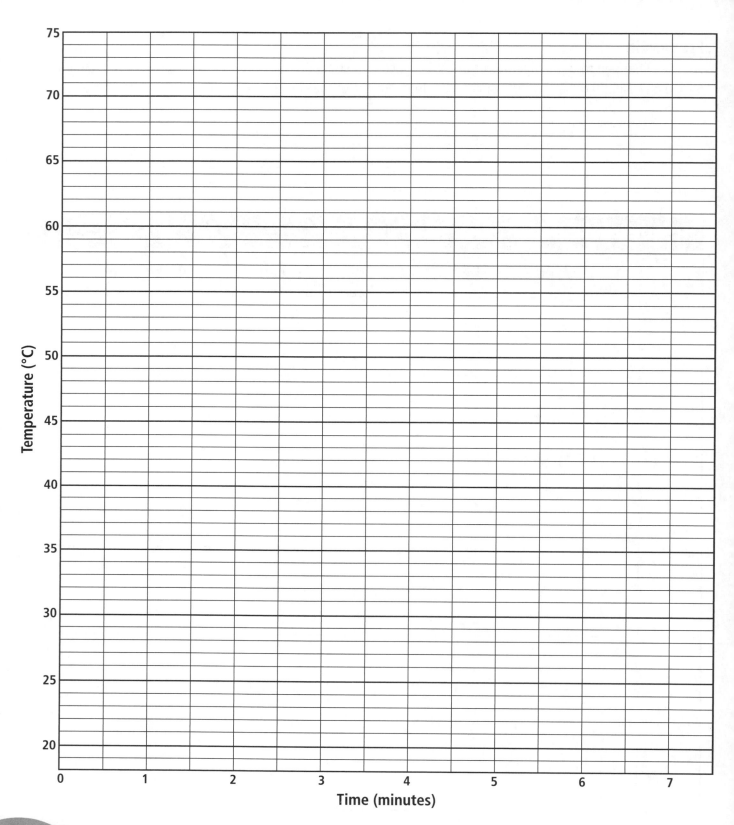

Which Gets Hotter: Light or Dark Surfaces?

What Is Happening?

Black surfaces appear black because they reflect very little of the light that strikes them. The fraction of light that is reflected is called the *reflectivity* of a surface. A completely white surface reflects 100% of the light that strikes it.

Light that is not reflected is absorbed. The fraction of light that is absorbed is called the *absorptivity* of a surface. A completely black surface absorbs 100% of the light that strikes it. A surface with a high absorptivity will have a low reflectivity, and vice versa.

The energy associated with light is called *radiation energy*. When light is absorbed, the radiation energy is converted to heat energy (also called thermal energy), and the object warms up. The more light that is absorbed, the faster the object heats up. Thus, the reason why darker surfaces heat up faster than lighter surfaces is the same reason why darker surfaces appear darker—more of the light that strikes black surfaces is absorbed.

As surfaces heat up, they can heat the air above them. In Activity 8, students will find that air becomes less dense as it warms up (assuming it can expand). Less dense air is buoyant, which makes it rise. Cooler air from the surrounding area then moves underneath. This is basically the mechanism for sea breezes that form on relatively calm, sunny, summer days as the wind comes off the cooler sea toward the warmer land (the wind blows the opposite way at night, when the land is cooler than the sea).

How Do We Know This?

How do we know that various types of surfaces warm up differently during the day?

Temperature data are collected from satellites that use Microwave Sounding Unit instruments and surface instruments such as thermometers, which can be placed on buoys and land-based weather stations. All of these data are fed to computers that can collect and plot the data across maps. Weather balloons are used for midaltitude data collection, and they can collect different temperatures above different surface features in the same general location.

Objective

Investigate how surface color affects heat flow when exposed to light.

Key Concept

II. Factors that contribute to weather

Materials

Each group of students will need:

- heat lamp or reflector lamp with 100-watt incandescent bulb
- one black metal cup or can (can be painted or covered with paper)
- one white metal cup or can (can be painted or covered with paper)
- two lids/covers with slits, one for each of the cups or cans, insulated if possible
- two thermometers
- ruler or meter stick

Time

30–40 minutes

Preconceptions

Students at this age may be confused about the meaning of energy, conservation of energy, and the sources of energy. The following are some possible preconceptions students might have:

- Heat is synonymous with energy.
- Heat and temperature are the same thing.
- Energy from an energy source is lost or used up.

What Students Need to Understand

- Heat is one type of energy.
- Temperature is the measure of the average kinetic energy of the particles in a substance, whereas heat energy is the total energy of all the molecules.
- The total energy is conserved; it is just converted from one type to another.
- Dark surfaces absorb more light (reflect less light) and heat more rapidly than light surfaces.

Time Management

The setup of the experiment requires 5 to 10 minutes. Allow 5 minutes for students to record their predictions. The data collection will take from 5 to 6 minutes, with about 10 additional minutes for graphing.

Preparation and Procedure

The cups, lids, and thermometers can be purchased from a scientific supply company as a kit or as separate pieces. The thermometers should be alcohol-based, not mercury-based. The cups are generally sold as black and silver. Silver cups work as well as white ones. A cheaper alternative is to make the materials yourself. Paint 12- to 16-ounce cans black or white ahead of time, or tape white or black construction paper around them. Many hot drink lids will fit onto 12- to 16-ounce cans. Insulated lids can be made from Styrofoam. Most craft stores sell 1.25 cm–thick Styrofoam sheets. Use one of the cups or cans as a cookie cutter and trace and cut the Styrofoam to size. Slits can be cut into the Styrofoam. Make sure the slits are large enough that students do not have to force the thermometers through the lids.

If you are using a light source other than a 100-watt incandescent bulb, it is important that you try this Activity first to determine which distances from the light give the best results. A compact fluorescent bulb, for example, will not produce as much heat as an incandescent bulb.

SAFETY ALERT

1. Urge students to use caution to avoid breaking the fragile thermometers. Do not force the thermometers through the slits in the lids as the glass bulbs may break.

2. The reflector lamps may become hot to the touch.

Extended Learning

- Students do not have to stop at five minutes of data collection in the experiment. Students can continue to take measurements over a longer time period to investigate whether both cans will eventually reach the same temperature.

- Students can repeat the experiment with their own selection of surface materials of different colors. Encourage students to make predictions about the temperature changes they will observe when the reflector lamp is directed toward surfaces of different colors.

- Have students investigate the term *snow blindness* and how it relates to this Activity.

- Have students investigate the panels used in solar heating. These panels use very dark surfaces to absorb the maximum amount of sunlight.

- The high absorptivity of dark surfaces can explain why densely populated cities often have higher temperatures than the suburban and rural areas surrounding them. This is partly due to the heavy concentration of asphalt roads (also known as "blacktop") in cities as compared to suburban and rural areas. Encourage students to investigate this phenomenon by locating such cities and examining the temperature differences.

- If students have already completed Activity 8, they can investigate why glider pilots sometimes look for large, paved areas (or fields that have been plowed recently) to fly over (a glider is a kind of airplane, one without an engine), and/or how wind can be created on a bright, sunny day between a large, light-colored area of land and a nearby dark-colored area of land.

- Many factors impact how much an object will warm when exposed to light. The color of the object (and its absorptivity/reflectivity) is just one factor. Another factor is the material's *specific heat*, which is related to how sensitive an object's temperature is to the quantity of energy that is absorbed. Some objects have a high specific heat, meaning they will warm only a little for a given absorption of energy. A third factor is how quickly the material is able to conduct energy away from the surface. For example, aluminum is a better conductor of heat than wood. That is why an aluminum pot handle will warm up quicker than a wood pot handle. It is also why, if they are the same temperature, a bathroom floor feels colder than a rug. A fourth factor is the amount of material that is actually absorbing the energy. For example, since water is partially transparent, sunlight is absorbed over a much deeper layer than for soil. For that reason, a much larger mass of water is absorbing the energy and thus does not warm as much. A fifth factor is the presence of water. Evaporation is a cooling process, which can counter the warming due to energy absorption. To assist students in investigating these different factors, consider having additional cups filled with various materials, like water, sand, grass clippings or leaves, and dark organic-rich soil.

Interdisciplinary Study

The tranfer of energy is a major theme in science and can be found in all domains of science, from chemistry and biology to oceanography and physics. For example, chemical reactions, metabolic pathways, ocean currents, and motion all involve the movement and changing of energy from one type to another.

- Have students study the Kreb's Cycle in the human body. Ask them to share how energy is conserved.
- Have students explore how electrical energy is converted to heat energy.
- Have students explore how scientists convert the Sun's energy into electric energy using photovoltaic cells.

Differentiated Learning

For students who completed this Activity quickly, invite them to explore how heat islands can be viewed and researched using satellites at *www.nasa.gov/topics/earth/features/heat-island-sprawl.html*.

Answers to Student Questions

1. The temperature of the black cup rose faster. Responses to how the temperatures of the two cups compare with their predictions will vary among students.

2. White reflects all of the light hitting it, and it appears bright when you look at it.

3. Black absorbs most of the light hitting it, and it appears dark when you look at it.

4. A dark surface should heat more quickly because dark surfaces absorb more of the light. Yes, this answer should agree with students' observations (see answer 1).

5. A white shirt would be preferable because it would reflect the sunlight rather than absorb it. By reflecting sunlight, the white shirt keeps you cooler.

6. In a cold climate, a house should have a darker roof to help absorb heat. The house in the warmer climate should have a light-colored roof to help reflect sunlight rather than absorb it.

7. The green cup will appear black because it absorbs the red light, whereas the red cup reflects the red light. Based on this, the green cup should be warmer since it is absorbing the light.

Assessment

- At the beginning of the Activity, have students complete a K-W-L chart in groups or as a class. Ask students to list what they know about how color affects the way in which heat is absorbed. Ask them to think about the color of clothes they prefer to wear or the color of surfaces they prefer to walk on with bare feet in the summer. Then have students record as questions what they want to learn about how different colors affect the way in which heat is absorbed in the W column of the chart. At the end of the Activity, revisit the K-W-L chart with students, and in groups or as a class record what they learned in the L column of the chart.

- During the Activity, ask students about the relationships between heat energy, reflection, and absorption. For example, "Which cup feels warmer just above the surface of the outside and which one feels warmer on the inside?" Informally evaluate their understanding of how these three items relate to one another. For example, what happens when heat is absorbed by a substance and not released through reflection? What happens to the temperature of a substance when the heat is reflected? What is the flow of heat when heat is reflected and absorbed?

- During the Activity, observe students to ensure they set up the apparatus and materials correctly, record the temperatures of the thermometers accurately and without disturbing the thermometers, and graph the temperatures from the thermometers correctly on the graph.

- At the end of the Activity, you can assess the answers to student questions.

Resources

www.nasa.gov/topics/earth/features/heat-island-sprawl.html

Activity 8 Planner

Activity 8 Summary

Students investigate how the density of air is affected by increasing or decreasing temperature.

Activity	Subject and Content	Objective	Materials
Up, Up, and Away!	Density and temperature	Investigate the effect of temperature on air density.	Each group of students will need: balloon; empty 475 ml or 600 ml glass bottle with a small opening; bucket of ice water; bucket of hot water; safety goggles for everyone

Time	Vocabulary	Key Concept	Margin Features
30 minutes	Air density	II: Factors that contribute to weather	Safety Alert!, Fast Fact, What Can I Do?, Connections

Scientific Inquiry	Unifying Concepts and Processes	Technology	Personal/Social Perspectives	Historical Context
Applying and using scientific knowledge	Cause and effect: mechanism and prediction; energy and matter: flows; stability and change: conditions and factors	Creativity and innovation	Scientific perspective of data	Evidence supporting a theory

National Science Teachers Association

Up, Up, and Away!

Background

A hot air balloon, as shown in **Figure 8.1**, uses hot air. You may have heard that hot air rises. In this Activity, you will explore what it is about hot air that makes it rise.

During this exploration, you will find that the concept of density is important. Everything is made up of atoms and molecules, and the density of something depends on how tightly packed together the atoms and molecules are (and how tightly packed together the subatomic particles are that make up the atoms and molecules). Styrofoam, for example, is not very dense; its molecules are not very tightly packed. In comparison, a lead block is much more dense; its atoms are more tighly packed.

Because they have different densities, a piece of Styrofoam that weighs the same as a piece of lead would have to be *much* larger.

Whether something rises or sinks when immersed in water depends upon its density. A lead block is more dense than water and so it sinks. A piece of Styrofoam is less dense than water and so it rises. Air is even less dense than Styrofoam, so bubbles of air in water also rise.

> ### Vocabulary
> **Air density:** The concentration of air molecules within a certain volume.

Topic: gas laws
Go to: *www.scilinks.org*
Code: PSCM 004

> ### Objective
> Investigate the effect of temperature on **air density**.

Activity 8

Materials

Each group of students will need:

- balloon
- empty 475 ml or 600 ml glass bottle with a small opening
- bucket of ice water
- bucket of hot water
- safety goggles for everyone

Time

30 minutes

Figure 8.1
A hot-air balloon uses hot air to rise.

SAFETY ALERT

The glass bottle may break when you transfer it from the hot water to the cold water. Wear safety goggles.

Procedure

Trial 1

1. Place the uncovered bottle in the bucket of hot water for three minutes. Do not submerge the bottle or allow water to get into the bottle. You will probably have to hold it in place to keep it upright.

2. While the bottle is still in the hot water, place the balloon over the mouth of the bottle. (See **Figure 8.2**.) You may need your laboratory partner to help you hold the bottle. You have now isolated a mass of air inside the bottle. It is important to remember throughout this trial that the amount, or mass, of air will remain constant. In the box marked "Trial 1 Prediction" on **BLM 8.1**, record what you think will happen to the balloon when the bottle is placed in a bucket of ice water. Explain your prediction.

3. There is a small chance the bottle may break when placed in the ice water. *It is important that everyone wears safety goggles.* Place the bottle in the bucket of ice water. (See **Figure 8.2**.) In the box marked "Trial 1 Observation" on **BLM 8.1**, describe what has changed, keeping in mind that the balloon over the mouth of the bottle has remained in place so the mass of the air in the bottle has remained constant (that is, it remains the same).

Trial 2

1. Take the balloon off the bottle and place the bottle in the bucket of ice water for three minutes. Do not submerge the bottle or allow water to enter it.

84

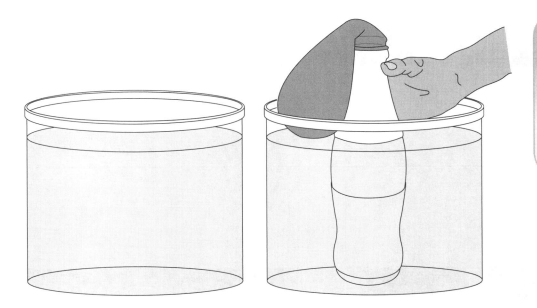

Fast Fact
The density of air at 5,000 feet gives the Colorado Rockies and visiting teams an advantage when hitting home runs. Baseballs travel 10% farther because the air is 15% less dense than at sea level.

Figure 8.2
The balloon keeps the amount, or mass, of air in the bottle constant.

2. Place the balloon over the mouth of the bottle. As in Trial 1, you have isolated a mass of air. Again, it is important to remember throughout this trial that the amount, or mass, of air will remain constant. In the box marked "Trial 2 Prediction" on **BLM 8.1**, record what you think will happen to the balloon when the bottle is placed in a bucket of hot water. Explain your prediction.

3. As with Trial 1, there is a small chance that the bottle may break when placed in the hot water. *Everyone should wear safety goggles.* In the box marked "Trial 2 Observation" on **BLM 8.1**, describe what changed when the bottle was placed in the hot water, keeping in mind that the mass of the air has remained constant.

Questions and Conclusions

1. As air is heated, what happens to its density? In other words, do the molecules of air move closer together or farther apart? How do you know?

2. As air is cooled, what happens to its density? In other words, do the molecules of air move closer together or farther apart? How do you know?

3. Gases such as helium, which are less dense than air, will rise in air. Based on this, what would you expect to happen to air in the atmosphere that is warmed? What would happen to air that is cooled? Explain.

4. Based on your observations and your answers to these questions, where would you place a warm-air vent in a room: near the floor or the ceiling? Where would you place an air conditioning vent? Explain your answers.

What Can I Do?
Determine if air in a balloon is the same density as air outside the balloon. Tie a piece of string to the center of a small diameter dowel rod that is about 40 cm long. Blow up two balloons approximately the same size, tie them, and tape them to the ends of the dowel rod. Place a small piece of tape on one balloon. Balance the dowel rod by moving the center string so that the balloons are at the same level. Prick a hole in the balloon through the piece of tape and see what happens. The piece of tape allows air to flow out of the balloon without having the balloon pop. If the density in the balloon is the same density as the air outside the balloon, then the dowel rod will remain balanced. Does it?

Hot Water to Ice Water	
Trial 1 Prediction	
Trial 1 Observation	
Ice Water to Hot Water	
Trial 2 Prediction	
Trial 2 Observation	

Up, Up, and Away!

What Is Happening?

The relationship between density, temperature, and volume can be somewhat confusing to students. This Activity is designed to help students investigate the relationship between these three important variables. A key point in this Activity that students must understand is that once the balloon is placed on the bottle, the amount, or mass, of air has been isolated. (The mass of the air used in each trial remains constant.) Second, by using a bottle covered with a balloon instead of a sealed container with a pressure gauge, the pressure inside the bottle will, for the most part, be held constant and will be equal to the air pressure outside the bottle. The pressure will be held constant because the balloon allows the volume of the air to change. The two variables being manipulated in this Activity are temperature and volume.

Objective
Investigate the effect of temperature on air density.

Key Concept
II. Factors that contribute to weather

Materials
Each group of students will need:

- balloon
- empty 475 ml or 600 ml glass bottle with a small opening
- bucket of ice water
- bucket of hot water
- safety goggles for everyone

Time
30 minutes

How Do We Know This?

How do we know how temperature affects the density of air?

Many scientists have studied the relationship among temperature, density, and pressure of gases. The relationship between temperature and volume (for a fixed pressure) is known as Charles's Law (or sometimes called the law of volumes), and was first identified by Jacques Charles in 1787 (and then published by Joseph Gay-Lussac in 1802). When included with pressure, the relationship is called the ideal gas law, a relationship identified in 1834 by Emil Clapeyron. The finding that hot air is less dense and consequently rises can be traced to Archimedes' principle (identified by Archimedes during the third century BCE), which states that there is a buoyant force exerted on an object equal to the volume of fluid it displaces (i.e., how much space it takes up within the fluid).

Scientists release large helium-filled balloons into the atmosphere where they monitor the air's temperature as high as 98,000 feet. The instruments on the balloon send signals back to the station via radio transmissions. NOAA's Earth System Research Laboratory has a Global Monitoring Division (NOAA/ESRL/GMD) that uses digital thermometers on balloons to determine the temperature in the atmosphere. Satellites are also used to measure temperature at different levels of the atmosphere. For example, infrared cameras are used to determine the temperature of Earth's surface and at different levels of the atmosphere.

When temperature is increased, as it is in Trial 2, the volume of the air increases. Increasing volume, while mass is held constant, results in decreasing density. In the same way, when air in the atmosphere is heated, it expands, becoming less dense than surrounding air and rising relative to the surrounding air. Conversely, when air is cooled, it contracts, becoming more dense than surrounding air and sinking relative to the surrounding air (see Reading 5: Weather and the Redistribution of Thermal Energy).

Many students will be familiar with the relationship between increasing temperature and increasing pressure. However, in the atmosphere, warmer temperatures tend to be associated with lower surface pressure. There are two reasons for this apparent conflict. First, the increasing temperature/increasing pressure relationship assumes that volume is held constant, which is not the case in the atmosphere. Within the atmosphere, when air temperature is increased, the air mass expands—the pressure remains the same. Second, the air mass, being less dense, rises, leading to a region at the surface that has a lower pressure than the surrounding areas. Consequently, a lower surface pressure is associated with the warmer temperature. Conversely, when air temperature is decreased, the contracting air mass sinks, creating a region that has a higher pressure than the surrounding areas. This relationship between the temperature of an air mass and the surface pressure is counter to most people's understanding of temperature and pressure. It is important to make this distinction clear. What is true in this Activity and in the atmosphere is that as air is heated, it becomes less dense; and as air is cooled, it becomes denser.

Preconceptions

Students sometimes confuse the relationship among temperature, density, and volume. Many students are familiar with the relationship between increasing temperature and increasing pressure. However, this relationship assumes a constant volume, which does not hold true in the atmosphere. The behavior of air, such as compressibility and expansion due to temperature, should be investigated using qualitative explanations. Students may have the following preconceptions:

- All atoms are the same.
- The structure of atoms is unknown.
- Atoms in an object are in fixed positions and do not move.

What Students Need to Understand

- As the temperature of a given mass of air increases, its volume increases and its density decreases. As the temperature of a given mass of air decreases, its volume decreases and its density increases.
- Less dense air rises relative to surrounding air. More dense air sinks relative to surrounding air.

Time Management

The Activity alone requires less than 15 minutes to complete and works well as a station with other activities dealing with air pressure. Thirty minutes will be required for student groups to conduct the two trials in the Activity and discuss and record their responses to Questions and Conclusions.

Preparation and Procedure

Aside from securing sources of hot water and ice for each group of students, no special preparations are required for this Activity. Using a thick-walled bottle will minimize the risk of the glass breaking when the bottle is transferred from hot water to ice water and vice versa. *However, to be safe, everyone involved should wear safety goggles during this Activity*. It is not essential that the bottle be of the volume specified in the Materials. Smaller and larger bottles will also work. What is important is the size of the opening. It must be small enough for the balloon to be placed over it. Plastic bottles should not be used, however, as they can deform under sudden temperature changes, perhaps confusing students and lessening the importance of the balloon.

Extended Learning

- In this Activity, students use only an intuitive definition of density. They do not use the mathematical definition of "density equals mass divided by volume." Depending on students' development, you may choose to give them this quantitative relationship and show them its applications. Guide students to devise a procedure and assemble the necessary apparatus to carry out relevant experiments. For example, density blocks can be purchased from many science supply stores. These density blocks can be massed on a balance, and the volume determined through measurement or submersion in a graduated cylinder. The density can be found for each density block, which is a different compound. Since the sizes of the blocks are the same, then the densities will be different due to the masses of the substances in each block.
- Have students research the lowest and highest air pressures that have been recorded on Earth. What weather conditions were associated with each?
- Have students relate what they learned in this Activity to hot air balloons.
- Have students relate what they learned in this Activity to what they learned in Activity 7. For example, on a bright, sunny day, why might a circulation be set up between a large, light-colored area of land and a nearby dark-colored area of land? Why do glider pilots sometimes look for large paved areas (or fields that have been plowed recently) to fly over? (A glider is a kind of airplane, one without an engine.) In both cases, the air above the dark surfaces (paved areas and plowed fields) will warm, expand, and—being less dense than the surrounding air—rise.

Interdisciplinary Study

The concept of density is important in geology and oceanography as well. Scientists hypothesize that density differences in Earth's mantle cause mantle convection, which in part is responsible for the movement of Earth's lithospheric plates. In oceanography, density is responsible for the global circulation of the ocean currents. The effects of density are more easily observed where dense ocean water comes in contact with less dense freshwater in estuaries.

Differentiated Learning

- Sketch what is happening to the air molecules inside the balloon in each trial to help ESL students understand how changing temperature increases or decreases the density of air. The sketches should show the molecules moving more rapidly and spreading apart.
- Students can search for the influence of hydrothermal circulation in the oceans and how this affects global climate and weather.

Answers to Student Questions

1. The density of the air decreases, and the molecules of air move farther apart because the volume increases but the mass remains constant.

2. The density of the air increases and the molecules of air move closer together because the volume decreases but the mass remains constant.

3. The warm air, being less dense than the surrounding air, will rise. The cold air, being denser than the surrounding air, will sink.

4. Heat vents go near the floor. This allows the warmer air to rise and circulate throughout the room. If the vents were near the ceiling, the warm air would have no place to rise and would remain trapped at the top of the room. It would be best to place air conditioning vents near the ceiling. This would allow the cool air to sink and circulate throughout the room rather than remain at floor level.

Assessment

- At the beginning of the Activity, gauge students' understanding of the concept of density, using questions such as the following: What does it mean for an object to be dense? Is there a difference between a very dense loaf of bread and one that is not? Given a rock and a piece of wood of approximately the same size, how would you determine which has the higher density? What if they were different in size? The key point with these questions is to evaluate whether students are confusing mass and density.

Connections

Density can perhaps be better understood by making an analogy to population and pollution. The amount of people in a certain area is called population density. Pollutants in water and in the air are measured by how many pollution particles are in a liter of water or a cubic liter of air. The number of pollution particles in a million particles of water or air is referred to as parts per million (ppm).

- To gauge students' understanding of how density is related to buoyancy, you can use questions such as the following: Have you ever seen a hot-air balloon? Why does it rise in the air? To gauge students' understanding of how density is related to temperature, you can use questions such as the following: Have you ever seen what happens when a sealed container is heated?

- During the Activity, make sure students record their predictions and observations on **BLM 8.1**. Students should be able to conclude or explain why their observations might be different than their predictions.

- At the end of the Activity, you can assess the answers to student questions.

Activity 9 Summary

Students explore how differences in air pressure create wind.

Activity	Subject and Content	Objective	Materials
Why Winds Whirl Worldwide	Air molecules, air pressure, and wind	Investigate how pressure differences create wind.	Each group of students will need: balloon (long balloons work better than round ones), string or fishing line (5 m), drinking straw (full length), clear tape, two chairs (optional)

Time	Vocabulary	Key Concept	Margin Features
15–20 minutes	Wind	II: Factors that contribute to weather	Fast Fact, What Can I Do?, Connections, Resources

Scientific Inquiry	Unifying Concepts and Processes	Technology	Personal/Social Perspectives	Historical Context
Modeling; asking questions	Cause and effect: mechanism and prediction; system and system models	Communication and collaboration	Science and technology in society	Changing knowledge of facts

Why Winds Whirl Worldwide

Background

Wind is an important part of everyone's daily lives. Have you ever flown a kite, thrown a disk, glided a paper airplane, or released a balloon into the air? All of these events have been affected by **wind** to some degree. If the wind blows rapidly, then an object in the air will be carried away quickly.

Wind has become so important that scientists are now harnessing its power to convert it into other more usable sources of energy. The total wind power of the atmosphere has been estimated to produce approximately 3.8 million kilowatts. Modern wind turbines can now harness between half a million and 1 million watts of electricity.

Wind can also cause great destruction. For example, hurricanes can have sustained wind speeds of greater than 240 kph. Port Martin, Antarctica, once reported an average wind speed of 108 mph for an entire day. Tornadoes can have wind speeds greater than 480 kph. Earth is not the only planet with wind. Space probes near Neptune have estimated wind speeds of 2,000 kph.

In this Activity, you will have an opportunity to explore how wind is related to differences in air pressure.

> **Vocabulary**
>
> **Wind:** The movement of air.

> **Fast Fact**
>
> The highest measurement of wind using an anemometer—a device that measures wind speed—was a 372 kph (231 mph) peak gust at the observatory atop Mount Washington in New Hampshire.

Topic: atmospheric pressure and winds

Go to: *www.scilinks.org*

Code: PSCM 005

> **Objective**
>
> Investigate how pressure differences create wind.

Activity 9

Materials

Each group of students will need:

- balloon (long balloons work better than round ones)
- string or fishing line (5 m)
- drinking straw (full length)
- clear tape
- two chairs (optional)

Time

15–20 minutes

Procedure

1. Thread the string through the straw.

2. Tie each end of the string to chairs (see **Figure 9.1**), or hold one end yourself and have someone else hold the other end.

3. Blow up the balloon but do not tie it.

4. With the help of another student, tape the balloon to the straw (see insert in **Figure 9.1** below).

5. Pull the string tight and move the straw to one end of the string, with the untied end facing as shown in **Figure 9.1**.

6. Let go of the balloon and observe what happens. Record your observations in the box marked "Trial 1 Observations" on **BLM 9.1**.

7. Repeat the process two more times, recording your observations each time.

Figure 9.1
When you blow up the balloon, the balloon squeezes the air inside the balloon. What happens to the pressure of the air inside the balloon? Does it increase or decrease?

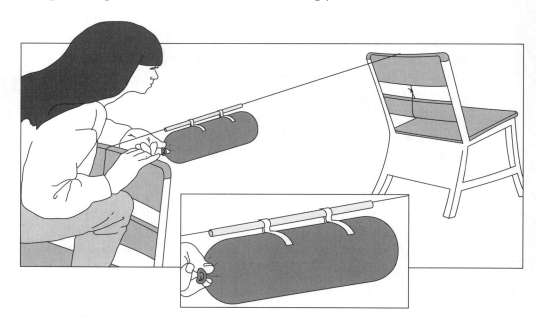

Questions and Conclusions

1. Prior to releasing the balloon, there is air inside the balloon. The air inside is being squeezed by the stretched elastic rubber of the balloon. The air outside the balloon is not being squeezed. Based on this, where is the air pressure greater: inside the balloon or outside the balloon?

2. Describe what happened to the air in the balloon when the balloon was released. Why did this happen?

3. How is what you did in this Activity similar to what happens when wind is created? How is it different?

What Can I Do?

Get a pinwheel or make one. Mark one of the flaps with a large dot or color marking. Take it outside and determine the relative speed of the wind in different locations around the school. Try open spaces, areas near black asphalt, and in between buildings.

94

Trial 1 Observations

Trial 2 Observations

Trial 3 Observations

Why Winds Whirl Worldwide

What Is Happening?

Wind is the movement of air. Wind results from pressure gradients, or differences in air pressure from one place to another. When air of high pressure is close to air of low pressure, air will be pushed from the high pressure area to the low pressure area, creating wind. Due to the rotation of Earth, the air will not move directly toward the low pressure area. Instead, it spirals in, creating a cyclone. A cyclone is any weather system with winds around a low pressure area. The wind will continue until the pressure between the areas is equalized.

How Do We Know This?

How do we measure wind speed?

Meterologists use two instruments to measure the wind: a wind vane measures the direction from which the wind comes, and an anemometer measures the speed of the wind. The arrow on a wind vane points in the direction from which the wind is blowing. The anemometer will measure the speed of the wind by turning faster or slower. Higher pressure pushes air toward the lower pressure. The wind speed depends on how close the high pressure center is to the low pressure center, as well as on the values of the pressures at the two centers.

Modern anemometers are quite sophisticated. A sonic anemometer uses sound waves traveling between a pair of transducers, a device that converts one type of energy to another type. The speed of air will affect the speed of sound, and this is measured by the change in energy of the detectors. This anemometer also is able to determine the direction of the wind by measuring the maximum and minimum sound that is detected in different locations. Ultrasonic and LASER Doppler anemometers use phase shifts of sound or light that are reflected off moving air molecules. Hot-wire anemometers use a very fine wire that is heated. When air flows past the wire, it cools the wire causing an electrical resistance, which can be measured.

Objective

Investigate how pressure differences create wind.

Key Concept

II. Factors that contribute to weather

Materials

Each group of students will need:

- balloon (long balloons work better than round ones)
- string or fishing line (5 m)
- drinking straw (full length)
- clear tape
- two chairs (optional)

Time

15–20 minutes

When a balloon is blown up, the air in the balloon is pressurized. The air around the balloon has a lower pressure than the air in the balloon. When the balloon is opened, the high pressure air rushes out to a region of low pressure. This is the same principle that governs wind.

There are, however, some differences between the model in this Activity and reality. There are no solid boundaries in the atmosphere such as the boundaries of the balloon. Further, the creation of wind is usually not so dramatic in the atmosphere as with the balloon being opened. The acceleration of wind occurs gradually, due to the uneven heating that creates differences in pressure (warm air rises, cool air sinks).

Wind speed is usually measured by a device called an anemometer using the Beaufort Wind Scale, which is a relative scale of 0–12. Reading 11: Scales in Meteorology explains the use of scales in meteorology in more detail, and the historical use of the Beaufort Wind Scale and how it has influenced current scales. Early instruments were disks placed facing the wind. The revolutions of the disk gave a relative speed for the wind. In the 19th century, the hemispherical cup anemometer was invented. This consisted of four hemispherical (half a sphere) cups attached to the ends of two crossed sticks. Each revolution was counted to measure the relative speed of the wind.

In the early 1800s, Sir Francis Beaufort developed what is now called the Beaufort Wind Scale, a standardized method of describing wind speed. This 0–12 scale related wind speeds to their effects on the sails and movement of a British man-of-war: 0 meant all sails would be up and the ship would be barely moving, 6 meant that only half of the sails would be up, and 12 meant that all sails would have been taken down (otherwise, they would be damaged). Eventually, anemometers were developed that give wind speed in km/h, and the Beaufort Wind Scale was quantified so that specific scale numbers equate to specific km/h (refer to Reading 11: Scales in Meteorology).

Preconceptions

Ask students, "How do we know there is air around us?" Students might have the following preconceptions:

- Wind is a supernatural thing caused by angels.
- Trees and bushes move to create wind.

What Students Need to Understand

- Wind results from pressure gradients (i.e., pressure differences from place to place).
- Air generally moves from an area of high pressure to an area of low pressure. (Over large distances, Earth's rotation causes the wind to spiral around the

98

low pressure center, counterclockwise in the northern hemisphere and clockwise in the southern hemisphere. This is known as the Coriolis Effect.)

• Wind continues until air pressure is equalized.

Time Management

This Activity will take 15–20 minutes.

Preparation and Procedure

Students often have preconceptions about wind and where it comes from. Before the lesson begins, discuss wind with the class. The object of the discussion is to reveal students' ideas of wind and its origins. Be sure that all materials are either centrally located or ready to be distributed to the student groups.

It has been suggested that this Activity may cause confusion among students because the same apparatus is used in studies of Newton's third law of motion as it applies to rocketry. The principle is identical in each situation. Gas moving from a region of high pressure to low pressure propels a rocket, and air (a gas) moving from high pressure to low pressure creates wind. Students, however, may not be ready developmentally to transfer learning across the two situations. If so, they may be confused by this Activity. As an alternative, the string and straw can be removed from the Activity, thus eliminating the resemblance to rocketry activities. By holding the blown-up balloon in one hand as the air is released, students can observe that air is moving out of the balloon by holding the other hand next to the opening. The force of the air on their hand is evidence that the air is escaping. In addition, the air escaping from the balloon feels like wind.

As suggested for Activity 3, you can also use the small plastic syringes (no needle) that are available at pharmacies. Have students pull the plunger almost all the way out, and then place their finger on the tip. Keeping their finger on the tip (to prevent air from leaking out), have them close the plunger. This increases the air pressure inside the syringe. If they then release their finger, the air will blow out the syringe.

Extended Learning

• Students may be interested in investigating storms, like tornadoes, in which pressure differences between two relatively close areas are very great. This would create an opportunity to talk about safety precautions that should be followed in tornadoes and strong wind storms. This Activity also provides a good opportunity to talk about the land and sea breezes that were mentioned in the Teachers' Guide to Activity 7.

- It might be appropriate to discuss the reason why the wind is directed around a low pressure center. It has to do with the rotation of Earth. When the wind is calm, the air is stationary with respect to Earth, but Earth is rotating around its axis. The air rotates with Earth. We do not see that rotation because the air rotates at the same rate as Earth. Forcing air toward the center of a low pressure area makes the rotation rate of the air faster, just as skaters rotate faster when bringing their arms in close to the body. We can then observe the rotating air because it is rotating faster than Earth. This is called the Coriolis Effect.

- For many years, both the Department of Energy and NASA have conducted research on wind as an alternative source of energy. Students can explore the history of wind machines, modern wind machines, the economics of wind power, and the environmental aspects of wind power.

- This Activity naturally leads into a study of rocketry and the propulsion of rockets. While this may not be strictly related to meteorology, it is still a topic students usually find very interesting and can be used to integrate a science curriculum. The topic of waves in oceanography is also relevant to wind. Most waves in the ocean are caused by wind.

Interdisciplinary Study

Wind has been a source of inspiration for literature and music. Both can provide ways to introduce topics to students and provoke class discussion. Poems about wind include "Who Has Seen the Wind?" by Christina G. Rossetti, which you can find at *www.poetryfoundation.org/poem/171952*, and "Wind Elegy" by Sara Teasdale, which you can find at *www.recmusic.org/lieder/get_text.html?TextId=59917*. Ask students to listen for references to wind in the music they enjoy and to share these with the class.

Differentiated Learning

- Sketch what happens as the balloon is released in each trial to help ESL students understand how the high pressure air inside the balloon rushes out to the lower pressure air around the balloon when the balloon is released.

- For students who have difficulty understanding the concept involved in this Activity, create a flow diagram that shows each step. This will emphasize the cause-and-effect connections at each step.

- Have students race different sizes, thicknesses (of rubber), and shapes of balloons by blowing them up and letting them go, so that the released air causes the balloons to move through the air. Challenge students to determine the major factors that allow a balloon to release the most air pressure.

Answers to Student Questions

1. The air pressure is greater inside the balloon.

2. Most of the air left the balloon. The air in the balloon rushed out because it was at a higher pressure than the air surrounding the balloon. Some students may also correctly realize that the elasticity of the balloon is a critical factor in this particular Activity.

3. Air moves from high to low pressure areas. The creation of wind is not usually as dramatic as with the balloon, and wind is not air that is escaping or is being forced from a container.

Assessment

- At the beginning of the Activity, gauge students' understanding of how wind is created. Ask students, "Where does wind come from? Why do we have wind? Why is wind sometimes stronger and other times weaker? Can you produce wind? If so, how?"
- During the Activity, make sure students record on **BLM 9.1** their observations for each trial.
- At the end of the Activity, you can assess the answers to student questions.

Resources

www.poetryfoundation.org/poem/171952

www.recmusic.org/lieder/get_text.html?TextId=59917

http://science.howstuffworks.com/environmental/green-science/wind-power.htm

Activity 10 Summary

Students will create a model of the hydrologic cycle.

Activity	Subject and Content	Objective	Materials
Recycled Water: The Hydrologic Cycle	Hydrologic cycle	Use the properties of water and water vapor to describe the parts of the hydrologic cycle.	Each group of students will need: clear plastic shoe box with lid, small plastic cup, sealed plastic bag filled with sand or soil, water, ice, heat lamp or reflector lamp with 100-watt incandescent bulb

Time	Vocabulary	Key Concept	Margin Features
50–60 minutes	Evaporation, Water vapor, Condensation, Hydrologic cycle	II: Factors that contribute to weather	Safety Alert!, Fast Fact, What Can I Do?, Resources

Scientific Inquiry	Unifying Concepts and Processes	Technology	Personal/Social Perspectives	Historical Context
Modeling; asking questions	Patterns; cause and effect: mechanism	Research tools: simulations; communication and collaboration	Populations, resources, and environments	Changing understanding of water

Recycled Water: The Hydrologic Cycle

Activity **10**

Background

When it rains, where does the water come from? You might say "clouds," but where was the water prior to there being any clouds?

As you might expect, the water in clouds came from water on Earth in the form of rivers, lakes, and oceans (a small fraction of the water on Earth is held in the ice caps and glaciers). Still, we have yet to describe how the water gets from Earth to the clouds. That involves evaporation.

During **evaporation**, liquid water turns into a gas we call **water vapor**. During **condensation**, water vapor turns back into liquid. The water molecules are still there—we just cannot see the water vapor, unlike the liquid water in lakes and rivers or as droplets in clouds and rain.

If we cannot see the water vapor, how do we know water vapor exists? In this Activity, you will examine the evidence regarding the presence of water vapor in the air and explore how water vapor plays a key role in the formation of clouds and rain.

Vocabulary

Evaporation: The transformation of water from a liquid into a gas.

Water vapor: Water that is in the gaseous phase.

Condensation: The transformation of water from a gas into a liquid.

Hydrologic cycle: The continuous movement of water from bodies of water to the air to the land and back to bodies of water. Water may change states among liquid, gas, and solid during this cycle.

Objective

Use the properties of water and water vapor to describe the parts of the **hydrologic cycle**.

Topic: water cycle
Go to: www.scilinks.org
Code: PSCM 006

Activity 10

Materials

Each group of students will need:

- clear plastic shoe box with lid
- small plastic cup
- sealed plastic bag filled with sand or soil
- water
- ice
- heat lamp or reflector lamp with 100-watt incandescent bulb

Time

50–60 minutes

Figure 10.1
You can use simple materials to create a model of the hydrologic cycle.

SAFETY ALERT

Be careful not to touch the lamp bulb when the lamp is turned on as it will become hot.

Procedure

1. Set up the apparatus as shown in **Figure 10.1**.

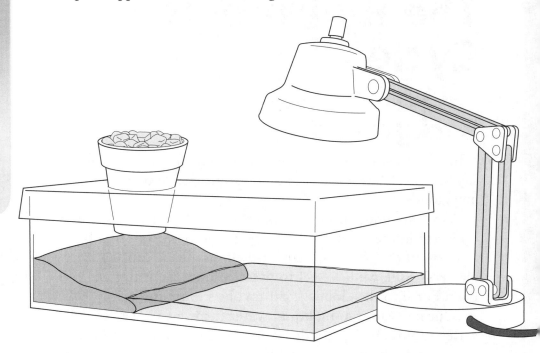

2. Cut a hole in one corner of the lid of the clear shoe box, just large enough for the cup to fit halfway through the lid.

3. Add enough water to cover the bottom of the shoe box to a depth of about 2–3 cm.

4. Position the sandbag at one end of the box, directly under the opening for the cup. The top of the sandbag should be above the surface of the water.

5. Fill the small plastic cup with ice and place it in the opening of the lid.

6. Position a gooseneck lamp so that its light shines down onto the water inside the box.

7. Every 10 minutes, record on **BLM 10.1** observations of what is happening in the shoe box.

8. Draw a diagram on **BLM 10.2** to illustrate the movement of the water through your model.

Questions and Conclusions

1. Based on your observations, what evidence is there that water vapor is present in your box? In your answer, consider where evaporation may be occurring and where condensation may be occurring.

2. Why do water droplets form on the outside of the cup in the shoe box?

3. The condensation of water on the outside of the cup is similar to the condensation of water in clouds. In both cases, water changes from a form we cannot see (water vapor) into a form we can see (liquid water). In nature, the liquid water is initially on land and in the oceans, and then it evaporates (the Sun helps by warming the water; more water evaporates if it is warmer). As the invisible water vapor rises into the atmosphere, it cools and condenses into liquid droplets that we can see (as clouds). Condensation continues, and these water droplets grow in size until they eventually fall back to the surface. Due to the cyclical nature of the process, this is called the hydrologic cycle, or water cycle.

   Compare the water cycle to your Activity apparatus. What role does the lamp serve? What role does the sandbag serve? What role does the ice serve?

4. Examine **Figure 10.2**, which illustrates the hydrologic cycle. Where in the figure is liquid water evaporated into water vapor? Where in the figure is water vapor condensed into liquid water?

5. Was any water lost in this Activity? Explain your reasoning.

Figure 10.2
Use the arrows to follow the movement of water as it changes states and moves from the sea to the air to the land and back to the sea in the hydrologic, or water, cycle.

Minutes	Observations
0	
10	
20	
30	
40	
50	
60	

The Hydrologic Cycle

Is about:

Essential Details					
Evaporation	**Condensation**	**Water Storage in the Atmosphere**	**Precipitation**	**Runoff**	**Groundwater Storage**
What is it?	What is it?	What is it?	What is it?	What is it?	What is it?
What occurs before this in the water cycle?	What occurs before this in the water cycle?	What occurs before this in the water cycle?	What occurs before this in the water cycle?	What occurs before this in the water cycle?	What occurs before this in the water cycle?
Give an example of when you have seen this occur.	Give an example of when you have seen this occur.	Give an example of when you have seen this occur.	Give an example of when you have seen this occur.	Give an example of when you have seen this occur.	Give an example of when you have seen this occur.

So What? (What's important to understand about this?)

Recycled Water: The Hydrologic Cycle

What Is Happening?

In nature, water is constantly changing from its liquid form (which we can see) to its vapor form (which we cannot see) and back again. The basic cycle is as follows. Water evaporates into the air, and as it rises, it encounters lower pressure and expands. During this expansion process, it cools, leading the water vapor to condense into liquid droplets (or, if it is cold enough, directly into snow crystals). With additional condensation, these water droplets grow in size until they eventually fall back to the surface.

In this way, water passes from bodies of water to air to land to bodies of water again in a cyclical pattern called the hydrologic, or water, cycle. (See **Figure 10.2.**) This continuous movement of water is central to meteorology. Water changes phases or places and may combine with other compounds, but water is essentially conserved.

In this Activity, students set up what is essentially a distillation apparatus. As far as water is concerned, Earth is basically a closed system that can be represented by the clear shoe box. A sandbag serves as a continent and water as the oceans. The cup of ice provides a mechanism for cooling the water vapor. In the atmosphere, cooling results from the expansion of air as it rises into regions of lower pressure. How cold it must get before condensation occurs depends on the concentration of water vapor that is present. The lamp serves as the Sun and enhances evaporation. Water evaporates at every temperature, day or night, but the evaporation rate is greater when the water is warmer.

Objective

Use the properties of water and water vapor to describe the parts of the hydrologic cycle.

Key Concept

II. Factors that contribute to weather

Materials

Each group of students will need:

- clear plastic shoe box with lid
- small plastic cup
- sealed plastic bag filled with sand or soil
- water
- ice
- heat lamp or reflector lamp with 100-watt incandescent bulb

Time

50–60 minutes

How Do We Know This?

How do we know that water vapor exists in the atmosphere?

Scientists monitor water vapor in the atmosphere in order to determine where water is and the atmospheric conditions related to the amount of water in the air. Scientists release large helium-filled balloons into the atmosphere where they monitor the air's vapor as high as 30,000 m. The instruments on the balloon send signals back to the station via radio transmissions. Geostationary and polar orbiting satellites and aircraft platforms monitor water vapor using multispectral instruments and infrared imaging.

Preconceptions

Ask students, "Can water exist as a solid? As a liquid? As a gas? How can you tell?" Students may have the following preconceptions:

- Water is not conserved.
- One water droplet cannot travel a large distance.
- When water evaporates, it is still liquid but it is in droplets too small to see.
- Water cannot evaporate if the temperature is less than 100°C, or water cannot exist as a gas below 100°C.

What Students Need to Understand

- The total amount of water on Earth is constant.
- Water vapor is invisible.
- The movement of water through the environment represents a complete cycle. There is little variation in the actual volume of ocean water.

Time Management

Building this demonstration requires a minimal amount of time. Once the lamp is turned on, the water droplets begin forming on the cup of ice within 15–20 minutes. As long as the cup is kept full of ice, the droplets will continue to form. Allow 50–60 minutes for this Activity.

Preparation and Procedure

Be sure that all materials are either centrally located or ready to be distributed to student groups. Ensure that students set up the apparatus as shown in **Figure 10.1**. Students will have to take care to cut the hole in the corner of the shoe box lid so that it is just large enough for the cup to fit halfway through the lid. If they cut the hole too large, their system will not be closed and the model will not work as it should. If the plastic lids are too thick, consider cutting the holes ahead of time so that students do not cut themselves. Plastic shoe boxes can be found at most stores and can be used for other activities and storage afterward. If you want to speed up the process, use warm water.

The ice should not be placed in a Styrofoam cup or any other type of insulating cup.

Alternative Preparation

You may wish to conduct this Activity as a demonstration of the hydrologic cycle. Between classes, or at intervals during the day, you may want to dry off the outside of the cup and replace the ice so that each class can see the initial formation of the water droplets. A cold can of soda or a glass of ice water can also be used if the air is humid enough, but you need to be careful that students do not infer that the water droplets on the outside of the cup originated from water inside the cup (and simply seeped through the cup).

Several class periods before you take up the topic of the water cycle in class, you may want to construct this model so that students can observe and informally investigate its operation.

Extended Learning

- Have students investigate what types of devices are used by countries to produce drinking water from ocean water. What issues does this bring to mind when thinking about oceanic pollution?
- You may want to construct a terrarium made out of a 2 L soda bottle. Cut the bottle near the top. Drill or make holes in the bottom and add the following layers: 5 cm of pebbles, 4 cm of charcoal, 4 cm of sphagnum or Spanish moss, and 10 cm of soil. Add some plants and grass seeds. Invert the top of the bottle that was cut off and place it onto the open part of the filled bottle. Water the soil and plants and let it sit in the Sun for a week or so. As you water daily, you will start to see condensation on the inside of the reversed top, especially if the terrarium is located in direct sunlight.

Interdisciplinary Study

- This demonstration stresses the fact that the water we have on Earth is constant. There is no new water coming in from outside the planet. The concepts of the hydrologic cycle and stewardship of the water we do have are therefore important for students to understand. This Activity demonstrates the hydrologic cycle, but students may come to appreciate it through more artistic forms. As a writing assignment, students might be asked to compose an essay on the implications for their own lives if there were no hydrologic cycle.
- Activity 11 is an interdisciplinary Activity in itself. The Activity leads students through a writing exercise in which they describe the journey of a water molecule through the hydrologic cycle.
- You may wish to use the poem "Our Hold on the Planet" by Robert Frost to initiate discussion about the nature and importance of the hydrologic cycle. You can find the text for Frost's poem at *http://writersalmanac.publicradio.org/index. php?date=2010/11/03*.

Differentiated Learning

- The visual nature of this Activity will enhance ESL students' understanding of the concepts. The use of diagrams to illustrate the concepts will also increase their understanding. Instead of recording written observations, ESL students could sketch what they observe happening in their models.

111

- For students who have difficulty understanding the hydrologic cycle, provide them with a detailed diagram of the hydrologic cycle and have them label the different parts.
- For students who finish this Activity early, have them use the internet or nonfiction print resources to find more information about the hydrologic cycle. Students can use an organizer such as the one shown on **BLM 10.3** to help them organize their thoughts and the content. (The correct responses for **BLM 10.3** are shown on the following page.)

Answers to Student Questions

1. Water vapor must be present in the box because droplets form on the cup. The only way this could happen is if the water in the bottom of the shoe box changes its state from the liquid phase to the gaseous phase, and then the vapor condenses (changes into water droplets) when it is cooled on the surface of the ice-filled cup.

2. Condensation causes water droplets to form on the outside of the cup in the shoe box. The warm water vapor rises and meets the cool sides of the cup. The vapor cools and changes back to the liquid form.

3. The lamp represents the Sun and the solar energy it transmits to Earth. The sandbag represents the land. The ice provides atmospheric low temperatures necessary for cloud formation (condensation).

4. *Evaporation*: From the ocean, rivers, lakes, ponds, puddles, anywhere there is liquid water exposed to the atmosphere.

   Condensation: Primarily in clouds, but also on the ground and other surfaces as dew.

5. Very little water should be lost in this Activity if the box is truly a closed system.

Assessment

- At the beginning of the Activity, gauge students' understanding of evaporation and condensation. Ask students what the different parts of the hydrologic cycle are.
- During the Activity, make sure students record their observations at regular intervals on **BLM 10.1**. You can assess their completed diagram on **BLM 10.2**. Monitor their development of a diagram. Make sure that the diagram labels the three different stages of water, the transitional processes between these phases, and the locations of where these processes occur.
- At the end of the Activity, you can assess the answers to student questions and the accuracy of the hydrologic cycle diagram. Focus your criteria on the phase changes, locations of water phases, and the overall accuracy of the diagram.

Resources

http://ww2010.atmos.uiuc.edu/ (Gh)/guides/mtr/hyd/smry.rxml

http://writersalmanac. publicradio.org/index. php?date=2010/11/03

The Hydrologic Cycle

Is about: the conservation of water and the processes of water phase changes on Earth. The hydrologic cycle conserves and regenerates all of the water. During the cycle, water changes into different states: liquid, solid (ice), and gas (vapor). Water moves on Earth, in the air, and below Earth's surface.

Essential Details

Evaporation	Condensation	Water Storage in the Atmosphere	Precipitation	Runoff	Groundwater Storage
What is it? Evaporation is the process water goes through when it changes from a liquid to a gaseous state. Evaporation is greater when water is warmer.	**What is it?** Condensation is the process water goes through when it changes from a gaseous to a liquid state. Condensation is greater when vapor is cooler.	**What is it?** Liquid water is "stored" as cloud droplets; water vapor is also "stored" in the atmosphere as part of the air.	**What is it?** Precipitation occurs when water falls from clouds. Cloud droplets grow with more condensation, eventually falling in the form of rain (liquid), ice (solid), sleet (liquid and solid), snow (solid), or hail (solid).	**What is it?** Runoff is precipitation that flows over the surface of Earth. It may be water running down the side of a mountain, a stream running into a river, or a river running into an ocean.	**What is it?** Groundwater is water stored below Earth's surface. It occurs when water seeps through fractures or spaces between rock particles below the soil.
What occurs before this in the water cycle? Water feeds into the ocean (from runoff) or collects on the ground after falling as precipitation.	**What occurs before this in the water cycle?** Water in the atmosphere must cool.	**What occurs before this in the water cycle?** Water vapor must cool and condense.	**What occurs before this in the water cycle?** Water has to be stored in the atmosphere.	**What occurs before this in the water cycle?** Water must fall as precipitation.	**What occurs before this in the water cycle?** Water must fall as precipitation and then seep below Earth's surface.
Give an example of when you have seen this occur. Drying your hands with a blow dryer	**Give an example of when you have seen this occur.** Water droplets on the outside of a glass of iced tea	**Give an example of when you have seen this occur.** Clouds, humidity	**Give an example of when you have seen this occur.** Thunderstorms	**Give an example of when you have seen this occur.** Rain runoff from the roof	**Give an example of when you have seen this occur.** Digging in the sand at the beach

So What? (What's important to understand about this?) If we understand the process (i.e., the water cycle), we can understand how to better use and protect our water supply.

Activity 11 Planner

Activity 11 Summary

Students write an original, creative story about the movement of a water molecule through the hydrologic cycle.

Activity	Subject and Content	Objective	Materials
Rainy Day Tales	Hydrologic cycle, or water cycle	Explore the ways water moves through Earth's hydrologic cycle.	Each student will need: notebook paper, blank white paper (for illustration)

Time	Vocabulary	Key Concept	Margin Features
Three class periods of 50–60 minutes	Molecule, Transpiration, Hydrologic cycle	II: Factors that contribute to weather	Fast Fact, What Can I Do?, Connections, Resources

Scientific Inquiry	Unifying Concepts and Processes	Technology	Personal/Social Perspectives	Historical Context
Communicating; applying and using scientific knowledge	Systems and system models	Research tools: simulations	Science and technology in society	Evidence supporting a theory

Rainy Day Tales Activity 11

Background

Mickey the Molecule fell to Earth as part of a raindrop with many other **molecules**. He landed in a tree, rolled over a leaf, then dripped to the ground. Mickey had plenty of company—molecules are so tiny that it took lots and lots of molecules to make up Mickey's raindrop. A short time after Mickey hit the ground, the Sun came out. This warmed the ground and the water molecules. Mickey evaporated back into the atmosphere and continued his travels around Earth as part of the water cycle. (See **Figure 11.1**.)

You see, water molecules are pretty tough, and it is not easy to destroy them. They are made up of three atoms that are tightly connected: two small hydrogen atoms and one larger oxygen atom. Water molecules do not change their appearance when they are cooled, warmed, or come under pressure. In ice, water, and water vapor (steam), water molecules are the same.

During Mickey the Molecule's travels in the water cycle, he may join other water molecules to become a water droplet in a cloud or freeze to fall to Earth as a snowflake. On Earth, he may be stored on the surface in glaciers or lakes, underground among rocks and soil, or in living things. He may return to the atmosphere through **transpiration** (given off as water vapor by plants and animals). Eventually, water flows to bodies of water and is evaporated directly back into the atmosphere. Throughout this cycle, the amount of water on Earth and in its atmosphere remains the same. It just changes form and travels.

Objective

Explore the ways water moves through Earth's **hydrologic cycle**.

Vocabulary

Molecule: The smallest unit of water that consists of one oxygen atom and two hydrogen atoms.

Transpiration: The process by which water that entered a plant, usually through roots, and moved through the plant, goes into the atmosphere through small openings in leaves.

Hydrologic cycle: The continuous movement of water from bodies of water to the air to the land and back to bodies of water. Water may change states among liquid, gas, and solid during this cycle.

Fast Fact

An average of 2.8 trillion gallons of water evaporates from the land each day. About 4.2 trillion gallons of water fall on the land daily. About 1.4 trillion gallons of water soak into the ground and run down rivers to the oceans each day.

Activity 11

Figure 11.1
Mickey's journey can vary among the different paths and processes of the hydrologic cycle.

Materials

Each student will need

- notebook paper
- blank white paper (for illustration)

Time

Three class periods of 50–60 minutes

Procedure

In this Activity, follow a water molecule and describe what happens to it on a trip through part of the water cycle. Select one of the following parts of the cycle:

1. river → ocean → evaporation
2. evaporation → condensation → precipitation
3. precipitation → groundwater → transpiration
4. precipitation → runoff → animal
5. snow → melting → evaporation
6. your own choice

In your story, you must do the following:

1. Have your water molecule travel through three steps of the water cycle.

2. Use five action verbs from a prewriting activity that capture the movement of your water molecule through different steps of the water cycle.

3. Write one paragraph per step of the water cycle and three or more sentences per paragraph.

4. Illustrate your water molecule's travels through the three steps of the water cycle.

Write a quick rough draft of your story and make sure it has the required components. To discuss your rough draft, your teacher will place you within a peer discussion group. After considering their comments, write a final version of your story. Be sure to polish your wording and refine your illustration.

Questions and Conclusions

1. Describe an overview of the water cycle.

2. How many different pathways exist through which water may cycle? Give an example of a particular pathway.

3. Why is it important that we understand the water cycle? In other words, why is it important to understand that the amount of water on Earth is constant and limited?

What Can I Do?

Go online and find out how you can help your local watershed district with its water conservation efforts by growing appropriate plants in your backyard. Go to *www.nrcs.usda.gov/feature/backyard/watercon.html.*

Author's Name: _____

Reviewers' Names: _____

Peer Evaluation Form

1. List all action verbs used.

2. Circle misspelled words.

3. What three steps of the water cycle does the water molecule travel through? Are they steps that follow one another in the water cycle?

4. Is there at least one paragraph per step? Are there three or more sentences per paragraph?

5. Are there good transitions between the paragraphs? Does each paragraph move smoothly into the next paragraph?

6. What did you particularly like about this story? (Make at least TWO positive comments.)

7. How can the author improve her/his work? (Give at least TWO helpful suggestions.)

BLM 11.2: Rainy Day Tales—Scoring Sheet

Date_____   Activity 11: Rainy Day Tales

Name: _____

Scoring Sheet		
	Points Possible	**Points Earned**
I. Three consecutive steps of the water cycle	10	
II. Five action verbs	5	
III. Illustration	10	
IV. Grammar, spelling, paragraph construction, etc.	15	
V. Overall creativity, originality	10	
VI. Rough draft	10	
Total Points Possible:	60	
	Total Grade:	

Teachers' Guide 11

BLM 11.3: Rainy Day Tales—Scoring Rubric

Date_____   Activity 11: Rainy Day Tales

Scoring Rubric			
Criteria	**Target**	**Acceptable**	**Unacceptable**
Steps of Hydrologic Cycle	The molecule travels through all three of the steps chosen.	The molecule travels through two of the steps chosen.	The molecule is described, and travels through one of the steps chosen.
Action Verbs	The action verbs used reflect knowledge of evaporation, condensation, transpiration, sublimation, and movement of water.	The action verbs used reflect knowledge of the movement of water.	The action verbs used only reflect a description of the water molecule's actions.
Paragraphs	Each paragraph accurately includes a step, action verbs to capture what the water molecule is doing, and a description of the state of the water molecule.	Each paragraph includes a step, action verbs for what the water molecule is doing, and a description of the water molecule.	The paragraphs do not have sufficient detail about steps, processes of the cycle, and state of the water molecule.
Science Content	The story uses correct scientific terms and the proper order of steps in the hydrologic cycle. The terms connect to one another and show how the system is closed and water is conserved.	The story uses correct scientific terms and the proper order of steps in the hydrologic cycle. The terms need to connect to one another and show how the system is closed and water is conserved.	The story describes the molecule without reference to the scientific steps or structure and state of the molecule.
Illustration	The illustration depicts the complete movement of the water molecule through all three steps chosen.	The illustration depicts the movement of the water molecule through two of the steps chosen.	The illustration shows the movement of the water molecule through one of the steps chosen.

Rainy Day Tales

What Is Happening?

The water cycle describes how water moves through the environment—a fundamental concept of weather. Activity 10 provides a model for students to explore the changing forms of water in the water cycle. This Activity combines learning this important science concept with creative writing skills, giving students a nontraditional way to consider the water cycle.

Before students begin writing, it may be useful to have a discussion about the weather patterns students are familiar with from television and radio. Discuss the origins of the moisture that falls as rain or snow, and be sure that students understand the terms *condensation, evaporation, precipitation,* and *transpiration*. The first three terms should be fairly well established from **Activity 10**.

Earth's supply of water is used over and over again and is considered to be conserved. Water moves in a cyclical pattern during which it is affected by a number of different processes. These processes include evaporation, sublimation, condensation, transportation, transpiration, and condensation. Evaporation is the transformation of water from a liquid into a gas. Sublimation is the transformation of water from solid ice to water vapor. Transportation is the movement of water through the atmosphere, along the surface of Earth, and underground. Transpiration is the evaporation of water from plants through stomata. Condensation is the transformation of water from a gas into a liquid.

Objective

Explore the ways water moves through Earth's hydrologic cycle.

Key Concept

II: Factors that contribute to weather

Materials

Each student will need:
- notebook paper
- blank white paper (for illustration)

Time

Three class periods of 50–60 minutes

How Do We Know This?

How do we know how much water exists on land and in the atmosphere?

Scientists use a variety of instruments to monitor and survey water on land. For example, Airborne Lidar Hydrography (ALH), echo sound sonar, Shallow Water Multibeam Sonars (SWMB), and digital side scan sonar are techniques and instruments used to survey the amount of water in oceans, lakes, rivers, and along coasts. Sonar can determine the depth of a pond or lake. Geometric calculations can then be used to determine the volume of water.

Scientists use other similar types of instruments to detect the amount of water vapor contained in the atmosphere. Water can exist in the atmosphere as liquid droplets, solid crystals or ice, or as vapor. Atmospheric water vapor can be detected using LIDAR sensors and GPS satellites using infrared sensors.

Preconceptions

Students may have the following preconceptions:

- Water is not conserved and it disappears or reappears magically.
- Supernatural events, such as angels crying, cause rain.
- Water molecules break apart and re-form during different steps of the hydrologic cycle.

What Students Need to Understand

- Water moves through the environment in a number of different pathways.
- The amount of water on Earth is constant and limited. Water that is used for drinking or bathing was at some point in time elsewhere in the environment.

Time Management

This Activity can be completed in three class periods of 50–60 minutes or less. A suggested schedule follows:

Day 1
Prewriting activity to generate a list of verbs that capture the movement of a water molecule through steps in the water cycle. Begin a rough draft.
Homework: Finish the rough draft.

Day 2
Peer Review: 3–4 students per group (Students can use **BLM 11.1** for this purpose.)
Homework: Make revisions and corrections to the rough draft based on comments from peer reviews.

Day 3
Prepare the final draft and illustration. (The final draft should be typed or in ink on one side of the paper.)
(The illustration should be colored and labeled.)
Share tales on a volunteer basis.

Preparation and Procedure

Ask students to read the background and procedure sections from the student materials. Discuss with students the steps of the water cycle that are depicted in the story at the beginning of the Activity. Explain to students that they will be writing their own story involving the water cycle.

As a prewriting activity, direct students to list 10 to 20 action verbs that capture the movement of a water molecule in different steps of the water cycle on a sheet of paper. These action verbs should reflect knowledge of evaporation, condensation, transpiration, sublimation, and movement of water. Some of these verbs will be used in students' stories. Provide an opportunity for students to share action verbs to build a bank of possible verb choices. You may wish to choose one of the parts of the water cycle listed in the Procedure section on the Student pages of this Activity and model the process of creating a story that follows a water molecule through the steps in this part of the water cycle. As you model the process, invite contributions from students to enhance their prewriting experience. Modeling the process and creating a rough draft with students will prepare them more effectively for their individual writing experiences and will ensure greater individual student success with this writing Activity. When the model rough draft is complete, review it to ensure that it has all the required components. As students participate in this group review of the necessary components, they learn how to check their own rough draft for these required elements.

When students have completed their rough drafts, divide the class into groups for peer review. A peer evaluation form is included as **BLM 11.1** for groups to use in reviewing each others' tales. On completion of the peer review, students should prepare their final drafts and illustrations. Illustrations should be in color.

Have students share their tales on a volunteer basis, and then have them turn in their final drafts as well as their rough drafts. A suggested scoring sheet and rubric are provided on **BLM 11.2** and **BLM 11.3**.

Extended Learning

- Students may wish to write other scenarios to trace water through alternative pathways.
- Have students investigate a local problem of water or air pollution and its effect on local and other water supplies. Encourage students to do research on how human activity affects the water cycle.
- Have students investigate the life cycle of a water droplet at their school. Students should go outside and imagine a water droplet falling from the sky and where it goes once it hits the roof. The students should diagram the movement of the droplet from the roof, through the downspouts, onto the ground, into the storm drain, down the culvert, into the receiving basin or pond, onto a field, into a stream that is part of a watershed, and finally down to the ocean. The idea is that the water and pollution at their school can end up miles away in someone else's backyard.
- Ditches, streams, and rivers connect with oceans even when the oceans are thousands of miles away. That means that any debris that begins in ditches, streams, and rivers can end up in the ocean and then onto a beach or in the gut of a marine mammal. Have students trace the potential path of a piece of trash from a nearby ditch or stream, downstream to the closest salt water. You may want to plan a cleanup of a beach or waterway near your school or in your local community. (See **Figure 11.2**.) If so, students can try to trace the likely path that particular items of debris may have taken prior to ending up along the beach or waterway.

Figure 11.2
Plan a cleanup program in your local community to pick up trash from beaches or along other bodies of water.

Interdisciplinary Study

This entire Activity is interdisciplinary as it involves teaching science through creative writing. It is also possible to involve literature in the Activity. For example, the poem "April Rain Song" by Langston Hughes may be used as an introduction to this Activity. You can find the text of Hughes's poem at *www.poemhunter.com/poem/april-rain-song*.

Differentiated Learning

- Provide students with options such as the following for depicting what happens to a water molecule on a trip through part of the water cycle:
  - creating a cartoon
  - creating a dramatization
  - creating an interview with a water molecule
  - creating an animated video
- Have students create an analogy between a water droplet in the water cycle with a water droplet going through the body, or a molecule within a rock going through the rock cycle.

Connections

Find out how analogies are used in geoscience. Read about the use of analogies and why they are good tools for learning at the following website: *http://serc.carleton.edu/NAGTWorkshops/metacognition/workshop08/participants/sibley.html*.

Answers to Student Questions

1. In the water cycle, water evaporates into the atmosphere and returns to Earth's surface as rain or snow. Here it may be temporarily stored in glaciers, lakes, underground reservoirs, or living things. Water then returns by the rivers to the oceans, or it is transpired or evaporated directly back into the atmosphere.

2. There is an almost infinite number of pathways through which water may flow in the environment. Expect some interesting answers to the second part of this question.

3. It is important to understand the water cycle because there is a finite amount of water on Earth. This results in an interdependence between people and the environment and a need to protect the cleanliness of the water supply.

Assessment

- At the beginning of the Activity, assess students' understanding of the water cycle by asking them questions about what they observed in their model of the hydrologic cycle in Activity 10.
- At the end of the Activity, you can assess the answers to student questions and students' stories using **BLM 11.2** and/or **BLM 11.3**.
- You can also assess students' understanding of the hydrologic cycle by presenting them with a copy of **Figure 11.1** and asking them to label the different processes in the cycle.

Resources

www.nrcs.usda.gov/feature/ backyard/watercon.html

www.poemhunter.com/poem/ april-rain-song

http://serc.carleton.edu/NAGT-Workshops/metacognition/ workshop08/participants/sibley. html

Activity 12 Planner

Activity 12 Summary

Students use hot water, ice, smoke, and aerosol to investigate what influences the formation of clouds in a jar.

Activity	Subject and Content	Objective	Materials
A Cloud in a Jar	Cloud formation	Investigate the conditions that must be present for clouds to form.	Each group of students will need: 1 L (or larger) clear glass jar with lid (large-mouth jars work best), ice cubes or crushed ice, hot water (very warm water will do), matches, can of aerosol spray (air freshener is suggested), black construction paper, safety goggles, flashlight (optional)

Time	Vocabulary	Key Concept	Margin Features
50–60 minutes	Cloud	II: Factors that contribute to weather	Safety Alert!, What Can I Do?, Fast Fact, Connections, Resources

Scientific Inquiry	Unifying Concepts and Processes	Technology	Personal/Social Perspectives	Historical Context
Modeling; asking questions	Cause and effect: mechanism; system and system models	Critical thinking, problem solving, and decision making	Populations, resources, and environments	Evidence of supporting a theory

A Cloud in a Jar

Background

Have you ever looked up in the sky and seen a cloud in the shape of an animal? Why are there so many different types of clouds that would allow you to make so many different animal shapes out of them? Clouds come in many shapes and sizes. Some clouds are rather flat and cover the entire sky; others may be small, white and fluffy; still others may be large, perhaps with lightning.

The names of clouds are determined by using Latin names, which describe the clouds in terms of their shape and height. For example, an altostratus cloud is a thin, layered cloud that forms between 2,000 km and 7,000 km above Earth. This particular cloud may have looked like a white lightning bolt flashing across the sky.

Regardless of the shape or size, certain conditions need to be present for a cloud to form. In this Activity, you will explore the conditions that must be present for clouds to form.

> **Vocabulary**
>
> **Cloud:** A large group of small water droplets and/or ice crystals in the atmosphere above Earth's surface.

Topic: clouds
Go to: *www.scilinks.org*
Code: PSCM 007

> **Objective**
> Investigate the conditions that must be present for clouds to form.

Activity 12

Materials

Each group of students will need:

- 1 L (or larger) clear glass jar with lid (large-mouth jars work best)
- ice cubes or crushed ice
- hot water (very warm water will do)
- matches
- can of aerosol spray (air freshener is suggested)
- black construction paper
- safety goggles
- flashlight (optional)

Time

50–60 minutes

SAFETY ALERT

1. Do not use water that is hot enough to burn your skin.

2. Be very careful when striking and using matches.

3. Wear safety goggles to protect your eyes when using matches and when using aerosol spray.

4. *Never* use matches around aerosol cans. Flames can cause aerosol cans to explode.

Procedure

1. Fill the jar with hot water and let it sit for about one minute.

2. Pour out most of the hot water, but leave about 2 cm of water in the bottom of the jar. Hold the black paper upright or prop it up against some books behind the jar. The black paper will make it easier to see the cloud.

3. Turn the lid of the jar upside down and fill it with ice.

4. Place the lid on the jar as shown in **Figure 12.1**. Observe the jar for three minutes. If you have a flashlight, darken the room and shine the flashlight on the jar while you observe it. You should find that a little cloud forms inside the jar. Record your observations in the box marked "Hot Water and Ice" on **BLM 12.1**.

5. Which aspects of the setup are needed to form the cloud? To find out, pour the water out of the jar and try the following variations:

   (a) Repeat steps 1–4, but do not place any ice on the lid. Record your observations in the box marked "Hot Water, No Ice" on **BLM 12.1**.

   (b) Repeat steps 1–4 with cold water instead of hot water and ice in the lid. Record your observations in the box marked "Cold Water and Ice" on **BLM 12.1**.

   (c) Repeat steps 1–4 with cold water instead of hot water and no ice. Record your observations in the box marked "Cold Water, No Ice" on **BLM 12.1**.

6. You will now investigate how the introduction of smoke impacts the production of the cloud. You will do this in two ways:

   (a) Pour out the water in the jar and repeat steps 1–3. Place the lid with ice on it within easy reach so that you can immediately cover the mouth of the jar during the next step.

   (b) Move all loose papers away from the jar. Put on your safety goggles, and then strike a match and drop the burning match into the jar. Cover the mouth of the jar immediately with the ice-filled lid. Record your observations in the box marked "Match" on **BLM 12.1**.

   (c) Repeat step 6a.

   (d) Spray a very small amount of the aerosol in the jar and immediately cover the mouth of the jar with the ice-filled lid. Observe what happens in the jar for three minutes and record your observations in the box marked "Aerosol" on **BLM 12.1**.

Figure 12.1
The black paper provides a dark contrast so that you can see the cloud forming.

Questions and Conclusions

1. Based on your observations, in which versions did a cloud form?

2. Based on your observations, was the ice needed to form a cloud?

3. Based on your observations, was hot water needed to form a cloud?

4. Do your observations support the notion that more water evaporates (from liquid to gas) when the water is warmer? Describe how your observations support your answer.

5. Do your observations support the notion that more water condenses (from gas to liquid) when the water vapor is colder? Describe how your observations support your answer.

6. What effect did the smoke and aerosol spray have on the formation of the cloud?

7. Look up the word *aerosol* in a dictionary and write the definition below the word on **BLM 12.1**.

8. Based on the definition of *aerosol*, would you classify smoke as an aerosol? Why or why not?

What Can I Do?

Clouds are very important in understanding the weather. Go online or use pictures of clouds and determine what each type of cloud means for impending weather. Clouds are typically divided into three different levels. Go to *www.srh.noaa.gov/jetstream/synoptic/clouds_max.htm*.

Fast Fact

The coldest temperature recorded at the top of a cloud was −102°C. This was recorded atop Tropical Cyclone Hilda east of Australia in 1990. The temperature 18,900 m below was 114°C warmer.

Trial	Observations
Hot Water and Ice	
Hot Water, No Ice	
Cold Water and Ice	
Cold Water, No Ice	
Match	
Aerosol	

A Cloud in a Jar

What Is Happening?

Three conditions are necessary for clouds to form: sufficient moisture in the air, cooling of the air, and suspended particles in the air. The first two conditions were investigated in previous Activities. The third condition requires a little more thought. Without suspended particles in the air, water vapor (moisture) will not condense to form the droplets that make up clouds because the evaporation rate from the curved surface of a tiny droplet is just too great. The suspended particles provide a condensation surface for the droplets. That is why they are called condensation nuclei.

At first glance, it may seem such nuclei are unnecessary, since it is possible to get a cloud to form without the introduction of smoke or other aerosols (airborne particulates). However, air is filled with many nuclei, even without the introduction of human-made aerosols. We just cannot see them.

How Do We Know This?

How do we know the conditions for cloud formation?

As mentioned in the Alternative Preparation section, the formation of clouds can be studied by using a chamber that is allowed to expand suddenly. The expansion lowers the temperature of the air inside the chamber because the air must expend energy to expand against the outside environment. Such expansion chambers have been used since 1875 when Paul Coulier, a French physician and chemist, used one to create water droplets from water vapor. He was also able to show that suspended dust particles aid in the formation of water droplets. Later, scientists used the chamber to show that droplet formation was much more difficult with dust-free air, reinforcing the view that both cooling and dust particles are necessary.

Nowadays, scientists can use satellite data to view cloud cover and atmospheric moisture. These data come from a variety of instruments, including regular cameras to multiangle imaging cameras that are based on NASA's satellite. This satellite uses nine viewing angles to measure the brightness, color, and contrast of reflected light. One result from the data collected is the regional and global impact of different types of particulate matter and clouds on climate. Researchers also use output from a chemical transport model to create images. The outputs from this instrument help scientists understand issues related to atmospheric composition such as particulate matter and cloud cover.

Objective
Investigate the conditions that must be present for clouds to form.

Key Concept
II: Factors that contribute to weather

Materials
Each group of students will need:
- 1 L (or larger) clear glass jar with lid (large-mouth jars work best)
- ice cubes or crushed ice
- hot water (very warm water will do)
- matches
- can of aerosol spray (air freshener is suggested)
- black construction paper
- safety goggles
- flashlight (optional)

Time
50–60 minutes

Condensation nuclei are small, usually about 0.1 micron in diameter. (A human hair is about 100 microns thick.) Common condensation nuclei include dust particles, salt from sea spray, pollen, and material ejected by volcanoes. Smoke can also act as condensation nuclei. That is why smog, a fog made up of industrial pollutants, is so common in industrial or highly populated areas.

For the most part, water droplets form only when the relative humidity reaches 100%, a point called saturation. To reach saturation, there needs to be a source of water vapor and a mechanism for cooling the water vapor. In this Activity, the source of water vapor is the hot water. Cold water also provides water vapor but not as much, since the evaporation rate is greater when the water is warmer. The mechanism for cooling is provided by the ice.

With certain particles, like the smoke, some condensation can occur when the relative humidity is a little less than 100%. This means that less cooling is needed to see the effect with the smoke particles, which enhances the effect. This is also why smog is greater when the humidity is higher.

Preconceptions

Students may have the following preconceptions:
- Clouds move because we move.
- Clouds come from somewhere above the sky.
- The Sun boils the sea to create water vapor.
- Clouds are made of cotton, wool, or smoke.
- Clouds are made of bubbles.
- Clouds are made of water vapor, not liquid or solid water.

What Students Need to Understand

- Three conditions are necessary for cloud formation: cooling of air, water vapor, and condensation nuclei.
- Water vapor must have something to condense on to form the droplets that compose clouds.
- Condensation nuclei are very small. We cannot see them.
- There are more than enough condensation nuclei in the atmosphere for clouds to form without human-made sources. Many things can serve as condensation nuclei. Some of the most common include dust, pollen, salt from ocean spray, and smoke.

Time Management

This Activity can be done in a class period of 50–60 minutes or less; however, the Activity should be conducted as two separate parts (steps 1–5, and then step 6). All students should complete the trial with matches, *and then the matches should be removed* before doing the trial with the aerosol can.

Preparation and Procedure

Before the lesson begins, discuss cloud formation with the class to determine students' ideas about how clouds form. Ask students what they think a cloud is made of; then ask them how a cloud forms.

Be sure that all materials are either centrally located or already distributed to the groups of students. Perhaps students could bring clear glass jars, such as mayonnaise jars, pickle jars, canning jars, and so on, from home. The jars do not have to all be the same shape, but clear glass works the best. The larger the mouth of the jar, the better the Activity works. If condensation on the inside of the bottle makes it difficult to observe the cloud, the lid can be removed after a minute or so, allowing the cloud to flow out of the jar. If no cloud is observed without the addition of smoke, you can try adding a few drops of isopropyl alcohol to the water. Alcohol evaporates quickly, enhancing the formation of the cloud.

Depending on students, you may choose to light all matches for them to reduce the risk of accidents and the temptation for horseplay. *Be careful. Flames and aerosol cans are an explosive combination. Students must never have access to both the matches and the aerosol at the same time*. If, in your opinion, this represents too great a risk for students, it is strongly recommended that the aerosol not be used at all. The important points of the Activity can still be made using only the smoke trial.

SAFETY ALERT

1. Do not use water that is hot enough to burn your skin.

2. Be very careful when striking and using matches.

3. Wear safety goggles to protect your eyes when using matches and when using aerosol spray.

4. *Never* use matches around aerosol cans. Flames can cause aerosol cans to explode.

Alternative Preparation

There are several other ways to carry out this Activity.

1. Use a plastic bottle. Put 2 cm of warm water into a 1–2 liter plastic bottle. Screw on the cap, squeeze the bottle hard, and release it to make the air contract and expand. Do this several times. You may see a cloud form as you release the bottle and let it expand. The air cools as the bottle expands, in much the same way that air cools as it rises into regions of lower pressure and expands. To illustrate the impact of smoke, unscrew the cap, put on goggles, light a match, and quickly drop it into the bottle. Again, seal the bottle and then squeeze and release the bottle several times. To remove condensation that forms on the bottle itself, slosh the water around inside the bottle while squeezing the bottle.

2. Instead of a plastic bottle, you can use a glass jar with a sheet of rubber or balloon placed over the opening (use a rubber band to seal it). By pressing into the rubber and releasing, you can compress and expand the air inside.

Extended Learning

• The jar in this Activity represents a small cloud chamber. Building a much bigger cloud chamber would make an excellent project. Students might also try using other things as condensation nuclei (e.g., chalk dust).

Connections

In the late 1940s, Nobel Laureate Irving Langmuir and atmospheric scientist Vincent Schaeffer demonstrated that humans could modify the weather by "seeding" clouds, forcing them to release precipitation. This can be done with dry ice, silver iodide, and sea salt. Cloud seeding is best used on clouds made up of supercooled water droplets (droplets that exist as water, even though the temperature is below freezing).

Resources

www.srh.noaa.gov/jetstream/synoptic/clouds_max.htm

www.ghcc.msfc.nasa.gov/GOES/goeseastconuswv.html

http://famouspoetsandpoems.com/poets/percy_bysshe_shelley/poems/12280

http://cloudappreciationsociety.org/category/cloud-poetry

www.osdpd.noaa.gov/ml/air/clouds.html

http://wvscience.org/clouds/Cloud_Key.pdf

• Students can view infrared water vapor images from satellites. These are real-time images at different times. Go to *www.ghcc.msfc.nasa.gov/GOES/goeseastconuswv.html*.

Interdisciplinary Study

• The poem "The Cloud" by Percy Bysshe Shelley could be used as an introduction to this Activity. You can find the text for this poem at *http://famouspoets andpoems.com/poets/percy_bysshe_shelley/poems/12280*.

You can find more cloud poems at *http://cloudappreciationsociety.org/category/cloud-poetry*.

Differentiated Learning

• To help ESL students understand the steps in the procedure, pair them with students who are proficient English language users. Model how students can read each step aloud and run their finger along under the text before completing the action required by each step so that ESL students can associate the oral sound of words with their written forms. Reading each step aloud and then performing the required task will enhance ESL students' understanding.

• The hands-on, visual nature of this Activity will help ESL students understand the concepts. When discussing the concepts involved in this Activity, sketch and label diagrams to enhance understanding. Have ESL students record their observations on **BLM 12.1** as sketches.

• For students who have difficulty understanding cloud formation, they should be directed to cloud types and their properties. They can develop their own cloud chart that depicts the different types. A graphic organizer would help them sort the different cloud types into groups by their properties.

• For students who finish this Activity early, they can research the different instruments and views of water vapor and clouds that scientists use to study the weather and atmosphere. Go to *www.osdpd.noaa.gov/ml/air/clouds.html*.

• For students who finish this Activity early, they can collect pictures from magazines that have clouds in them and classify them using a dichotomous key. Go to *http://wvscience.org/clouds/Cloud_Key.pdf*.

Answers to Student Questions

1. A cloud should have formed in the "Hot Water and Ice," the "Smoke," and the "Aerosol" versions.

2. Yes, if ice was not used, a cloud did not form.

3. Yes, if hot water was not used, a cloud did not form.

4. Yes, more water evaporates when the water is warmer, as the cold water trials did not produce a cloud. Apparently, not enough water vapor was produced.

5. Yes, more water condenses when the water vapor is colder, as the trials without ice did not produce a cloud. Apparently, the water vapor needs to cool to produce condensation.

6. The smoke and aerosol spray produced a thicker and more noticeable cloud.

7. Aerosol is a suspension of fine solid or liquid particles in gas.

8. Yes, smoke can be classified as an aerosol because it is made up of fine solid particles in gas.

Assessment

• At the beginning of the Activity, determine students' understanding of cloud formation by having them explain the conditions necessary for the cloud to form.
• During the Activity, make sure students record their observations for each trial on **BLM 12.1**.
• At the end of the Activity, you can assess the answers to student questions.

Activity 13 Planner

Activity 13 Summary

Students will learn how to measure the dew point of air.

Activity	Subject and Content	Objective	Materials
Just Dew It!	Dew point	Determine the dew point of the air.	Each group of students will need: Celsius thermometer (alcohol), shiny can with top removed (aluminum cans work well), glass stirring rod or wooden stirrer, water at room temperature, ice (crushed or cubes work best)

Time	Vocabulary	Key Concept	Margin Features
50–60 minutes	Humidity, Saturation, Dew point	II: Factors that contribute to weather	Safety Alert!, Fast Fact, What Can I Do?, Connections, Resources

Scientific Inquiry	Unifying Concepts and Processes	Technology	Personal/Social Perspectives	Historical Context
Collecting, analyzing, and interpreting data; asking questions	Cause and effect: mechanism; energy and matter: flows	Critical thinking, problem solving, and decision making	Scientific perspective of nature	Changing understanding of science

Just Dew It!

Background

If you watch the local news, you have probably heard meteorologists talk about the humidity as well as the temperature. In many locations, the **humidity** varies from day to day, with some days "humid" and other days "dry." In other locations, it is always humid or always dry. What does this mean?

The humidity represents the amount of moisture (in the form of water vapor) that is in the air. There is always some moisture in the air, even in the desert. Most of the water vapor gets into the air by evaporation, largely from the ocean, but also from lakes, rivers, ponds, and even puddles. Temperature is a major factor in determining how much and how rapidly water will evaporate from these places. The warmer it is, the more water will evaporate. Because of this, at any location, there will probably be more water vapor during warm weather than during cold weather.

There *is* a maximum amount of water vapor that can exist in the air. At that point, it can be stated that the air is "saturated" with water vapor. The amount of water vapor at **saturation** depends on the temperature. The warmer it is, the greater the amount of water vapor that can be present.

In this Activity, you will use the fact that the amount of water vapor at saturation depends on the temperature to determine how humid the air is. The method involves cooling the air. If you cool the air enough, the water vapor begins to condense and form water droplets. The temperature at which this happens is called the **dew point**.

The less water vapor there is in the air, the more it has to

> **Vocabulary**
>
> **Humidity:** A measure of the amount of water vapor.
>
> **Saturation:** The condition where the maximum amount of water vapor is present.
>
> **Dew point:** Temperature at which water vapor will condense if air is cooled.

Topic: clouds and fog
Go to: *www.scilinks.org*
Code: PSCM 008

> ## Objective
> Determine the dew point of the air.

Activity 13

Materials

Each group of students will need:

- Celsius thermometer (alcohol)
- shiny can with top removed (aluminum cans work well)
- glass stirring rod or wooden stirrer
- water at room temperature
- ice (crushed or cubes work best)

Time

50–60 minutes

Figure 13.1
Bromeliads are plants that have overlapping leaves that form a basin for dew to collect. The plant eventually absorbs the water that collects in the basin.

SAFETY ALERT

1. Be careful when working with thermometers. They are made of glass and may break.

2. The tops of the cans may have sharp edges. Be careful when handling them.

be cooled to make the water vapor condense. Because of this, the dew point provides a measure of the amount of water vapor in the air. On days when the air temperature and the dew point are very close to each other, we say that the air is "humid." If, for example, the air temperature is 30°C and the dew point is 25°C, there is much more water vapor in the air than on a day when the air temperature is the same, but the dew point is 5°C. We are most likely to notice water vapor on very humid, warm days, when we feel clammy or sticky because all the water vapor surrounding us prevents our perspiration from evaporating easily.

Procedure

1. Measure the air temperature with your thermometer. Record this value in the column labeled "Air Temperature (°C)" on **BLM 13.1**.

2. Fill the shiny can half full with water at room temperature. Allow the can to sit for one minute. If condensation forms on the outside of the can, replace the water with warmer water until no condensation forms.

3. Place the thermometer in the can with the water as shown in **Figure 13.2**.

4. Slowly add small pieces of ice to the can while using the glass rod or wooden stirrer to slowly and gently stir the ice in the water. Watch the outside of the can closely for the first sign of condensation.

5. When condensation begins, immediately record the temperature of the water in the can in the column labeled "Dew Point (°C)" on **BLM 13.1**.

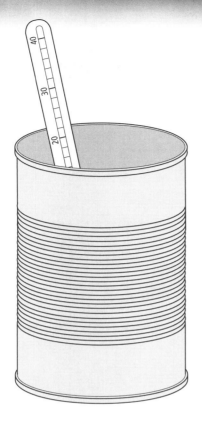

Fast Fact

When winter arrives, the cool air from the outside is heated inside our homes. The heated cool air from the outside may only have a relative humidity of 5%, which is as dry as the air in the Sahara Desert.

Figure 13.2
The setup uses an aluminum can and a thermometer.

6. If the temperature in the room is fairly constant, repeat steps 2 through 5 twice more. Record your data beside "Trial 2" and "Trial 3" on **BLM 13.1**. Before you begin each trial, wipe out the inside of the cans or use warm water to allow them to warm to room temperature.

7. Find the average dew point by adding the three individual dew points and dividing the sum by three. Record the result on **BLM 13.1**.

Questions and Conclusions

1. By how many degrees would the air have to cool to reach the dew point you just determined?

2. If you did this Activity again tomorrow and found that the dew point had increased, would this indicate that there was more or less moisture (water vapor) in the air? Why? (Assume the air temperature is the same.)

3. Under what conditions would the air temperature and the dew point be the same?

4. At what time of day are you most likely to find dew? Why?

5. Where do you normally see dew?

6. How does this Activity show that dew does not fall from the sky like rain?

What Can I Do?

Mapping regional dew points can give you insight about moving humid air and how this air may change with the passage of fronts and other weather systems. You can get dew point maps of the United States from the Weather Underground at *www.wunderground.com/ US/Region/US/Dewpoint. html*.

Dew Point Data Table

Air Temperature (°C)	Trial	Dew Point (°C)
	1	
	2	
	3	
Average Dew Point (°C)		

Just Dew It!

What Is Happening?

The amount of water vapor that can exist depends on the air temperature. For any given temperature, there is a maximum amount of water vapor that can be present before the vapor begins to condense. The maximum amount increases rapidly as temperature increases. (See **Figure 13.3**.)

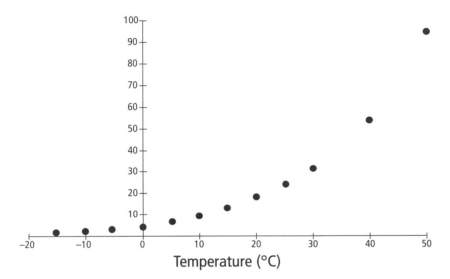

Figure 13.3
The maximum amount of water vapor that can exist varies with the temperature.

Objective
Determine the dew point of the air.

Key Concepts
II: Factors that contribute to weather

Materials
Each group of students will need:
- Celsius thermometer (alcohol)
- shiny can with top removed (aluminum cans work well)
- glass stirring rod or wooden stirrer
- water at room temperature
- ice (crushed or cubes work best)

Time
50–60 minutes

How Do We Know This?

How do we know there is water vapor in the air?

The first device for measuring humidity was invented by Cardinal Nicholas de Cusa in the 15th century. It used a piece of wool, which became heavier when it was humid due to the water that was absorbed by the wool. At the time, it was not recognized that water vapor was a distinct gas in the atmosphere. That insight did not come until Daniel Bernoulli's kinetic theory of gases in 1738 (although his theory was generally ignored until the following century). Nowadays, there are many different methods for measuring the water vapor content of the air. For example, the air can be sent through a wet cloth. The evaporation of the water into the air cools the air. The lower the humidity, the more the air is cooled. The humidity can be then be determined by comparing the temperature of the air passing through the wet cloth (called the wet bulb temperature) with the actual air temperature (called the dry bulb temperature).

More water vapor can exist when the air is warm than when the air is cool. Air is saturated when the maximum amount of water vapor is present. This saturation point can be obtained in two ways. One way is to continue evaporating water so that the amount of water vapor increases. The other more common way is to cool the air. The temperature at which air is then saturated is identified as the dew point. When the dew point is very close to the air temperature, the air's high humidity becomes easily noticeable.

In areas with many hot and humid days, the dew point is often given by meteorologists not only as a measure of the humidity, but also as a kind of "comfort index." On hot days when the air temperature and the dew point are close, working outdoors can be very uncomfortable because the air is nearly saturated. When air is nearly saturated, evaporation is slowed dramatically. As a result, perspiration from our bodies is prevented from evaporating, and our cooling mechanism is impaired.

If the air temperature and the dew point are known, "relative humidity" can be calculated. Relative humidity is the ratio of the amount of water vapor *actually* in the air to the maximum amount that could *possibly* be in the air at that temperature. When the dew point and the air temperature are close to each other, the relative humidity will be high. When they are the same, the relative humidity is 100%.

Dew forms by essentially the same process as clouds and raindrops. When moist air is cooled enough and condensation nuclei are present, water droplets will form in the atmosphere, creating clouds. Dew is the condensation of water vapor, not around nuclei in the air but on the surfaces of objects around us.

Dew typically starts to form after sunset when the air begins to cool. How dew forms was a puzzle for many years. It was solved when scientists realized that air contains water vapor, even the air in deserts. During the day, the Sun warms the ground and the air above it. At night, the ground cools by radiating its heat into the sky. On cloudy nights, this radiant heat is absorbed by the water in the atmosphere and radiated back to the ground, and no dew is formed. On clear nights, the radiant heat is lost to space and the ground cools quickly, cooling the air above it. If the temperature of the air reaches its dew point, then water vapor will condense.

Measuring how much water condenses as dew is difficult to determine because the quantity is so small. In dry climates like deserts, dew probably accounts for most of the precipitation in that area. Scientists have used a block of gypsum to measure the amount of water vapor in the air by weighing the dry block before dew formation, and then again after dew has formed. The difference is the amount of water absorbed as dew.

Preconceptions

Students sometimes have a difficult time understanding where dew comes from. The preconceptions may come from observing condensation on the outside of their cup or glass. Many students may think that the water passes through the container to the outside. Students may have the following preconceptions:

- Dew forms on grass every night.
- Dew is another form of rain or precipitation.
- Dew falls from clouds.
- If water vapor is in the air, you can see it. (Students think that water vapor is visible (like a cloud). Subsequently, they think that clouds are made of water vapor (as opposed to liquid).)
- The maximum amount of water vapor that can exist depends on how much air is present (i.e., it depends on how much "space" is available between the air molecules).

What Students Need to Understand

- The maximum amount of water vapor that can be present depends on the air temperature.
- Dew point is a measure of the amount of water vapor in the air. For a specific temperature, a higher dew point means more water vapor is present.
- Relative humidity is a measure of the actual amount of water vapor in the air relative to the maximum amount of water vapor that can be present at its temperature. When the relative humidity is 100%, the air is saturated.

Time Management

This Activity can be completed in 50–60 minutes or less. It can be done in one class period or conducted on different days over the course of several weeks, as the humidity conditions change due to outside weather and the presence of storm systems.

Preparation and Procedure

Prior to beginning the Activity, ask students what they know about dew and its formation. Ask students if they have seen any plants that collect water on the inside of their overlapping leaves. Show them pictures of bromeliads. Ask students if they have ever seen a spider web wet with droplets of water that glistened in the sunlight. Record students' background knowledge about dew and its formation in the K column of a K-W-L chart. (See **Figure 13.4**.) Be sure to accept all comments.

Ask students what they want to learn about the formation of dew and record their questions in the W column of the K-W-L chart. Return to the K-W-L chart at the conclusion of the Activity and record in the L column what students learned about the formation of dew and dew points. Correct any misinformation in the K column and see which questions they are able to answer from the W column.

Topic: _____		
What Do You *Know*?	**What Do You *Want* to Know?**	**What Did You *Learn*?**

Figure 13.4
Numerous KWL graphic organizers such as this are available online by searching for "KWL chart."

You should check the dew point yourself, especially during winter months. Indoors, the dew point in winter can be below 0°C at times. When the dew point is below 0°C, this Activity will not work.

Be sure the materials are centrally located so that each group of students can easily access them. Soup cans or fruit and vegetable cans work best. Since opened cans often are extremely sharp, you should carefully inspect each can before use and caution students to handle them carefully. Use alcohol-filled thermometers, and warn students about the dangers of breaking the glass surrounding the alcohol. Crushed or cubed ice will work for the Activity. It is somewhat easier to add small amounts of crushed ice. It is best to start with room temperature water because sometimes tap water is cold enough to cause condensation by itself.

Alternative Preparation

This Activity could be done as a demonstration. If so, have students observe and record the temperatures.

An alternate procedure can also be followed, as shown in **Figure 13.5**:

1. Place crushed ice in a small aluminum can (8 oz.).

2. Place the can inside another larger can, such as a coffee can. Place this can on top of a one-inch piece of cardboard or wooden block.

3. Place a thermometer inside the larger can.

4. When dew forms, record the temperature. This temperature is the dew point.

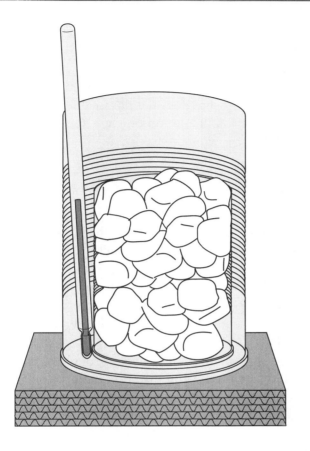

Figure 13.5
This setup uses one small can of crushed ice inside a larger can.

Extended Learning

• This Activity leads naturally into a discussion of relative humidity. Have students find the relationship between temperature, dew point, and relative humidity. For more information on this topic, see Activity 15. In fact, there are tables that allow you to determine the relative humidity of the atmosphere from the dew point and the air temperature. Try different methods of determining relative humidity and compare the results. Students could measure dew point and temperature and create their own tables.

• Have students determine the relative humidity from an online calculator. If students know the temperature and the dew point, the online calculator will give them the relative humidity. Go to *www.hpc.ncep.noaa.gov/html/ dewrh.shtml*.

• Have students look at relative humidity as a variable to use for weather forecasting. Go to *www.weather.gov/forecasts/graphical/sectors/conus.php*. If you click on the relative humidity tab, you can then click on the next tab to see the forecast for relative humidity.

Interdisciplinary Study

The poem "Snail" by Langston Hughes might be used to introduce the topic of dew point. Students can be asked to investigate whether snails actually drink dew. Also in the poem, what does the phrase "dew drop's mystery" mean? The text for the poem can be found on page 4 at *www.poetryfoundation.org/downloads/BHM_Elementary.pdf*.

Differentiated Learning

- Have students complete this activity at home. Set two pieces of black paper outside on the ground. Late in the day, when dew is likely to form, set up an umbrella so that it shades one of the black pieces of paper. At sunset, start checking the pieces of paper for any apparent signs of moisture. Continue checking every half hour. Dew may form on one but not the other—but which one? If this experiment is done on different and consecutive nights, there may be some nights that no dew is formed, so doing this experiment on several nights may be worthwhile.

- Patterns in weather are often displayed through maps. These maps are used to show patterns over time and distance. Patterns of data, such as temperature, dew point, wind speed, and pressure, show the presence and movement of storm fronts and other weather patterns. Have students locate maps of various weather data, including water vapor. Have students create a map of dew points across the United States at the National Weather Service JetStream Online School for Weather. This activity can also be used to allow students to develop the idea of isopleths, which show equal values for data. Go to *www.srh.noaa.gov/jetstream/synoptic/ll_analyze_dp.htm*.

Answers to Student Questions

1. This depends on students' data. The answer is obtained by subtracting the average dew point from the measured air temperature.

2. It would indicate that there is more moisture in the air because the air would not have to be cooled as much to reach the point where it would be saturated. This means that there must be more water vapor in the air to begin with.

3. Air temperature and dew point would be the same in a cloud or fog. It is a preconception that it rains every time the air becomes saturated with water vapor. It is also a preconception that the air at ground level is saturated every time it rains. Often, the air just beneath a raining cloud is not saturated.

4. You are most likely to find dew in the early morning because the objects on which dew collects have cooled overnight while the Sun is not shining on them. These cool surfaces lower the surrounding air temperature to their dew point, just like the can in this Activity.

5. You normally see dew on any surface on which it is cool enough for water vapor in the air to condense (for example, grass, cars, metal railings, spider webs).

6. Dew formed on the can without any water "falling" from the air. It simply condensed there from water vapor in the surrounding air.

Assessment

- At the beginning of the Activity, assess students' background knowledge about dew and its formation by using a K-W-L chart. (See **Figure 13.4**.)
- During the Activity, make sure students record the temperature data properly. If students have varying temperatures on their trials, have them start over with a dry, clean can.
- At the end of the Activity, you can assess the answers to student questions.
- At the end of the Activity, you might also want to take two to three concepts from the K column of the K-W-L chart and have students determine if the statement is correct.

Resources

www.wunderground.com/US/Region/US/Dewpoint.html

www.hpc.ncep.noaa.gov/html/dewrh.shtml

www.weather.gov/forecasts/graphical/sectors/conus.php

www.poetryfoundation.org/downloads/BHM_Elementary.pdf

www.airbestpractices.com/industries/medical/importance-dewpoint-medical-air-systems

www.srh.noaa.gov/jetstream/synoptic/ll_analyze_dp.htm

Activity 14 Planner

Activity 14 Summary

Students investigate why snow forms as crystals.

Activity	Subject and Content	Objective	Materials
Let's Make Frost	Water vapor and frost	Relate the formation of crystals to the phase change from vapor to solid.	Each group of students will need: aluminum or tin can (8 oz.) with the top removed (black cans work best), 10 g table salt, 4 oz. crushed ice

Time	Vocabulary	Key Concept	Margin Features	
30 minutes	Frost, Snow, Deposition	II: Factors that contribute to weather	Safety Alert!, What Can I Do?, Fast Fact, Connections, Resources	

Scientific Inquiry	Unifying Concepts and Processes	Technology	Personal/Social Perspectives	Historical Context
Collecting, analyzing, and interpreting data; asking questions	Cause and effect: mechanism; energy and matter: flows	Critical thinking, problem solving, and decision making	Scientific perspective of nature	Changing understanding of science

Let's Make Frost

Background

Snowflakes are made of ice. We think of ice as being frozen water. However, if you have ever seen a snowflake, chances are you have noticed that snowflakes do not look like most examples of frozen water we are used to seeing (e.g., ice cubes, icicles, ice skating rinks). Instead, they look like little crystals. In fact, if you were asked to draw a picture of a snowflake, you would probably draw a six-sided star, rather than a frozen drop of water.

Snow looks like it is made up of little crystals because they are indeed crystals. In this Activity, you will investigate why snow is made up of crystals. You will do this by forming frost. The process for forming **frost** is the same as the process for forming snowflakes, except that frost forms on surfaces (like leaves and windows) whereas **snow** forms on very tiny particles in the air.

To form the frost, you need to have a very cold surface. It has to be so cold that the temperature of the surface is below freezing. As you know from previous Activities, water vapor exists in the air. When the water vapor is cooled, it can condense and form droplets. If the droplets form on surfaces, it is called dew. What happens if the water vapor is cooled to a temperature below the freezing point?

> ### Vocabulary
> **Frost:** Ice crystals produced by the **deposition** of water vapor directly upon a surface at or below the freezing point of water.
>
> **Snow:** Ice crystals produced by the **deposition** of water vapor directly upon a particle in the air.
>
> **Deposition:** The process by which water changes phase directly from a vapor into a solid without first becoming a liquid.

Topic: phases of matter
Go to: *www.scilinks.org*
Code: PSCM 009

> ### Objective
> Relate the formation of crystals to the phase change from vapor to solid.

Activity 14

What Can I Do?

Prepare for an early or late frost or freeze by preparing your house and yard. Search for "Preparing for a Frost" at *www.hgtv.com*.

Fast Fact

Certain valleys can be markedly colder than surrounding areas because cold air, being more dense, routinely drains into them. The colder air results in a different climate (called a microclimate) with different plants than the surrounding areas. These valleys are called frost hollows (or frost pockets) because they are more likely to experience frost than surrounding areas.

Procedure

1. Fill a can halfway with crushed ice and add approximately 10 g of salt (the salt is used to keep the temperature below the freezing point of water).

2. Observe the outside of the can for the first signs of frost. When the first signs appear, describe what they look like and record your observations. Is the frost liquid or solid?

3. Continue observing the outside of the can for several minutes. Is the frost growing? Describe what you observe.

Questions and Conclusions

1. Where did the moisture come from that formed on the outside of the can?

2. Did the moisture first appear as solid or as liquid? Why do you think this happened?

3. As the frost grew, did it seem to first appear as a liquid that then froze, or did it first appear as a solid?

4. Why is frost not the same as frozen dew? What would frozen dew look like? (Think about the phase changes involved.)

5. What might happen if the same process of frost formation occurs high up in the atmosphere?

6. Compare and contrast the difference between dew and frost by completing the graphic organizer on **BLM 14.1**.

1. Overall Concept

2. Concept

2. Concept

3. Characteristics

3. Characteristics

4. Like Characteristics

5. Unlike Characteristics

5. Unlike Characteristics

6. Summary

Let's Make Frost

What Is Happening?

Dew or frost will form when the air cools to the point at which the air is saturated with water vapor (gas). The air temperature will determine whether dew (liquid) or frost (solid) will form. In the example of dew, the temperature is at or above 0°C. The process starts when the invisible air vapor molecules slow their movement. Some water molecules move slowly to combine with other vapor molecules to start forming tiny, visible drops of water. Water molecules still evaporate, but more vapor molecules condense resulting in a net creation of liquid.

In the example of frost, the temperature is 0°C or colder. Salt was added to the ice to lower the melting point of water and allow the temperature of the ice/water mixture to stay below 0°C. This is the difference between this Activity and **Activity 13**. The process starts when the invisible air vapor molecules slow down enough to form ice crystals, a process called deposition. Water molecules still transition from solid back to vapor (a process called sublimation), but more vapor molecules undergo deposition leading to a net creation of ice crystals, which begin to form on leaves and other cold objects. In comparison, when dew freezes, it creates solid ice drops or a glaze of clear ice. This process is shown in **Figure 14.1**.

Objective
Relate the formation of crystals to the phase change from vapor to solid.

Key Concept
II: Factors that contribute to weather

Materials
Each group of students will need:
- aluminum or tin can (8 oz.) with the top removed (black cans work best)
- 10 g table salt
- 4 oz. crushed ice

Time
30 minutes

How Do We Know This?

How do we predict when frost will form?
   Weather sensors are used to collect a myriad of data about the local weather. These sensors collect precipitation amounts, temperature, humidity, wind speed and direction, and barometric pressure. Collectively, the data can determine if frost will form.

Preconceptions

Students sometimes think that frost falls from the sky as solid particles. Ask students, "Do you remember cutting out a snowflake from paper? What did it look like? How do you think actual snowflakes are formed?" Students may have the following preconceptions:

- Frost is frozen dew.
- Frost and dew are forms of precipitation.
- Frost and dew fall from the sky.
- Snow is the result of raindrops freezing.

What Students Need to Understand

- Frost, like dew, is not a form of precipitation and therefore does not fall from the sky.
- The crystalline appearance of frost and snowflakes is due to the fact that they form when water vapor, a gas, deposits as ice crystals, a solid. This is a phase change.
- For frost to form, the air must be saturated with moisture and the temperature must be at or below the freezing point of water.

Time Management

This Activity can be done in 30 minutes

Preparation and Procedure

Before the lesson begins, discuss the formation of frost with the class to determine students' ideas about how frost forms. Ask questions such as the following: Where does frost come from? What is the difference between frost and snow? Do you know what a frost fern or a frost hoar is? (These are the shapes that frost makes when water vapor cools to form ice crystals on glass surfaces.) You may wish to begin with a K-W-L chart. Record students' background knowledge about frost and its formation in the K column of the chart. Be sure to accept all comments. Ask students what they want to learn about the formation of frost and record their questions in the W column of the chart. Return to the K-W-L chart at the conclusion of the Activity and record what students learned about the formation of frost in the L column. Correct any misinformation in the K column and see which questions students are able to answer from the W column.

This Activity will work best on a day with a relatively high humidity. In the middle of winter, particularly if it is very cold outside, there may not be sufficient water vapor in the air to produce enough frost on the sides of the can. Along the same lines, dehumidifiers (like those used with air-conditioning in the summer) may remove the moisture needed to show a lot of frost formation.

Soup cans work well for this Activity. Remove the tops with a can opener. Use care when removing the tops, and cover or remove sharp edges. A can that is painted black works well to enhance the observations of the frost formation, but unpainted cans work well, too. Make sure you add enough salt to lower the melting point of the ice.

SAFETY ALERT
The tops of the cans may have sharp edges. Be careful when handling them.

Alternative Preparation

Crystals can be formed when salts and minerals "condense" out of a solution, a process that can be illustrated using Epsom salts. In this Activity, Epsom salts will crystalize and appear like "frost" on a piece of glass. You will need access to a stove and the following materials:

- 1 cup Epsom salts (available at your local pharmacy)
- 1 cup water
- 1 quart heat-proof container
- liquid dishwashing detergent
- small paintbrush
- piece of glass or a window
- spoon

Follow these steps:

1. Add 1 cup of water to a heat-proof container.

2. Heat the water to boiling.

3. Gradually add Epsom salts and stir while keeping the solution boiling.

4. Add Epsom salts and stir until the Epsom salts will no longer dissolve and can be seen settling to the bottom of the container. This makes a supersaturated solution.

5. Remove the container from the heat, add some liquid dishwashing detergent, and stir.

6. Let the mixture cool.

7. "Paint" the solution on a window or piece of glass with a paintbrush. When the solution dries, needlelike crystal fan patterns will appear, looking like "frost" on the window.

Extended Learning

- Challenge students to determine the conditions at which dew would form on the can, and compare the results with the conditions at which frost forms on the can.
- Have students investigate the saying, "It is too cold to snow."
- Have students determine why Antarctica is considered a desert.
- Have students explore the differences between snow, sleet, freezing rain, and hail.
- The process of sublimation (the reverse of the process examined in this Activity) can be illustrated with "dry ice." Dry ice is solid carbon dioxide, and it goes from the solid phase directly to the gas phase. No puddles of liquid carbon dioxide are left on the table when it sublimates.
- The addition of salt to ice lowers the melting point of ice so that the ice/water mixture can exist at temperatures below 0°C. The same principle is used to make ice cream. The salt added to the ice cools the cream faster and to a lower temperature so that the ice cream can form. The following ice cream–making activity is a fun activity to highlight the phase change of water and begin a discussion on colligative properties of solutions. Colligative properties are properties of a solution that depend mainly on the relative numbers of solute particles, and not on the detailed properties of the molecules themselves. Whole cream works the best for making ice cream. The formation of ice cream will take approximately 10–15 minutes. The more salt and ice added to the bag, the quicker the cream will freeze. You will need the following materials:

- sandwich-size plastic bag
- gallon-size plastic bag
- 3 oz. of sugar
- 15 ml half-and-half (half cream and half milk) or milk
- flavoring (such as vanilla)
- ice (enough to half fill the gallon-size plastic bag)
- 15 g salt or rock salt

1. In a plastic sealable sandwich bag, add 3 oz. of sugar and 50 ml of milk or half-and-half. Add some flavoring if you have it. Seal the bag.

2. In a larger gallon-sized bag, add 15 g of salt or rock salt and fill the bag halfway with ice.

3. Place the smaller sealed plastic bag inside the larger bag.

4. Shake and roll the bag over and over until the contents of the inside bag freeze. *Be careful not to push down or squeeze the bag too hard.*

Interdisciplinary Study

The weather is intimately tied to other science disciplines. Many educators integrate content from different disciplines so that students learn concepts in the context of nature rather than learning concepts in isolation. In this activity, students will simulate the process of frost shattering or wedging. Water seeps into tiny cracks in rocks and freezes. When water freezes, it expands with enough force to shatter boulders. Frost shattering helps create smaller fragments of rocks and can ultimately lead to soil development. Have students complete this simple activity to show how weather impacts and integrates with geologic processes.

- Take a small stone that has crevices (granite, conglomerate, or sandstone) and place it in a cup of water to soak overnight.
- Place the soaked rock into a plastic bag, seal it, and place it in the freezer. Let it sit in the freezer overnight.
- Remove the bag and let the rock defrost. Once the ice has melted and the rock is at room temperature, empty the contents of the bag onto a sheet of paper. See if the freezing of water in the crevices did anything to the rock. Are there smaller pieces of broken rock?

Connections

Builders use the air freezing index (AFI) to determine the ground freezing potential of a given climate. The air freezing index allows builders to plan how to construct a foundation for a house or building in an area where freezing often occurs. These data are used to establish building code regulations for builders in areas where there are extensive air temperatures below freezing. Go to *www.ncdc.noaa.gov/oa/fpsf*.

Differentiated Learning

- For students who experience difficulty understanding how frost forms, have them complete Activities 13 and 14 side by side. Ask students what the difference is between the setups and the temperature inside the cans. These differences should help them understand the concepts.

Teachers' Guide 14

Resources

www.hgtv.com

www.ncdc.noaa.gov/oa/fpsf

www.ncdc.noaa.gov/oa/
climate/freezefrost/frost-
freemaps.html

- For ESL students, **BLM 14.1** will help them organize the important content for dew and frost formation while distinguishing between them.
- For students who finish the Activity quickly, ask them to explore maps of frost formation and seasonal planting. Annual plants, such as wheat, must produce seeds between the last frost in spring and the first frost in the fall. Plants fail to reproduce if frost damages them before seeds form. These maps will show the probability of freeze and frost across the United States. Go to *www.ncdc.noaa.gov/oa/climate/freezefrost/frostfreemaps.html*.

Answers to Student Questions

1. The frost that deposited on the can came from water vapor in the air.

2. The moisture first appeared as a solid because the temperature of the can was below the freezing point of water.

3. The frost first appeared as a solid.

4. After water vapor has condensed to a liquid, dew freezes when the temperature drops below 0°C. Frozen dew looks like tiny frozen water droplets.

5. Water vapor deposits on tiny particles to form ice crystals that can grow into snowflakes.

6. A completed version of **BLM 14.1** appears on the following page.

Assessment

- At the beginning of the Activity, assess students' background knowledge about frost and its formation by using a K-W-L chart.
- During the Activity, make sure students measure the correct amounts of salt and ice. The data collection should reflect the first appearance of frost.
- At the end of the Activity, you can grade the answers to student questions and their completed comparison of dew and frost on **BLM 14.1**.
- At the end of the Activity, you might also want to take two to three concepts from the K column of the K-W-L chart and have students determine if each statement is correct.

BLM 14.1: Comparing Dew and Frost

Date_____

Activity 14: Let's Make Frost

1. Overall Concept

Phase changes of water.

2. Concept

Dew

2. Concept

Frost

3. Characteristics

Dew is water that has condensed on the surface of different objects.

This occurs above 0°C.

3. Characteristics

Frost is ice crystals produced from the deposition of water vapor.

This occurs below 0°C.

4. Like Characteristics

Water molecules in the air slow down when the temperature drops.
Water molecules in the form of gas particles undergo a phase change.
Air cools to the point at which the air is saturated with water vapor.

5. Unlike Characteristics

The temperature is at or above 0°C.
The phase change is water vapor to liquid.
The phase change is called condensation.

5. Unlike Characteristics

The temperature is at or below 0°C.
The phase change is water vapor to solid.
The phase change is called deposition.

6. Summary

Dew and frost are similar forms of water. They both start as water vapor. Depending upon the air temperature, water vapor will form either dew or frost.

Activity 15 Summary

Students make a hygrometer and use the measurements from the thermometers on the hygrometer to calculate relative humidity in the classroom and outdoors.

Activity	Subject and Content	Objective	Materials
It's All Relative!	Relative humidity	Use evaporative cooling to determine relative humidity.	Each group of students will need: 6 cm × 6 cm piece of gauze, clear plastic tape, two indoor/outdoor alcohol thermometers, water, two sturdy paper plates or pieces of cardboard

Time	Vocabulary	Key Concept	Margin Features
50–60 minutes	Relative humidity	II: Factors that contribute to weather	Safety Alert!, Fast Fact, What Can I Do?, Connections, Resources

Scientific Inquiry	Unifying Concepts and Processes	Technology	Personal/Social Perspectives	Historical Context
Asking questions; collecting, analyzing, and interpreting data	Cause and effect: mechanism	Critical thinking, problem solving, and decision making	Science and technology in society	Evidence supporting conclusions

It's All Relative! Activity **15**

Background

Have you ever heard the word "muggy" used to describe the weather? How about the phrase "hazy, hot, and humid"? These phrases are used to describe times when there is considerable moisture in the air. Of course, there is always moisture in the air, but the amount varies.

At every temperature, there is a limit to the amount of water vapor that can exist. The warmer the air, the higher is this limit. When the amount of water vapor is at the limit, we say that the air is "saturated." Usually, there is less water vapor present in the air than this.

In this Activity, you will measure humidity. In **Activity 13**, you measured the humidity by determining how cold the air could be cooled before some of the water vapor condensed to form droplets. The closer the air was to "saturation," the less the air had to be cooled before droplets formed.

In this Activity, you will explore an alternative way of measuring humidity. Rather than cooling the air, you will evaporate water into the air. The more water you can evaporate into the air, the less water vapor that is present initially.

How do we know how much water is evaporating into the air? Evaporation is a cooling process, so the more water that evaporates, the cooler the air will get. You can measure the cooling with a thermometer. You may already be familiar with how evaporation cools you—that is why you sweat. The sweat evaporates and you feel cooler. When the **relative humidity** is high, perspiration does not easily evaporate. This means that your body's cooling mechanisms are less effective. As a result, you become uncomfortable.

Vocabulary

Relative humidity: A measure of how much water vapor is *actually* in the air compared to the maximum amount of water vapor that can be in the air.

Topic: atmospheric moisture
Go to: *www.scilinks.org*
Code: PSCM 010

Objective

Use evaporative cooling to determine relative humidity.

Activity 15

Materials

Each group of students will need:

- 6 cm × 6 cm piece of gauze
- clear plastic tape
- two indoor/outdoor alcohol thermometers
- water
- two sturdy paper plates or pieces of cardboard

Time

50 to 60 minutes

Figure 15.1
The two thermometers are taped parallel to one another onto a sturdy piece of cardboard or a paper plate.

SAFETY ALERT !

Be very careful when handling the thermometers to avoid breaking them.

Procedure

1. Wrap a piece of gauze around the bulb of one thermometer.

2. Tape the thermometers upright and parallel to each other on a piece of cardboard or a paper plate about 10 cm apart. (See **Figure 15.1**.)

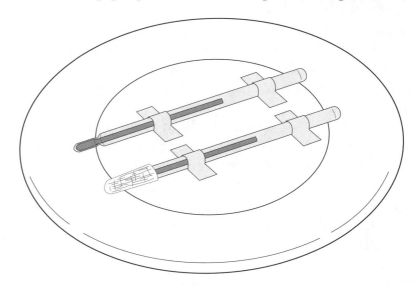

3. Moisten the gauze around the bulb of one thermometer with 10–12 drops of water. It is fine if there is water dripping down the plate. The water should be at room temperature.

4. Use the following procedure to find the relative humidity in your classroom:

    (a) On **BLM 15.1**, record "Classroom" as your location and the time of day that you are measuring the relative humidity.

    (b) Read the temperature of the thermometer without the gauze on the bulb. Call this the "dry bulb temperature" and record it on **BLM 15.1**.

    (c) Hold the piece of cardboard or paper plate with the thermometers upright, or lean them vertically against a stack of books. Fan both thermometers with the other paper plate for three minutes and record the lowest temperature reached by the thermometer with the gauze on the bulb. Call this the "wet bulb temperature" and record it on **BLM 15.1**. Also, record the dry bulb temperature after three minutes of fanning.

    (d) Subtract the wet bulb temperature from the dry bulb temperature and record the difference on **BLM 15.1**.

    (e) From your calculation of the difference between dry and wet bulb temperatures, determine the relative humidity using **Table 15.1**. Record the relative humidity of your classroom on **BLM 15.1**.

Table 15.1 Percent Relative Humidity

To determine relative humidity, find the column for the observed dry bulb temperature; then move down the column to the row for the difference between the observed dry and wet thermometers. The number in that square is the percent relative humidity. For example, if the dry bulb temperature is 20°C, and the difference between the two temperatures is 10°C, then the relative humidity is 24%.

Dry Bulb Temperature (°C)

Diff.	5	6	7	8	9	10	11	12	13	14	15	16	17	18	19	20	21	22	23	24	25	26	27	28	29	30	31	32	33	34	35
1	86	86	87	87	88	88	89	89	90	90	90	90	90	91	91	91	92	92	92	92	92	92	92	93	93	93	93	93	93	93	94
2	72	73	74	75	76	77	78	78	79	79	80	81	81	82	82	83	83	83	84	84	84	85	85	85	86	86	86	86	87	87	87
3	58	60	62	63	64	66	67	68	69	70	71	71	72	73	74	74	75	76	76	77	77	78	78	78	79	79	80	80	80	81	81
4	45	48	50	51	53	55	56	58	59	60	61	63	64	65	65	66	67	68	69	69	70	71	71	72	72	73	73	74	74	75	75
5	33	35	38	40	42	44	46	48	50	51	53	54	55	57	58	59	60	61	62	62	63	64	65	65	66	67	67	68	68	69	69
6	20	24	26	29	32	34	36	39	41	42	44	46	47	49	50	51	53	54	55	56	57	58	58	59	60	61	61	62	63	63	64
7	7	11	15	19	22	24	27	29	32	34	36	38	40	41	43	44	46	47	48	49	50	51	52	53	54	55	56	57	57	58	59
8				8	12	15	18	21	23	26	27	30	32	34	36	37	39	40	42	43	44	46	47	48	49	50	51	51	52	53	54
9						6	9	12	15	18	20	23	25	27	29	31	32	34	36	37	39	40	41	42	43	44	45	46	47	48	49
10									7	10	13	15	18	20	22	24	26	28	30	31	33	34	36	37	38	39	40	41	42	43	44
11											6	8	11	14	16	18	20	22	24	26	28	29	31	32	33	35	36	37	38	39	40
12														7	10	12	14	17	19	20	22	24	26	27	28	30	31	32	33	35	36

Difference Between Dry Bulb and Wet Bulb Temperature (°C)

Activity 15

Fast Facts

- During the cold winter months, the heated air inside your home or school can have a relative humidity under 5%, unless a humidifier is operating and adding water vapor to the air.

- At 100% relative humidity, a cubic meter of air at 25°C and standard sea-level pressure has about one-tenth of a cup of water (if all of the water could be condensed out).

What Can I Do?

Go online and determine the relative humidity using temperature and dew point data. NOAA's Relative Humidity Calculator will give you the humidity if you have the temperature and dew point data. Go to *www.hpc.ncep.noaa.gov/html/dewrh.shtml*.

5. Use this method to determine the relative humidity outdoors. Record "Outdoors" as the location and the time of day that you are measuring the relative humidity on **BLM 15.1**. Also, record the dry bulb temperature before fanning, the wet and dry bulb temperatures after fanning, the difference between the wet and dry bulb temperatures, and the relative humidity outdoors.

Questions and Conclusions

1. What did you notice about the wet bulb temperature as you fanned the thermometer with the paper plate? How can you explain what you observed?

2. Relative humidity indicates how much water vapor is *actually* in the air compared to the maximum possible amount. According to your measurements, is the air in your classroom saturated (i.e., is the water vapor present equal to the maximum possible at that temperature)?

3. Was there a difference between the classroom and outdoor relative humidity? If there was, how could you explain the difference?

4. If relative humidity was measured throughout the day, was there a difference in the indoor relative humidity as the day progressed? Was there a difference in the outdoor relative humidity? How could you explain the differences?

5. Some people's hair curls when the relative humidity is high. Can you think of a way to use this fact to measure relative humidity?

6. Do water puddles evaporate faster on days when the humidity is high or on days when the humidity is low?

7. Sometimes people say phrases such as, "It's the humidity that makes us feel so hot, not the heat." What do they mean?

Relative Humidity Data Table						
Location	Time	Dry Bulb Temp. (°C) (before fanning)	Wet Bulb Temp. (°C)	Dry Bulb Temp. (°C) (after fanning)	Difference (°C)	Relative Humidity

It's All Relative!

What Is Happening?

As discussed in Activity 13, when the maximum amount of water vapor is present for a given temperature, the air is said to be saturated, and the water vapor will begin to condense as clouds, fog, or dew. The amount of water vapor at saturation is determined by the temperature of the air. The warmer the air, the greater the amount of water vapor that can be present. When the amount of water vapor actually in the atmosphere is measured and divided by the value needed for saturation at that temperature, relative humidity is obtained. Saturated air has a relative humidity of 100%. Clouds or fog form when, and where, the air is saturated.

The same relative humidity at two different temperatures actually represents different amounts of moisture present in the air. What relative humidity measures is the actual amount of water vapor in the air relative to the maximum possible amount of water vapor. In other words, the relative humidity not only depends on the amount of water vapor in the air; it also depends on the temperature. This means that the relative humidity decreases during the morning (as the temperature increases), and then rises in the evening into the early morning hours (as the temperature decreases), since the amount of water vapor typically does not change much during the day. This also means that the relative humidity on hot and humid days may not be much different from what it is during cold days. However, a more humid hot day will have more water vapor present than a less humid hot day.

High relative humidity has some noticeable consequences for humans. Some people's hair will curl. Static electricity is reduced. On warm, humid

Objective
Use evaporative cooling to determine relative humidity.

Key Concept
II: Factors that contribute to weather

Materials
Each group of students will need:
- 6 cm × 6 cm piece of gauze
- clear plastic tape
- two indoor/outdoor alcohol thermometers
- water
- two sturdy paper plates or pieces of cardboard

Time
50–60 minutes

How Do We Know This?

How do we measure how much water vapor is in the air?

Modern hygrometers use electronic sensors that measure the difference in conductance of electricity at two points to calculate the humidity. To measure the humidity above the surface, these hygrometers are carried upward through the atmosphere by balloons (called radiosondes) that can radio the information back to meteorologists. Satellites can also measure water vapor by monitoring infrared radiation. Water vapor specifically absorbs certain bands of infrared radiation. Consequently, the less infrared radiation sensed by the satellite, the more water vapor must be present.

days, sweat does not readily evaporate, thereby hindering the body's cooling mechanism. This last consequence has led to the saying: "It's not the heat; it's the humidity." Likewise, there are consequences of low humidity. When such a condition persists for a long period of time, brush and forest fires are more likely. Also, our skin becomes dry and chapped, and our clothes are more subject to "static cling." Mouth and nasal membranes dry out, and this may make it easier for viruses to enter our bodies. It has been suggested that this is why we are more likely to have colds during winter.

In this Activity, students measure relative humidity with an instrument called a psychrometer, which is a particular type of hygrometer (an instrument that measures humidity). A psychrometer uses the cooling that occurs when water evaporates to determine the relative humidity. By covering a thermometer with wet gauze, water is allowed to evaporate into the air prior to the air reaching the thermometer. The more water that evaporates, the cooler the air is that reaches the thermometer.

The reason why evaporation is a cooling process is because it takes energy to evaporate water. Evaporation is essentially the breaking of the bonds that bind the water molecules together. It takes energy to break these bonds, much like it takes energy to break apart two magnets that are attracted. When evaporation occurs, the energy is taken from the air, cooling it down. We use a thermometer to measure how cold the air gets when we evaporate the water. (See **Figure 15.2.**)

Figure 15.2.
The amount of water vapor at saturation depends on its temperature.

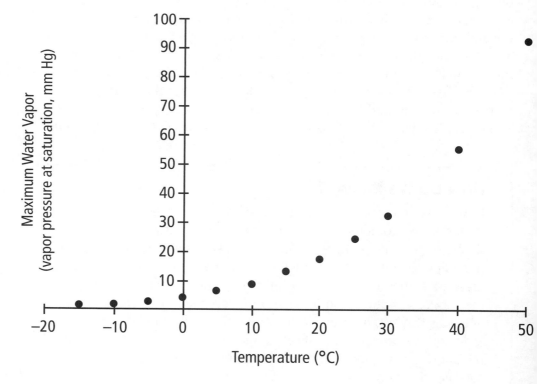

Preconceptions

At the beginning of the Activity, ask students, "Does the air feel dry today? Did any of you feel like your hair is more curly today? If you were to describe the air as 'muggy,' what does that mean?" Students may have the following preconceptions:

- Water droplets cannot exist in the air.
- Desert air does not contain water.
- Heat is contained in the water vapor that evaporates.
- The wet bulb temperature is lower than the dry bulb because the water is cooler than the air.
- Evaporation and condensation depend on the amount of "space" there is between air molecules.

What Students Need to Understand

- Air is saturated with water when the maximum possible water vapor is present at a given temperature.
- Evaporation is a cooling process.
- The maximum possible amount of water vapor increases with the temperature.
- Relative humidity is calculated with the formula

$$\text{Percent Relative Humidity} = 100 \times \frac{\text{Amount of water vapor actually present}}{\text{Maximum amount of water vapor that can be present at that temperature}}$$

- Humidity affects us in observable ways.

Time Management

This Activity can be completed in 50–60 minutes. The time-consuming parts of this Activity will be constructing the hygrometer and moving outdoors. Taking the measurements requires only a few minutes. Answering the questions may take about 10 minutes.

Preparation and Procedure

Before the lesson begins, discuss humidity with the class. Ask questions such as the following: What is humidity? When people say the air is humid, what do they mean? When meteorologists refer to relative humidity, what do you think they mean? You may wish to begin with a K-W-L chart. Record students' background knowledge about humidity in the K column of the chart. Be sure to accept all comments. Ask students what they want to learn about humidity and record their questions in the W column of the chart. Return to the K-W-L chart at the conclusion of the Activity and record what students learned about relative humidity in the L column. Correct any misinformation in the K column and see which questions students are able to answer from the W column.

All materials should be either centrally located or already distributed to the groups of students. Use alcohol-filled thermometers for this Activity, and urge students to use caution to avoid breaking the thermometers.

Some advance coordination will be required if the Activity is to be conducted throughout the day or over a number of days. You need to decide if every class will construct the hygrometers or if only one class will make them. If only one class makes them, the other classes may use these hygrometers. This may simplify keeping track of data collected between classes and over a period of days.

Alternative Preparation

An alternative method for preparing a psychrometer is to create a sling psychrometer. Instead of fanning the thermometers, students can attach each thermometer to a block of wood that is attached to a piece of heavy string. Once the wet bulb is moistened, students can "sling" or rotate the psychrometer around in the air. The slinging motion serves the same purpose as fanning the wet bulb thermometer with the paper plate. If students build one of these, it is essential that the thermometers are firmly attached to the board and that the string is sufficiently strong. *The sling psychrometer has been known to produce airborne thermometers, which is extremely dangerous!*

Extended Learning

- The hygrometer is easily transportable. Students may find it interesting to measure relative humidity in a variety of locations to study variations.
- Track relative humidity throughout the day and for several days, and then graph the results. Do the students see consistent trends in relative humidity as the day progresses? Do they see trends over a period of several days?
- Investigate the relationship between relative humidity and the dew point. See Activity 13.
- Encourage students to investigate the reasons for the consequences of high and low humidity mentioned in the What Is Happening? section of this Activity.

Interdisciplinary Study

- Students could research further effects on humans of prolonged high relative humidity and low relative humidity. They could also explore ways in which humans adapt to living in regions that are known to experience extremes of relative humidity (e.g., the desert and a tropical rain forest). For example, students could correlate the increase in human population in the southeast of the United States with the invention of air conditioning.
- Students could research how athletes use mist-producing devices to cool off.
- Students could research why they do not feel as cold coming out of a pool when it is indoors (high humidity) as opposed to outdoors (lower humidity).

Differentiated Learning

- For ESL students, have them work in pairs or groups to record the data, complete the mathematics, and find the relative humidity in **Table 15.1**, so that they can follow what their partners or group members are doing.
- For students who have difficulty understanding relative humidity, use analogies or examples of water vapor in the air. An analogy to illustrate when evaporation occurs and why it is associated with cooling is to have students in school represent water molecules in the liquid state. To leave the school, they have to expend energy to open the door. That loss of energy is analogous to the cooling that occurs when the water molecules break their bonds with other water molecules during evaporation. Warmer water means students are more energetic, leading to more students opening the door and leaving (i.e., more water evaporating). For example, when someone breathes on their glasses to clean them, little droplets of water are produced on the lens. This means that our breath contains water vapor. Another example may be that on hot humid days, usually in the summer, the feeling of humidity is increased.
- For students who finish the Activity early, have them research how humidity affects how sweat is evaporated from the body, and how high humidity does not allow for a person to cool off as quickly as when the humidity is low.

Connections

Students could research the effect of temperature and humidity on humans. Meteorologists use the Heat Index to provide a comfort index for humans. The Heat Index takes into account the air temperature and the relative humidity, and creates a number that describes a comfort factor. Students could explore how the Heat Index has altered events. For example, a high Heat Index has occurred at times of higher than normal numbers of deaths in many northern cities. This has become a public health issue, and studies have determined, for example, that a "heat alert" should be issued in New York City when the Heat Index is 38°C (100°F) or higher for two consecutive days.

Answers to Student Questions

1. The temperature of the wet bulb thermometer dropped. As the thermometer was fanned, the water evaporated. Evaporation is a cooling process so the temperature dropped. The temperature of the dry bulb thermometer does not change after fanning it with the paper plate.

2. The relative humidity inside the classroom should be less than 100%, which means the air is not saturated.

3. This will depend on students' data. In general, because of heating and air conditioning, the relative humidity will be lower indoors. Answers will vary by student.

4. Each of these answers will depend on students' data and the weather conditions for that day. In schools with closed ventilation systems, outdoor relative humidity will be more variable, and indoor relative humidity will be more uniform. Outdoor relative humidity will generally reach a low in mid-afternoon and then begin to rise again. This trend happens because the day's highest temperatures generally occur in midafternoon, but the water vapor content is roughly steady throughout the day.

5. You could just look at someone that this happens to on a regular basis and judge whether the humidity is high or not. Humidity note: Instruments have actually been constructed to measure relative humidity based on this fact. (See **Figure 15.3**.)

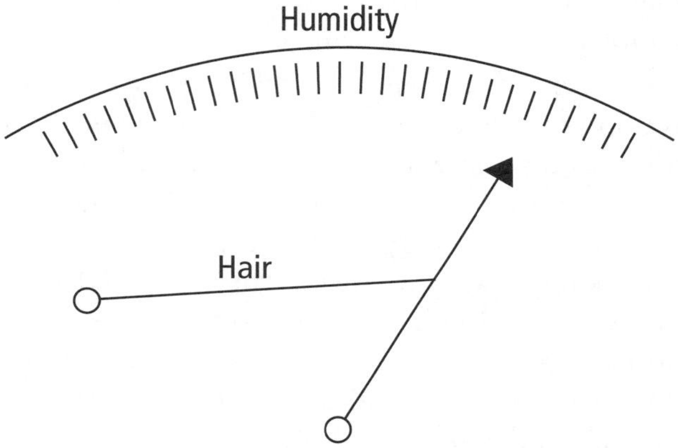

Figure 15.3
A hair hygrometer works on the fact that hair changes its length when humidity varies. The scale shows the contraction or extension of the hair when it is dry or humid, respectively.

6. When other conditions are the same (e.g., wind speed, brightness of the Sun, etc.), water puddles evaporate faster on days when the relative humidity is low. (Challenge students to explain why, and to consider what other elements affect evaporation rate.)

7. Just as high relative humidity prevents puddles from evaporating, it prevents sweat from evaporating from our skin. It is through the evaporation of sweat that our bodies are cooled. When sweat cannot evaporate, we lose the ability to cool ourselves, and we get hotter than we would in dry air. (For this reason, athletic events are sometimes canceled when both the temperature and the relative humidity are very high. Strenuous exercise in such weather can lead to heat exhaustion, heat stroke, and other dangerous physical conditions.)

Assessment

- At the beginning of the Activity, assess students' background knowledge about humidity by using a K-W-L chart.
- During the Activity, make sure students record the temperatures on the dry bulb and wet bulb thermometers accurately. Ensure that they fan the thermometers for the time suggested, and that they watch the wet bulb thermometer for the lowest temperature reading during that time.
- At the end of the Activity, you can assess the Answers to Student Questions.
- At the end of the Activity, you might also want to take two to three concepts from the K column of the K-W-L chart and have students determine if the statements are correct.

Resources

www.hpc.ncep.noaa.gov/html/ dewrh.shtml

Activity 16 Planner

Activity 16 Summary

Students use a cutout model to observe what types of clouds form when warm air meets cold air.

Activity	Subject and Content	Objective	Materials
Moving Masses	Interactions between air masses	Learn what types of clouds form when a cold front moves into an area of warm air.	Each student will need: scissors, blue crayon, tape or glue, paper or thin cardboard (letter-size)

Time	Vocabulary	Key Concept	Margin Features
30–40 minutes	Air mass, Front	III: The interaction of air masses	Fast Fact, Safety Alert!, What Can I Do?, Connections, Resources

Scientific Inquiry	Unifying Concepts and Processes	Technology	Personal/Social Perspectives	Historical Context
Modeling; applying and using scientific knowledge	Patterns: organization; system models	Research and information fluency	Scientific perspective of variables	Changing knowledge of observations

Moving Masses

Activity **16**

Background

The air inside a cloud can be very different from the air outside the cloud, not only because of the presence of cloud droplets and increased water vapor, but also in terms of density and temperature. Just as the air inside the cloud can be different from the air outside, the properties of air vary across the globe. **Air masses** are large bodies of air that have distinctly different temperatures and relative humidity.

Sometimes there is a dramatic boundary between two adjacent air masses. It is similar to the clear edge one sees between the air inside a cloud and the air outside (it is particularly dramatic with white fluffy clouds). These boundaries exist because it takes a relatively long time for air to mix over such large distances.

The boundary that forms between warm and cool air masses is called a **front**. At the boundary, the more stable air mass sinks. Since cool air is typically more stable than warm air, cooler air masses wedge themselves underneath warmer air masses, and warmer air masses ride over cooler air masses. Air that rises at the front expands as it encounters lower pressure at high altitudes. This expansion cools the air, and the moisture in the air condenses, forming clouds. If the air continues to rise and expand, rain or snow may form.

Such clouds and precipitation are a visible result of the interactions of air masses.

Vocabulary

Air Mass: A large body of air that has a distinct temperature and relative humidity.

Front: The boundary that forms between a warm and a cool air mass.

Fast Fact

Red and blue barbed lines were first used on weather maps to identify warm and cold fronts in the mid-1930s.

Topic: fronts and severe weather

Go to: www.scilinks.org

Code: PSCM 011

Objective

Learn what types of clouds form when a cold front moves into an area of warm air.

Activity 16

Figure 16.1
A folded piece of paper with vertical cuts creates the viewer for this simulation.

Procedure

1. Cut along the dotted lines on **BLM 16.1** to separate the three strips. Also cut out the "City."

2. Color the cold air blue.

3. Tape or glue the three large strips together by matching up the letters. For example, match up the letters A, and tape or glue the edges together. Then match up the letters B, and tape or glue the edges together.

4. To make the viewer itself, fold a letter-size piece of paper or thin cardboard in half lengthwise and make a vertical 6 cm cut about one-third of the way across the paper and about 2 cm above the bottom edge. Then make another cut about 7.5 cm away from the first one, as shown in **Figure 16.1**.

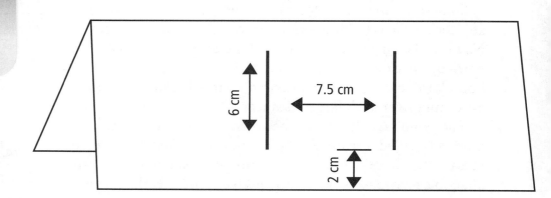

5. Tape or glue the "City" below the two slits.

6. Feed the strip through the two slits. Pull from the right so that you start with Monday morning, as shown in **Figure 16.2**.

Figure 16.2
The cutout weather strips form a weather timeline when they are passed through the viewer.

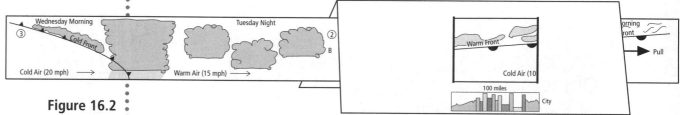

Questions and Conclusions

1. Describe the first type of cloud to appear on Monday morning.

2. What did the clouds look like by Tuesday morning when they were producing rain?

3. Why did the warm air rise up over the cold air on Monday?

4. Describe the type of clouds present as the cold front moved in on Wednesday morning.

5. If you see thin wispy clouds followed by lower layered clouds, what type of weather might you expect in the near future?

What Can I Do?

Vilhelm Firman Koren Bjerknes is considered one of the founding fathers of modern meteorology. He discovered the existence of distinct air masses that did not mix. He called the boundary a front. You can read more about the life of Bjerknes at *www-history. mcs.st-and.ac.uk/history/ Biographies/Bjerknes_ Vilhelm.html*.

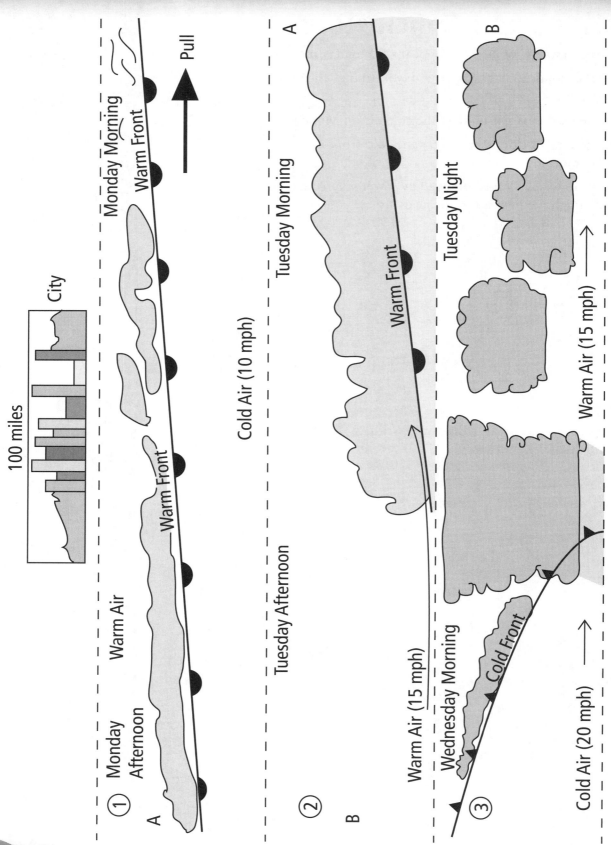

① Monday Afternoon

Monday Morning

Warm Front

Warm Front

Warm Air

Pull

City

100 miles

A

② Tuesday Morning

Cold Air (10 mph)

Tuesday Afternoon

Warm Front

A

B

③ Wednesday Morning

Cold Front

Warm Air (15 mph)

Tuesday Night

Warm Air (15 mph)

Cold Air (20 mph)

B

Moving Masses

What Is Happening?

Fronts are responsible for much of the clouds, rain, and snow in the United States, especially in the winter. A front is a boundary that exists between air masses of different temperature and humidity. The boundary exists because it takes a relatively long time for air to mix over such long distances. The warmer air, being less dense, rides up over the cold air. As this happens, the moisture in the warm air will condense and form clouds, rain, or snow because the warm air expands and cools into regions of lower pressure.

There are various types of fronts, and they are named according to their direction of movement. The two types of fronts discussed in this Activity are warm and cold fronts. In a warm front, warm air advances, replacing cooler air. In a cold front, cold air advances, replacing warmer air. In each case, characteristic clouds form, which allow the prediction of coming weather. The model in this Activity is designed to help students recognize these characteristic types of clouds. A representation of what the cutout model might look like on a weather map is shown in **Figure 16.3**.

The cutout model is only two-dimensional. Fronts and airflow are three-dimensional. The fronts and their movement are actually into and out of the page in addition to across it. It is important to convey to students that the sequence of clouds presented in this Activity represents an *idealized* front.

Objective

Learn what types of clouds form when a cold front moves into an area of warm air.

Key Concept

III: The interaction of air masses

Materials

Each student will need:
• scissors
• blue crayon
• tape or glue
• paper or thin cardboard (letter size)

Time

30–40 minutes

How Do We Know This?

How do we know the location of fronts?

Identification of the location of a front arises from an interpretation of multiple data. For example, the location of a front can be determined by observing weather data that includes atmospheric pressure, temperature, and humidity. These data are collected across the country at different locations. When the data are different over a small geographic location, one interpretation is that there is a front approaching. Other weather data—wind speed and direction—will help meteorologists determine when and where the front will occur.

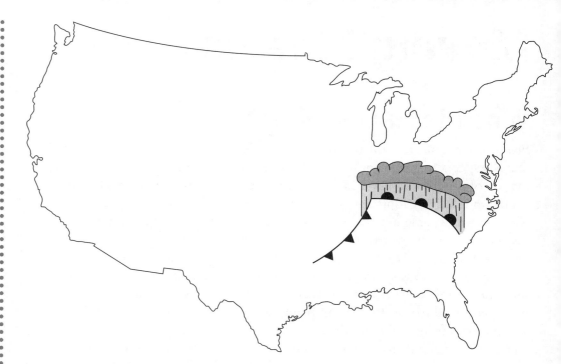

Figure 16.3
A weather map will show multiple curved lines and symbols to represent where different air masses meet each other and the resulting weather from these interactions.

Preconceptions

Ask students, "What happens before a storm approaches? What do you notice about the change in temperature before and after a storm? What do the clouds look like before, during, and after a storm?" Students may have the following preconceptions:

- Storms occur when clouds blow into the area.
- Only dark clouds produce rain.
- The clouds of a front produce the wind.
- Cloud type cannot predict the weather.

What Students Need to Understand

- Air masses of different temperature and humidity do not readily mix.
- The boundary between air masses of different temperatures is called a front.
- When warmer air meets colder air, the warmer air is forced to rise and cool. The moisture in the warmer air may condense forming clouds, and eventually rain or snow.

Time Management

This Activity can be done in 30–40 minutes.

Preparation and Procedure

Be sure that all supplies are centrally located or already distributed to groups. There are a variety of posters and charts with photographs of cloud types (see the annotated Resources). These visual aids may assist the discussion of cloud types. The viewers can be made ahead of time and used in different classes.

> **SAFETY ALERT** !
>
> Use caution when working with sharp items such as scissors. They can cut or puncture skin.

Alternative Preparation

There is no alternative preparation for this simulation, but the concept of a warm front riding over a cold front, or a cold front coming in lower than a warm front, can be achieved using simple demonstrations:

- First, take a 2 L plastic container and construct a plastic divider that will fit vertically across its diameter. Place the vertical divider in the center of the container and mold clay into the seam where the divider contacts the container so that water cannot flow between the two sides. On one side, pour two cups of hot water and mix it with blue food coloring. On the other side, pour two cups of ice water and mix it with yellow food coloring. Slowly lift the divider and watch how the colored water masses interact with one another. Make sure students understand that air masses move in a similar manner as the water.

- The second demonstration illustrates how cold air sinks relative to warm air and, in so doing, can displace the warm air. Measure the room temperature with a thermometer. Make sure all doors and windows are closed so that there is no air movement. Place a tray filled with ice on a medium-size box. The cold air above the medium-size box should sink and flow down the sides of the box. Place the thermometer in a shoe box that is open on top. To the side of the medium-size box, place the shoe box so that the cold air can flow down the side of the medium box and into the shoe box. Make sure the shoe box is lower than the medium-size box. Record the temperature in the shoe box every two minutes for about ten minutes. The cold air displaces the warm air out of the shoe box.

Extended Learning

- The names for the different types of clouds were not discussed in this Activity. Encourage students to investigate these names on their own. Have separate classes do class predictions of the weather and compete with each other for the most accurate prediction (see Activity 1).

- Students can make predictions about weather by looking at the weather maps in newspapers. Other sources of weather maps include local television weather reports and The Weather Channel. These usually include the cold and warm fronts across the nation. This is also a good opportunity for students to learn the symbols used to represent the different types of fronts.

181

Interdisciplinary Study

- Clouds can provide the motivation for a writing exercise. Most people have imagined that clouds look like people, animals, or other things. Students can be asked to write a poem or a descriptive paragraph about what they imagine they see in the clouds.
- Sayings and folklore about weather can be found in almost every culture. Some of the sayings that predict weather are based on careful observation and are fairly accurate. Encourage students to research the origins of weather sayings and folklore, and have them think about how to test the validity of these sayings through observations and experiments.

Connections

Students can determine if General Eisenhower was given a good weather prediction for the invasion of D-Day by looking at the weather maps prior to the invasion. Go to *www.ecmwf.int/research/era/dday* and read the article. Students can determine if a front was approaching, how they knew a front was approaching, and what the cloud types may have been. What would students have advised the general to do?

Differentiated Learning

- For ESL students, have them learn about the various types of weather fronts: warm front, cold front, stationary front, and occluded front. A quick animation can demonstrate current fronts to students. The animation can be found at *www.atmos.washington.edu/~ovens/loops/wxloop.cgi?fronts_ir+/48h*.
- For students who have difficulty understanding fronts, have them complete a comparison chart that identifies the main features, conditions, and cloud types associated with each type of front.
  - **Cold Front:** A boundary between colder air and warmer air. The cold air pushes the warm air up, like a wedge (usually pushing to the south and east).
  - **Warm Front:** A boundary between warm air and a retreating wedge of cold air. The warm air usually travels to the north and east.
  - **Stationary Front:** A front between warm and cold air masses that is moving very slowly or not at all.
  - **Occluded Front:** A line along which warm air is lifted by opposing wedges of cold air, causing precipitation.
- For students who finish the Activity early, have them develop their own cloud chart and dichotomous key for identifying cloud types.

Answers to Student Questions

1. Thin, wispy, featherlike clouds (cirrus clouds) are the first type of cloud to appear on Monday morning.

2. By Tuesday morning, the clouds looked much thicker and gray.

3. The warm air rose up over the cold air on Monday because it was less dense.

4. As the cold front moved in on Wednesday morning, tall, towering, billowing clouds in various shades of white, gray, or black appeared.

5. If you see thin wispy clouds followed by lower layered clouds, you would expect a warm front moving in with increased cloudiness and rain or snow likely.

Assessment

- At the beginning of the Activity, assess students' understanding of air masses and fronts by asking them, "Who has seen a weather map and heard meteorologists say something about a cold front moving into the area? Were there any observations you made about the onset of a cold front and the atmospheric conditions, such as cloud types?"
- At the end of the Activity, you can assess the answers to student questions.
- At the end of the Activity, you can also assess students' understanding of what happens when a warm front moves in by asking them to illustrate what happens in a flow diagram.

Resources

www-history.mcs.st-and.ac.uk/history/Biographies/Bjerknes_Vilhelm.html

www.ecmwf.int/research/era/dday

www.atmos.washington.edu/~ovens/loops/wxloop.cgi?fronts_ir+/48h

Activity 17 Planner

Activity 17 Summary

Students learn weather map symbols and use them to interpret a weather map of the United States.

Activity	Subject and Content	Objective	Materials
Interpreting Weather Maps	Interpreting weather maps	Interpret a basic weather map and understand weather station symbols.	Each student will need: colored pencils, pencil

Time	Vocabulary	Key Concept	Margin Features
50 minutes	Weather forecast, Station model	III: The interaction of air masses	What Can I Do?, Fast Fact, Connections, Resources

Scientific Inquiry	Unifying Concepts and Processes	Technology	Personal/Social Perspectives	Historical Context
Modeling; applying and using scientific knowledge	Patterns; system and system models; stability and change	Digital citizenship, research and information fluency	Teamwork; natural hazards	Historical methods of science

Interpreting Weather Maps

Background

Meteorologists collect data from multiple weather stations and instruments on Earth's surface. These data allow them to make **weather forecasts**. Airports, broadcast stations, schools, private citizens, and the National Oceanic and Atmospheric Administration (NOAA) maintain the weather stations and collect data. Surface weather maps usually outline an interpretation of all of the data. The weather maps seen online and on TV are analyzed pictures that are produced after the data analyses have been completed. Weather maps usually show the area being surveyed and symbols that represent the weather data. These weather symbols express a lot of information in a concise way. If you combine information from many stations on a map, the map will give you a picture of the large weather systems across the nation.

Figure 17.1 shows an example of the symbols used to indicate the weather at each station, and the information given by each symbol. The arrangement of the data around the station location is called a **station model** and is standardized by international agreement. Following **Figure 17.1** is an explanation of each type of information. As of this writing, weather station symbols in the United States are still expressed in the English system of measurement.

Vocabulary

Weather forecast: The prediction of the weather for a certain area based upon previous conditions.

Station model: A pictorial representation of the current weather conditions. A station model usually describes wind speed and direction, temperature, dew point, pressure, and sky cover.

Objective

Interpret a basic weather map and understand weather station symbols.

Topic: weather maps
Go to: www.scilinks.org
Code: PSCM 012

Activity 17

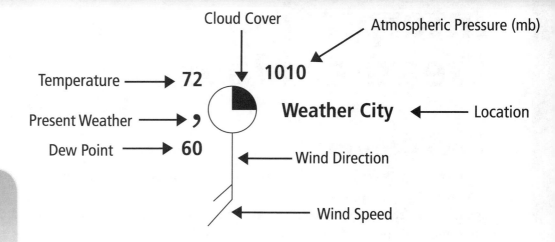

Atmospheric Pressure (mb)

Cloud Cover

Temperature → **72**

1010

Present Weather → **,**

Weather City ← Location

Dew Point → **60**

← Wind Direction

← Wind Speed

Materials

Each student will need:
• colored pencils
• pencil

Time

50 minutes

Atmospheric pressure: This is the atmospheric (or air) pressure measured in millibars (mb). Air pressure at sea level averages about 1013 mb (14.7 lb/in² or 1.04 kg/cm² or 760 mm Hg or 29.92 in. Hg). Weather maps report the last two digits of pressure in mb, plus the tenths of mb. For example, a pressure of 1013.2 mb is recorded on the station model as 132. Many weather maps have curved lines called isobars (literally "equal bars"). These lines are drawn by connecting locations of equal pressure on the map.

Wind speed: The small lines that look like barbs represent the wind speed. Each full line represents 10 knots (kt) of wind speed (1 kt = 1.8 kph = 1.15 mph). Shorter lines represent wind speeds of 5 kt. If there is more than one line, the total wind speed is the sum of all the lines. **Figure 17.2** shows several examples.

Figure 17.2
Wind speed and direction are represented by arrow orientation, and by number and size of feathers.

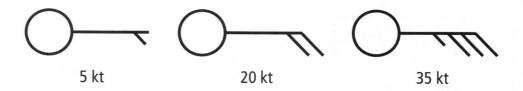

5 kt   20 kt   35 kt

Wind direction: If you think of the wind speed lines as feathers on an arrow, the circle represents the arrowhead. The arrow points in the direction that the wind is blowing, and wind direction is designated as the direction from which the wind is blowing. Therefore, if an arrow points to the east, the wind direction is actually referred to as "from the west." In **Figure 17.1** above, the arrow points north and the wind direction is from the south. See Figure **17.3** for the principal wind directions.

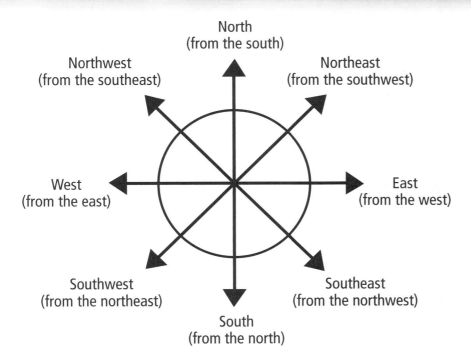

Figure 17.3
The wind direction is represented by eight standard labels indicating the direction from which the wind is blowing. The wind barb on a weather map, representing the tail of the arrow, points opposite to the direction indicated in the figure.

Temperature: This is the temperature measured in °F every hour.

Dew Point: This is the temperature in °F that the air would have to be cooled to for the air to become saturated and for water vapor in the air to condense.

Cloud Cover: The amount of cloud cover is represented by the amount of the circle that is shaded. **Figure 17.4** shows some examples.

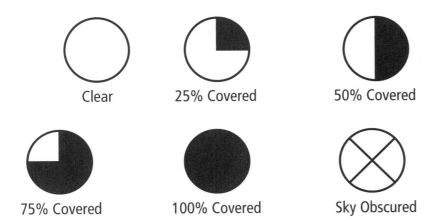

Figure 17.4
The shaded portion of the circles represents how much of the sky is covered with clouds.

Present weather: **Figure 17.5** shows a list of symbols used to designate some of the different types of weather.

Activity 17

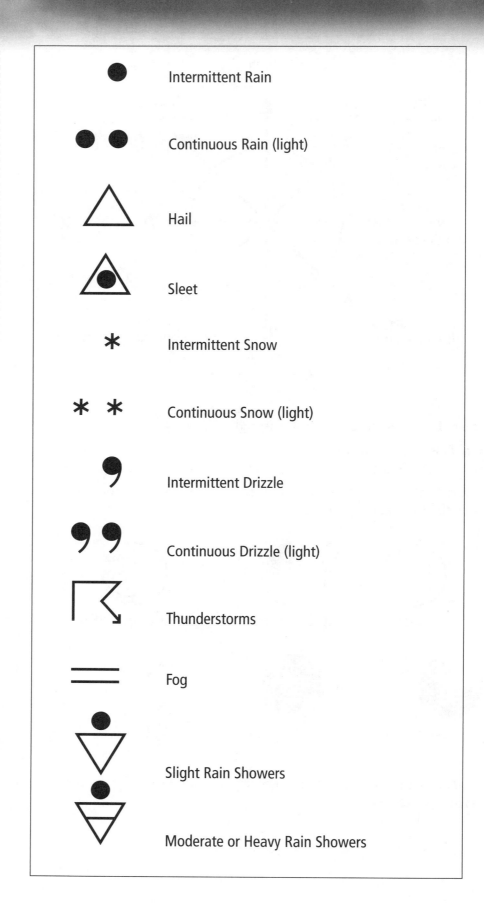

Figure 17.5
These symbols are used to represent the current conditions at the station's location.

Intermittent Rain

Continuous Rain (light)

Hail

Sleet

Intermittent Snow

Continuous Snow (light)

Intermittent Drizzle

Continuous Drizzle (light)

Thunderstorms

Fog

Slight Rain Showers

Moderate or Heavy Rain Showers

National Science Teachers Association

Questions and Conclusions

1. Answer the following questions referring to the weather map on **BLM 17.1**:

   (a) What is the "present" weather in Dallas, Texas?

   (b) What is the atmospheric pressure in Kansas City?

   (c) From which direction is the wind blowing at Hatteras, North Carolina, and what is its speed?

   (d) What is the temperature in Pueblo, Colorado?

   (e) What is the cloud cover in Miami, Florida?

   (f) What is the atmospheric pressure in Roswell, New Mexico?

   (g) What is the "present" weather in Chicago, Illinois?

   (h) What is the cloud cover in New York City?

   (i) From which direction is the wind blowing in Helena, Montana, and what is its speed?

   (j) What region of the nation appears to be generally cloudy? What region appears to be generally clear?

2. In Weather City, the atmospheric pressure is 1010 mb. The temperature is 54°F, and the dew point is 40°F. The wind speed is 15 kt from the southeast. The cloud cover is 50%. Draw the weather symbols that represent the data recorded at Weather City.

3. Use a colored pencil to shade lightly all areas on **BLM 17.1** that are experiencing 100% cloudiness or precipitation.

4. Why is it important to be informed about weather conditions?

5. Of all the weather conditions that occur in your area, which pose threats to life and property?

What Can I Do?

Look at a weather report on the TV or internet. Look at the symbols and see if you can tell what data were used to develop them. Go to *www.weather.gov* and click on all of the weather tabs to see different weather maps.

Fast Fact

A 40% chance of precipitation means that the weather forecaster is 40% confident that precipitation will occur somewhere in the forecast area.

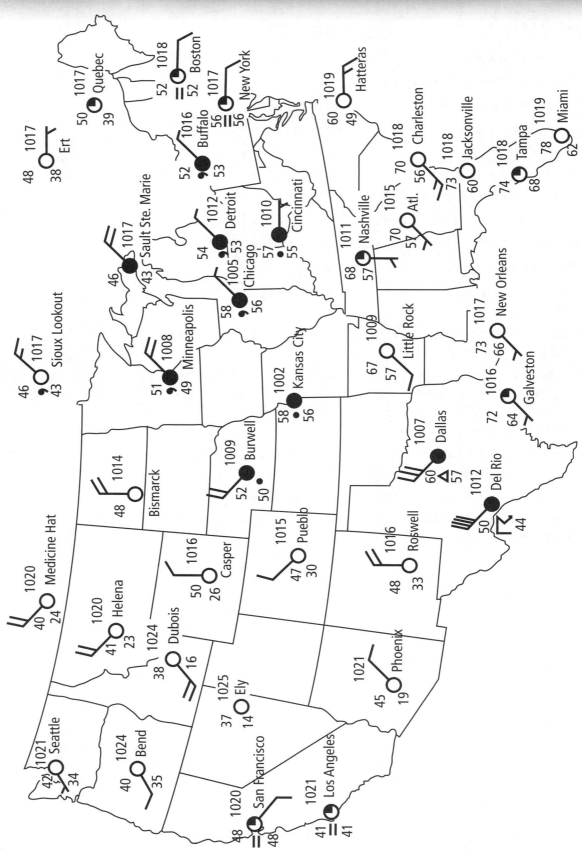

Interpreting Weather Maps

What Is Happening?

By combining the information from many stations, an accurate picture of large weather systems can be obtained. As a result, these surface weather maps hold an enormous amount of information about weather systems and about the movement of weather over the continent. Those skilled in weather map reading can make accurate forecasts and will be able to adjust their lives accordingly: severe weather can be anticipated, travelers can be appropriately clothed, and schedules can be altered to accommodate weather changes.

How Do We Know This?

How do we use weather data and symbols to predict the weather?

Meteorologists use previous data and weather patterns to predict future weather patterns. Meteorologists interpret satellite imagery and maps of weather observations, not only the surface maps discussed in this Activity, but also maps at levels above Earth's surface, to predict the weather. In addition, meteorologists use powerful computers that take the observations (both at the surface and above the surface) and incorporate them into computer programs that simulate the evolution of the atmosphere. Several different computer programs can be used. The programs (called models) might incorporate different observations, use different ways of solving certain equations, have different ways of modeling certain physical processes, simulate a different region (e.g., a continent versus the globe), and/or have different resolutions (i.e., number of data points being simulated). The different computer programs usually produce similar forecasts, but they can differ in ways that allow experienced forecasters to modify their forecast appropriately. The computer program that has the highest resolution (i.e., the most data points for a given region) usually makes the best forecast.

Satellites collect quantitative and qualitative data that help meteorologists interpret the ground data. An infrared satellite image can show where clouds are located across a region. The shape of clouds from above can indicate the type of weather and the direction in which it is moving. A storm system might appear as a comma-shaped cloud, which results when moisture wraps around a low pressure center.

Objective

Interpret a basic weather map and understand weather station symbols.

Key Concept

III: The interaction of air masses

Materials

Each student will need:
• colored pencils
• pencil

Time

50 minutes

Preconceptions

Begin the Activity by asking students, "How many of you have seen a weather map and can use it to predict the weather for the next day? What symbols were on that weather map that helped you understand the current weather and predict the weather for the next day?" Students sometimes think that weather maps are constructed from a computer, with no understanding that many data points have gone into the creation of one map. They may have the following preconceptions:

- Weather maps are based on information from one location.
- Weather forecasting is always accurate for many days ahead.
- Weather forecasts are done by using historical records of weather events.

What Students Need to Understand

- There is a network of weather reporting stations across the nation and the world.
- The symbols used in weather maps are a form of shorthand, which makes it possible to represent a large amount of information in a small space.
- Each symbol has a very specific meaning.

Time Management

This Activity can be completed in 50 minutes.

Preparation and Procedure

The only preparation necessary to do this Activity is for you to become familiar with the symbols and terminology used on weather maps. The descriptions of the symbols used are provided in the student section. (The scope of this Activity does not include some important but difficult to understand features of weather maps—e.g., isobars and fronts—except as suggestions for further study.)

Alternative Preparation

An alternative way to address these concepts is to provide each student with a photocopy of the weather map from a local newspaper. This weather map may be more regional and have fewer symbols representing the weather conditions. Have each student answer questions for the local map similar to the ones in this Activity. It is still important for students to understand the symbols included in a station model.

Extended Learning

- While fronts, isobars, and isotherms are difficult to understand and to construct, they are not beyond the capabilities of most middle school students. Students may be interested to learn how to draw them on their own. Drawing the isobars at four-millibar intervals (996 mb, 1000 mb, 1004 mb, 1008 mb, etc.) can give them additional insight into pressure systems. Also, by using wind shifts and temperature changes, the fronts can be located. A diagram showing the isobars and the fronts for the weather map in this Activity is given in **Figure 17.6**.

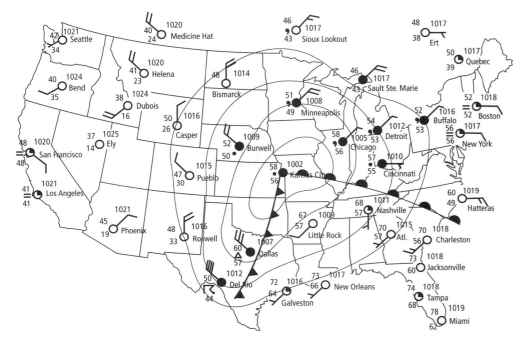

Figure 17.6
This is the same weather map as that in **BLM 17.1**, except that isobars and fronts have been added.

- Encourage students to apply what they have learned in this Activity to weather maps in the newspaper and to the ones they see on television weather reports. A topic that may interest students is weather satellites. These satellites make possible the global pictures of weather systems that are shown on television news reports.

- Weather forecasting can be done just by looking at Doppler radar images over time. Search for your local radar on the website of a local news station. Click on the radar image and then the three- or six-hour time loop, if available. This will show the previous three- to six-hour rainfall, if precipitation has occurred. Some sites will have a three-hour forecast, which will predict what will happen with precipitation in the future. Click on this button, if available, to see the forecasted rainfall.

- Have students investigate the profession of a TV meteorologist. What do these people have in common? What type of education do you need to be a TV meteorologist? Go to *www.ametsoc.org/pubs/careers.html*.

Fast Fact

Previous forecasts were not as scientific as the models and predictions we have today. More than 4,000 years ago in Babylonian time, priests used the positions of stars and planets and developed predictions of weather based largely upon myth. During the Greek era 2,000 years ago, scientists based their predictions on experience and observation. The Romans included weather "signs" or "symbols" in handbooks prepared for farmers. This use of zodiacal signs continues today in the popular *Farmer's Almanac*, which has been published in the United States for the past 167 years.

Teachers' Guide 17

• Have students explore the tsunami forecast center at *http://nctr.pmel.noaa. gov/tsunami-forecast.html.*

Interdisciplinary Study

Weather forecasting combines the ideas of models, prediction, and patterns. When many data are collected and transferred to a map, the map becomes a model or a representation of collected data. The model represents what is currently happening. The data may contain patterns, which indicate where strong winds, rain, or pressure may be. If these patterns persist, then the model represents a continuum. If you extend this continuum, then you can predict the pattern in the future using the past information.

• Have students investigate different types of patterns in weather forecasting.
• Have students research the "scientific" validity of weather forecasting. For example, see if they can find a court case in which the weather forecast was considered to be objective and reliable, or subjective and unsure.

Differentiated Learning

• For ESL students, a game can be created in which many station models are developed using the symbols, and students describe the conditions represented by the symbols. Another method for involving ESL students is to have them research the local weather conditions in their hometown or country. They can find these online at NOAA or The Weather Channel.
• For students who have difficulty understanding weather maps and forecasting, have them compile a list of symbols from the station model and match them to the word and description of the symbol. Flash cards will also help students align a picture or symbol to a weather condition. Forecasting can also be associated with "if/then" statements. Develop a list of actions that have a logical conclusion. This will help students realize that what is presented now may lead to something later.
• For students who have completed this Activity early, invite them to explore significant weather events such as historical winter storms, summer floods, hurricanes, freeze warnings, wind advisories, or tornadoes. Go to *www.spc. noaa.gov.*

Answers to Student Questions

1. (a) The "present" weather in Dallas, Texas, is hail.
   (b) The atmospheric pressure in Kansas City is 1002 mb. This is the low pressure center on the map.
   (c) The wind is blowing from the east at Hatteras, North Carolina, and its speed is 15 kt.

Connections

The National Hurricane Center has a Tropical Forecast Center where they track and predict when and where a hurricane will be. Go to *www.nhc.noaa.gov/HAW2/ english/forecast_process. shtml.*

Resources

www.weather.gov

www.ametsoc.org/pubs/ careers.html

http://nctr.pmel.noaa.gov/ tsunami-forecast.html

www.nhc.noaa.gov/HAW2/ english/forecast_process.shtm

(d) The temperature in Pueblo, Colorado, is 47°F.

(e) The skies are clear in Miami.

(f) The atmospheric pressure in Roswell, New Mexico, is 1016 mb.

(g) The "present" weather in Chicago, Illinois, is intermittent drizzle.

(h) The cloud cover in New York City is 25% covered.

(i) The wind is blowing from the northwest at 20 kt in Helena, Montana.

(j) The midwest and northeast appear to be generally cloudy. Most of the western United States appears to be generally clear.

2.

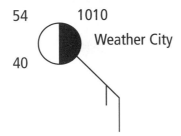

3. Students should color in the midwest and northeast regions of the United States.

4. It is important to be informed about weather conditions to dress appropriately, to make travel plans, and to prepare for hazardous weather.

5. Answers will vary with location. For example, some parts of the nation are particularly susceptible to tornadoes. Some have dense fog on a regular basis, which may cause traffic accidents.

Assessment

- At the beginning of the Activity, show a weather map and ask students what outdoor activities they should do based on what they see on the weather map. Use a local or regional map to determine if students know where they are located on the map, and if they understand some of the basic weather map symbols and how they apply to their daily activities.

- During the Activity, make sure students are able to match the symbols with the proper conditions. Monitor their ability to locate the different cities and then interpret the station model symbols.

- At the end of the Activity, you can assess the answers to student questions.

- At the end of the Activity, you can also project a weather map on a screen or whiteboard, and have students act like TV meteorologists and give a weather forecast. Analyze their presentation based on their knowledge of the symbols and current conditions.

Activity 18 Summary

Students investigate what happens to water when it is cooled below the freezing point.

Activity	Subject and Content	Objective	Materials
Water Can Be Supercool!	Phases of Water	Investigate the properties of water below the freezing point.	Each group of students will need: crushed ice, large test tube, 400–600 ml beaker or similar size jar, salt, water, thermometer, stirring rod

Time	Vocabulary	Key Concept	Margin Features
50 minutes	Supercooled, Hail	II: Factors that contribute to weather	Safety Alert!, What Can I Do?, Fast Fact, Connections, Resources

Scientific Inquiry	Unifying Concepts and Processes	Technology	Personal/Social Perspectives	Historical Context
Collecting, analyzing, and interpreting data; asking questions	Cause and effect: mechanism	Digital citizenship	Scientific perspective of nature	Changing understanding of science

Water Can Be Supercool!

Background

Even though we cannot see it, water vapor is almost always present in the air, regardless of the temperature. This means that water vapor can exist at any temperature.

What about ice? Can ice exist at any temperature? Ice can exist only when its temperature is at or below freezing. If the surrounding temperature is above freezing, the ice will warm up, but only up to 0°C. At that point, any energy that is absorbed is used to break the bonds between the water molecules that make up the ice. When this happens, the ice melts. Large quantities of ice, such as a glacier, will simply take a much longer time to melt; this is why they may survive for many years, even when surrounding temperatures are sometimes above freezing.

What about liquid water? Can water exist as a liquid at any temperature? You will investigate that question in this Activity. You will also learn about what it means for a liquid to be **supercooled**, and how this property is used in the formation of **hail**.

Vocabulary

Supercooled: A description of a liquid that has a temperature below the melting point of its solid phase.

Hail: A form of solid precipitation in the form of balls or irregular lumps of ice.

Topic: phases of matter
Go to: www.scilinks.org
Code: PSCM 009

Objective
Investigate the properties of water below the freezing point.

Activity 18

Materials

Each group of students will need:

- crushed ice
- large test tube
- 400–600 ml beaker or similar size jar
- salt
- water
- thermometer
- stirring rod

Time

50 minutes

SAFETY ALERT

Stir the water gently with the stirring rod to avoid breaking the glass thermometer.

Figure 18.1
The setup includes a beaker, ice water, a test tube, and a thermometer.

What Can I Do?

Search for online videos about **supercooled water**.

Procedure

1. Fill the beaker three-quarters full with equal amounts of ice and cold water.

2. Pour in enough salt so that even after stirring, you can still see salt on the bottom of the beaker.

3. Wash the test tube and make sure that no dust or dirt remain inside it. Fill the test tube with cold water so that the level of water in the test tube is the same as the level of water in the beaker when the test tube is placed in the beaker. (Remember to allow for a small increase in the water level in the beaker as the test tube is placed in it.)

4. Put the thermometer in the beaker. Then put the test tube in the beaker, as shown in Figure **18.1**.

5. Allow the test tube and beaker to sit for 10 minutes, stirring inside the beaker occasionally with the stirring rod. *Stir gently to avoid breaking the thermometer*.

6. At the end of 10 minutes, remove the thermometer and record the temperature for Trial 1 on **BLM 18.1**.

7. Remove the test tube and immediately drop a small piece of crushed ice into it. Record your observations for Trial 1 on **BLM 18.1**.

8. Empty the test tube and repeat steps 3 through 7. Record the temperature and observations for Trial 2 on **BLM 18.1**.

Questions and Conclusions

1. According to a reference like an encyclopedia, what is the freezing point of water in °C?

2. What was the temperature of the water in the test tube at the end of 10 minutes? (Assume that the temperature of the water in the test tube is the same as the water in the beaker.)

3. What happened when the piece of ice was dropped into the test tube?

4. The water in the test tube was below water's freezing point before the piece of ice was inserted. Why do you think the water did not freeze before the ice was inserted?

5. Why do you think it was important to clean the test tube so well before you used it for this Activity?

6. Liquid cloud droplets have been observed in clouds even when the temperature is below 0°C. Is this supported by your observations as well? Why might such a cloud be hazardous to descend through on a plane, given that the plane itself is likely to be below 0°C?

Fast Fact

Hail is solid precipitation that can be produced as balls of ice in severe thunderstorms. These balls of ice can grow quickly when they collide with supercooled water droplets, which then freeze on the ever-growing hailstone. Hailstones can be as small as a pea, but hailstones larger than baseballs also have been recorded. The largest hailstone ever recorded fell in Nebraska. It was 18 cm in diameter, which is bigger than a softball. Whole fields of crops have been wiped out by a single hailstorm. In the United States alone, hail causes nearly $1 billion of damage annually to crops. A hailstorm in Denver in 1990 caused over $600 million of damage.

Properties of Water Data Table

Trial	Temperature (°C)	Observations
1		
2		

Water Can Be Supercool!

What Is Happening?

Supercooled water is liquid water cooled below 0°C. In the absence of something to crystallize on, liquid water surrounded by a gas such as air can be cooled to as much as –39°C without freezing. In the atmosphere, then, clouds of supercooled water droplets can exist (most likely between 0°C and –20°C). With the introduction of something to initiate freezing, the water can quickly solidify into ice. In this experiment, the freezing is initiated by the introduction of a small piece of ice. In the atmosphere, it can be initiated by contact with objects like the ground, an airplane, airborne particulate matter, or a hailstone.

Supercooled water droplets provide just one of the ingredients for hail

Objective

Investigate the properties of water below the freezing point.

Key Concept

II: Factors that contribute to weather

Materials

Each group of students will need:
- crushed ice
- large test tube
- 400–600 ml beaker or similar size jar
- salt
- water
- thermometer
- stirring rod

Time

50 minutes

How Do We Know This?

How do we know that liquid water droplets can exist below 0°C?

Cloud droplets can be observed by probes on specially equipped aircraft as they fly through the cloud. Along with temperature measurements, these probes can determine when the droplets consist of supercooled water.

Hail, cloud droplets, raindrops, and snowflakes can also be detected using radar. Radars send out short bursts of radio waves called pulses. The pulses bounce off particles in the atmosphere, and the pulses are then reflected back to the radar dish, which receives or catches the signals. A computer uses an algorithm and processes the returned signals. Hail generally sends a return signal that looks like extremely heavy rainfall. (In fact, a Hail Detection Algorithm (HDA) has been incorporated, using high-resolution sensors to diagnose which portions of storms contain large hail.) The development of hail seems associated with the presence of supercooled water droplets.

Clouds with supercooled water droplets can be "seeded" by introducing some material that can act to initiate freezing. Once created, ice crystals are more likely to grow than water droplets in such an environment. Consequently, the ice crystals grow and the water droplets evaporate. Eventually, the ice crystals grow enough to fall to the ground as precipitation.

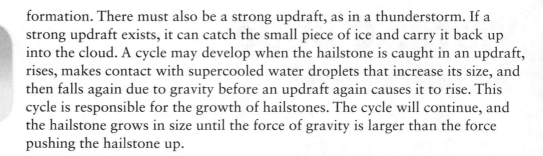

formation. There must also be a strong updraft, as in a thunderstorm. If a strong updraft exists, it can catch the small piece of ice and carry it back up into the cloud. A cycle may develop when the hailstone is caught in an updraft, rises, makes contact with supercooled water droplets that increase its size, and then falls again due to gravity before an updraft again causes it to rise. This cycle is responsible for the growth of hailstones. The cycle will continue, and the hailstone grows in size until the force of gravity is larger than the force pushing the hailstone up.

Preconceptions

Ask students at the beginning of the Activity, "Can water vapor exist at temperatures below 100°C? Can water exist below 0°C?" Students may have the following preconceptions:

- Hail is the same as sleet.
- Hail occurs in the winter along with snow.
- Water vapor can only exist at temperatures greater than the boiling point of water (100°C at standard sea-level pressure).
- Water can only exist at temperatures greater than 0°C.
- When water is supercooled, it is simply taking a long time to freeze, just like when ice is raised to a temperature greater than 0°C and it takes a while to melt.

What Students Need to Understand

- If something (dust, etc.) is present for water to freeze or crystallize on, it forms ice at 0°C; in the absence of something to freeze on, water can remain a liquid to –39°C.
- Water droplets can exist in clouds, even though the temperature is less than 0°C (down to about –20°C).

Time Management

This Activity requires 50 minutes to complete.

Preparation and Procedure

Have all materials either centrally located or already distributed to student groups. Be sure that ice can be acquired on the day of the Activity. It is very important that the test tubes be as clean on the inside as possible. If they are not, particles may be present that will allow ice to form when the water reaches its freezing point. Use alcohol-filled thermometers for this Activity, and urge students to use caution to avoid breaking the thermometers.

Alternative Preparation

If supplies are not available or you would like to do this as a "dry lab," then the construction of a flow chart using diagrams and pictures can be used to show how hail is formed in the cycle. Each diagram can have the conditions labeled for hail formation.

Extended Learning

- Encourage students to try this Activity with other "particles" besides the piece of ice.
- This Activity might also motivate students to investigate the field of crystal growth. Encourage them to research the advantages of growing crystals in outer space, a project that NASA is currently conducting as an integral part of the space shuttle missions.
- Students may mistakenly think that cloud seeding by humans to make rain is a myth. The practice has gone on for decades and has become increasingly more refined. Related to this practice are the many different efforts at hail suppression that began in the late 1800s and were popular until the 1970s. Until the late 1970s, the United States government funded research in hail suppression. An interesting research project would be to investigate the different methods that have been used in attempts to prevent hail and why such research was stopped.

Interdisciplinary Study

- Have students write a story about being caught in a hailstorm. Students can use their knowledge of how cumulonimbus clouds form and the conditions before, during, and after a severe thunderstorm.
- Hail does a great deal of damage to crops. Small hail can destroy crops, slicing corn and other plants to ribbons in a matter of minutes. Farmers can purchase insurance to cope with the hail hazard. In the United States, hail is most common in the area where Colorado, Nebraska, and Wyoming meet, known as "Hail Alley." Parts of this region average between seven and nine hail days a year. As an interdisciplinary project, have students research where hail occurs the most and where it does the most damage. They can explore the types of damage that hail has done on houses, crops, and cars. See if students can find details about the record for the largest hailstone ever found. The record-setting hailstone is mentioned in the Fast Fact section of this Activity.
- Students can investigate the impact of weather on historical events. For example, hail caused damage to crops in France in the summer of 1788. The loss of food and other factors contributed to the civil unrest and the French Revolution.
- Students can investigate situations where supercooled water droplets may have resulted in airplane accidents (a process called "icing").

Connections

Students need to be aware of hailstorms and how to prepare for them. They can learn how to predict them with incoming storms and how to prepare their home. Students can also find out the latest severe weather prediction that includes hail. Go to *http://aftermathreport. com/2010/04/how-to-prepare-for-a-hail-storm* and *www.spc.noaa.gov/climo/ online*.

Teachers' Guide 18

Resources

http://aftermathreport. com/2010/04/how-to-prepare- for-a-hail-storm

www.spc.noaa.gov/climo/online

http://cdn.gotoknow.org/assets/ media/files/000/315/320/ original_diagram-Hail_ Formation-1.jpg?1285631318

www.weathermod-bg.eu/ pages/obr_en.php

Differentiated Learning

- For ESL students, they can use a computer to see pictures of how hail forms. Visit the following websites: *http://cdn.gotoknow.org/assets/media/ files/000/315/320/original_diagram-Hail_Formation-1.jpg?1285631318* and *www.weathermod-bg.eu/pages/obr_en.php*.
- For students who have difficulty understanding the formation of hail, diagram the process in a flowchart that illustrates the conditions and stages in the formation of a hailstone before it falls to the ground. View the pictures at the websites listed above.
- For students who finish the Activity early, have them research insurance costs for hail damage. For example, how much damage does one hailstorm cost an insurance company, and how much does an average person report in lost items to an insurance company?

Answers to Student Questions

1. The freezing point of water is 0°C.

2. This answer will vary for each student or group of students. The temperature should be below 0°C.

3. When the piece of ice was dropped into the test tube, the top portion of the water froze instantly.

4. Before the ice was inserted, there was nothing for the water to crystallize on. The piece of ice provided the particle on which the water could crystallize and form ice.

5. It was important to clean the test tube very well to get rid of any particles capable of serving as sites for growth of ice crystals. If particles were present, the water would have frozen before the piece of ice was added.

6. Yes, the observation of cloud droplets below 0°C is supported by the observations here since the water remained as liquid even as it was cooled below 0°C. The plane, being below 0°C, can act to initiate the freezing, leading to ice on the aircraft.

Assessment

- At the beginning of the Activity, ask students if liquid water can exist at temperatures below 0°C. Determine if students have any prior knowledge of what phases of water can exist at different temperatures.
- During the Activity, make sure students are making accurate observations and following the directions. The data must be recorded, and two trials should reproduce the same conditions and conclusions.
- At the end of the Activity, you can assess the answers to student questions.

Activity 19 Summary

Students will track the path of a hurricane and issue watches and warnings based upon weather conditions.

Activity	Subject and Content	Objective	Materials
Riding the Wave of a Hurricane	Components and path of a hurricane	Track the position of Hurricane Ike and distinguish between a hurricane watch and a hurricane warning issued by the National Weather Service.	Each student will need: pencil and eraser, ruler

Time	Vocabulary	Key Concept	Margin Features
50 minutes	Hurricane, Storm surge	III: The interaction of air masses	What Can I Do?, Fast Fact, Connections, Resources

Scientific Inquiry	Unifying Concepts and Processes	Technology	Personal/Social Perspectives	Historical Context
Asking questions; modeling; collecting data	Patterns and similarity (organization); system models	Digital citizenship, research and information fluency	Populations, resources, and environments; natural hazards	Changing understanding of observations

Riding the Wave of a Hurricane

Activity 19

Background

Hurricanes are the most destructive storms on Earth. They develop from tropical storms (cyclones) and are classified as hurricanes when their winds reach 64 kt (about 119 kph or 74 mph). Hurricanes have a small central region known as the eye, where the winds are light and there are few clouds. Moving out from the eye, there is a narrow band of intense thunderstorms, heavy rains, and strong winds. This first band is called the eye wall. Beyond the eye wall are strong but diminishing winds and thunderstorms. Hurricanes are very large storms that can reach 500 km in diameter. The strength or intensity and duration of these storms depend upon many meteorological variables such as mid-level wind speed, water temperature, humidity, position of fronts, and upper level winds.

Hurricanes contain tremendous amounts of energy. They gather this energy from warm ocean waters in the tropics. As the warm, humid air rises, it cools and condenses, releasing heat (called latent heat). Latent heat is the heat released or absorbed when substances change phases. This heat warms the surrounding air, making it lighter and causing it to rise farther. As the warm air rises, cooler air flows in to replace it, causing wind. The ocean warms this cooler air, and the cycle continues. The heat from warm ocean water is the fuel for hurricanes. For this reason, hurricanes diminish and die when they move inland or move into colder water.

Vocabulary

Hurricane: A weather phenomenon in which a storm is made up of winds greater than 119 kph or 74 mph directed around an area of low pressure.

Storm surge: The rise in sea level caused by wind and pressure associated with a hurricane.

Objective

Track the position of Hurricane Ike and distinguish between a hurricane watch and a hurricane warning issued by the National Weather Service.

Topic: hurricanes
Go to: www.scilinks.org
Code: PSCM 013

Activity 19

Materials

Each student will need:
- pencil and eraser
- ruler

Time

50 minutes

In addition to the high winds—gusts up to 172 kt (about 320 kph or 192 mph)—and the torrential rains, hurricanes produce what is known as a **storm surge**. The circular winds, together with the low-pressure eye and high-pressure outer regions of a hurricane, create a mound of water in the center of a hurricane. The storm surge causes considerable flooding and is responsible for most hurricane damage and deaths.

Weather satellites in orbit above Earth can easily detect hurricanes. Satellite data, along with data from radar and aircraft, are used to follow developing hurricanes. Through tracking, we can tell where a hurricane has been. We also can estimate where it will go in the near future. When it appears that a hurricane is moving toward land, the National Weather Service (NWS) issues hurricane watches and warnings. A hurricane *watch* means that hurricane conditions are likely in the watch area within 36 hours. A hurricane *warning* means that hurricane conditions are likely in 24 hours. People living in low coastal areas that could be affected by a storm surge need to evacuate as soon as watches and warnings are issued.

Procedure

1. Look at **Table 19.1**. It contains four types of data, three of which are the following:

   (a) *Date/Time*: Data in **Table 19.1** were collected on Ike every six hours beginning September 5 through 15, 2008. Time is given using a 24-hour clock; for example, 1200 is 12:00 noon and 1800 is 6:00 p.m.

   (b) *Position*: Longitude and latitude coordinates show the position of the eye of the hurricane. The storm is much larger than the eye, and hurricane force winds may extend out from the center about 250 km in all directions (about one-half the area of one 5° longitude-latitude square on the map).

   (c) *Wind Speed*: This is the maximum speed of the winds in the hurricane, not the speed at which the hurricane is actually moving. Wind speed is given in knots (kt). 1 kt = 1.85 kph = 1.15 mph.

2. Using the latitude and longitude coordinates on **Table 19.1**, plot the changing position of the eye on **BLM 19.1**. Make a dot for each position of Ike, and then connect the dots to show the path of Hurricane Ike.

3. For each position at the beginning of a day (time = 0000), draw a small star or asterisk over the dot.

4. For each of the dates and times on **BLM 19.2**, issue hurricane watches and warnings for specific locations. Base your decisions for locations affected by watches and warnings on how far and in which direction the storm traveled in the previous 24 hours.

5. **Table 19.2** contains the storm surge data for Hurricane Ike in two different states. What does this data tell you about the landfall of Hurricane Ike in that area?

Table 19.1 The Track of Hurricane Ike, September 5–15, 2008

Date/Time (UTC)	Latitude (°N)	Longitude (°W)	Pressure (mb)	Wind Speed (kt)
05 / 0600	23.6	60.4	949	115
05 / 1200	23.5	61.9	954	105
05 / 1800	23.2	63.4	959	100
06 / 0000	22.8	64.9	962	100
06 / 0600	22.4	66.3	964	100
06 / 1200	21.9	67.7	965	95
06 / 1800	21.5	69.0	950	115
07 / 0000	21.2	70.3	947	115
07 / 0600	21.1	71.6	947	115
07 / 1200	21.0	72.8	947	110
07 / 1800	21.0	74.0	946	105
08 / 0000	21.1	75.2	945	115
08 / 0600	21.1	76.5	950	100
08 / 1200	21.1	77.8	960	85
08 / 1800	21.2	79.1	964	75
09 / 0000	21.5	80.3	965	70
09 / 0600	22.0	81.4	965	70
09 / 1200	22.4	82.4	965	70
09 / 1800	22.7	83.3	966	65
10 / 0000	23.1	84.0	968	65
10 / 0600	23.4	84.6	964	70
10 / 1200	23.8	85.2	959	80
10 / 1800	24.2	85.8	958	85
11 / 0000	24.7	86.4	944	85
11 / 0600	25.1	87.1	945	85
11 / 1200	25.5	88.0	946	85
11 / 1800	25.8	88.9	952	85
12 / 0000	26.1	90.0	954	85
12 / 0600	26.4	91.1	954	90
12 / 1200	26.9	92.2	954	90
12 / 1800	27.5	93.2	954	90
13 / 0000	28.3	94.0	952	95
13 / 0600	29.1	94.6	951	95
13 / 1200	30.3	95.2	959	85
13 / 1800	31.7	95.3	974	50
14 / 0000	33.5	94.9	980	35
14 / 0600	35.5	93.7	985	35
14 / 1200	37.6	91.0	987	40
14 / 1800	40.3	87.2	988	50
15 / 0000	43.3	81.5	988	50
15 / 0600	45.8	75.3	986	40
15 / 1200	47.2	71.1	986	35
15 / 1800	Incorporated into another low weather system.			

Activity 19

What Can I Do?

Find a local and reliable news station to monitor a hurricane's track.
Learn about the stages of development for a hurricane. Go to *www.weather.com/outlook/wxready/articles/id-36.*

Fast Fact

During the 2008 Atlantic Basin Hurricane Season:
- Bertha was a tropical cyclone for 17 days (July 3–20), making it the longest-lived July storm on record in the Atlantic Basin.
- Fay is the only storm on record to make landfall four times in the state of Florida.
- Paloma reached Category 4 status with winds of 145 mph and was the second strongest November hurricane on record.

Table 19.2 Storm Surge for Hurricane Ike During Landfall

Location	Minimum Sea Level Pressure		Maximum Surface Wind Speed			Storm Surge (ft)	Storm Tide[a] (ft)
	Date/Time (UTC)	Press. (mb)	Date/Time (UTC)	Sustained (kt)	Gust (kt)		
Port Arthur, Texas	13/0856	962.8	13/0654	47	73	11.25	11.93
Texas Point, Texas	13/0609	972.2	13/0406	57	80	11.79	13.37
Shell Beach, Louisiana	12/0948	1005.5	12/1012	23	30	7.51	7.81
Grand Isle, Louisiana	12/2030	1006.4	12/1730	29	45	3.84	5.22
Calcasieu Pass, Louisiana	13/0936	989.5	13/0818	61	75	10.40	11.94

a. Storm tide refers to the total rise in water level due to storm surge plus tides.

Questions and Conclusions

1. Where did Ike do the most damage before striking the United States? Why?

2. Refer to **BLM 19.1** and describe how the storm moved from the first point you plotted to the last.

3. Where did Ike go after making landfall on the Texas coast?

4. What type of severe weather might have occurred in other states that were in the path of the storm?

5. Judging from wind speed, when did Ike downgrade to a tropical storm?

6. Based on the data about storm surge in selected Louisiana and Texas cities, what can you conclude about the relationship between wind speed and surge, and why some areas received different size storm surges?

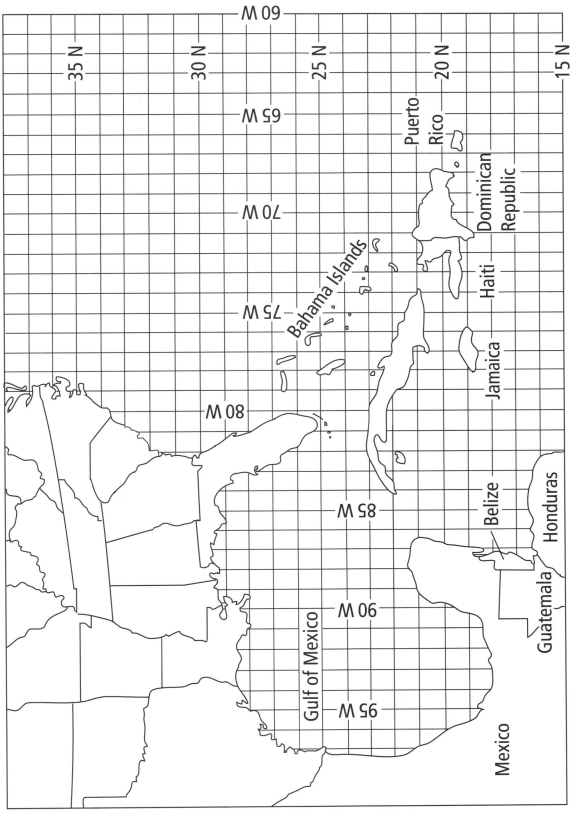

For each of the dates and times below, for which locations would you issue hurricane watches and warnings? Base your decisions on how far and in which direction the storm traveled in the previous 24 hours.

Date / Time	Where Is the Hurricane Watch?	Where Is the Hurricane Warning?
07 / 1800		
09 / 0000		
12 / 1800		
13 / 0900		

Riding the Wave of a Hurricane

What Is Happening?

This Activity introduces students to the topic of hurricane tracking and the distinction between hurricane watches and warnings, which are issued by the National Weather Service. Weather satellites, radar, and aircraft provide data about hurricane conditions for analysis. By plotting the data that are gathered with these methods, the paths of hurricanes can be determined. Combining the data of a hurricane with the data of weather conditions to the north and west of a hurricane helps meteorologists predict the intended path of a hurricane. Hurricane watches and warnings accompany the path predictions. People who live closest to the storm surge are in the most precarious situations and are ordered to evacuate.

Hurricanes form from thunderstorms or disturbances in the atmosphere. These storms can evolve into hurricanes with the proper conditions of warm ocean water, weak wind shears, high relative humidity, and high latent heat release. The warm, moist air rises and causes an area of low pressure. Due to the rotation of Earth, the rising air circulates in a counterclockwise direction in the Northern hemisphere (clockwise in the Southern hemisphere). (See Figure 19.1.)

Objective
Track the position of Hurricane Ike and distinguish between a hurricane watch and a hurricane warning issued by the National Weather Service.

Key Concept
IIII: The interactions of air masses

Materials
Each student will need:

• pencil and eraser
• ruler

Time
50 minutes

How Do We Know This?

How do we predict the path of a hurricane?

The National Hurricane Center uses a myriad of computer-generated models using multiple data sources. Meteorologists use information from all of these models to come up with the best prediction of the hurricane path. Dynamical models solve equations of atmospheric motion and thermodynamics to simulate the evolution of the hurricane. Statistical models use historical data to create relationships and make predictions. Since the 1990s, dynamical models have provided consistently better predictions than the statistical models.

Figure 19.1
This flowchart shows the development of a hurricane.

(a) Hurricanes start as thunderstorms over tropical waters, and then become a tropical depression with winds near 34 kt and a lower air pressure in the center.

(b) High winds spiral inward, rise to the upper portion of the stratosphere, and cool.

(c) Next, the tropical depression reaches the stage of a tropical storm, which is characterized by sustained winds of 35–64 kt, a recognizable rotation of wind, and a more organized center of circulation. The storm grows as warm air continues to rise and condense. Most of the air is propelled outward, making room for more warm moist air to rise.

(d) Finally, the tropical storm becomes a hurricane with minimum winds of 64 kt, a pronounced center of rotation around an eye, and a low pressure. Some of the air sinks back into the center of the storm, creating the eye.

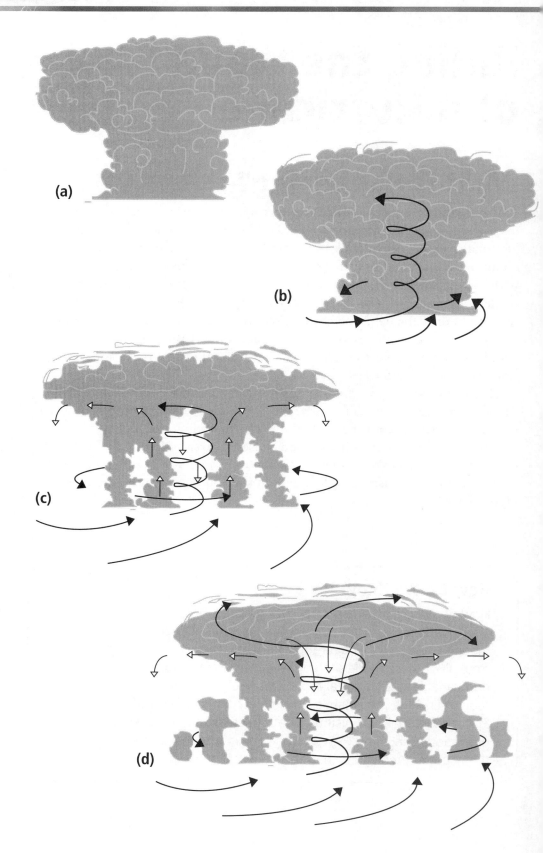

Preconceptions

Students sometimes think that a hurricane is located only at the position of the coordinates that are given. In fact, the hurricane is a large system in which the outer band of winds and rain can extend up to 250 km from the eye. Students might have the following preconceptions:

- Hurricane winds typically affect only very small areas.
- Hurricane force winds are found only in the eye of the hurricane.
- Hurricanes repeat their path every season.

What Students Need to Understand

- Satellites, aircraft, and radar give data as to where hurricanes are and where they are going.
- Tracking a hurricane helps meteorologists develop models of the intended path so that they can issue hurricane warnings and watches.
- People who live in the areas where hurricane warnings and watches are issued need to evacuate and are in the most danger of a storm surge.

Time Management

The entire Activity should take about 50 minutes. It should take students 15–20 minutes to plot Hurricane Ike's path on **BLM 19.1**, about 15 minutes to prepare their lists of warnings and watches on **BLM 19.2**, and about 10–15 minutes to answer the questions. If you use the introduction described in Preparation and Procedure, you will need an additional 20–25 minutes.

Preparation and Procedure

You may wish to use the following steps as an introduction to Activity 19:

1. Tell students that you just heard on the radio that a hurricane warning has been issued for their city. That means they have 36 hours to prepare and/or evacuate.

2. Have students work in groups of four or five, called family units, to prepare a hurricane preparedness kit and a list of the items they will take from their home when they evacuate. Limit the possessions they can take with them to those that will fit in a large SUV with five family members.

3. Have each family unit make a list of how they will prepare their home for the hurricane. Students can do some preliminary research by going online and searching for hurricane preparedness guides (e.g., *www.nhc.noaa.gov/HAW2/ english/disaster_prevention.shtml* and *www.hurricanesafety.org/hurricanesafety- checklists.shtml*).

4. Give students 15 minutes to prepare their lists.

Once students have finished their lists, discuss with them the main characteristics of a hurricane and the resulting knowledge needed to understand a hurricane warning versus a hurricane watch. Typically, hurricane force winds extend about 100 km in all directions from the eye. You may want to choose a city that is 100 km from your school to help students understand how close a hurricane eye can be. You may need to review or introduce students to the concepts of longitude and latitude. Plotting the first few latitude and longitude coordinates with students as a class will help ensure their success with the mapping Activity.

This Activity is best done in the months of September and October when the hurricane season is most active. Whether you live in the west, central plains, or northeast, hurricanes can affect the weather in these areas. It is most likely during these months that there will be some hurricanes or tropical storms that students can monitor. Once students complete this Activity, they can use a large class map to collectively track a newer, current hurricane with real-time data.

Alternative Preparation

Take students to a computer lab and find a recent hurricane in the Atlantic or Pacific Basins. Ask students to collect the coordinates of the hurricane in a table, plot its track, and determine the damage caused by the hurricane. They can get hurricane data from local weather stations, the Weather Underground, or the National Hurricane Center.

Extended Learning

- With the use of Smartphones and the internet, people can get hourly updates about the path and coordinates of a hurricane. For example, some applications will give you storm-centered satellite images, forecast image maps, tropical storm bulletins, radar, and data feed. These applications use public domain information from the U.S. National Oceanic and Atmospheric Administration (NOAA) and National Hurricane Center (NHC).

- Weather services provide many different images for the purpose of documenting a hurricane. This website is a graphic archive of Hurricane Katrina. You can view the three- and five-day cone of the projected path and warnings, strike probability, wind swaths, wind speeds, and wind table at *www.nhc.noaa.gov/archive/2005/KATRINA_graphics.shtml*.

- You can view the history of any Eastern Pacific or Atlantic Basin hurricane at *www.nhc.noaa.gov/pastall.shtml*. From this website, you can download a PDF file, which summarizes the development of the storm, and gives the tracking coordinates, wind speed, and stages of a hurricane. You can also find sea level pressure, surface wind speed, storm surge, and total rain for different monitoring stations for each hurricane. Different images are also included.

You can also download a KMZ file, which can be directly opened in Google Earth. A KMZ file is a compressed image that can be opened using a geobrowser software application like Google Earth.

Interdisciplinary Study

Models have been used to describe many weather patterns and types of data presented in this book. Models make up a very important aspect of science. Even though science is not completely objective, models provide the best possible representation of data that scientists have collected.

- Have students look at the historical tracks of hurricanes in a certain location for the past 10 years. Can they find any patterns and predict what will happen in the coming hurricane season?
- Have students compare and contrast the destruction and devastation of a tornado and a hurricane. Each severe weather storm uses a different wind scale. See if students can find pictures from a hurricane, tornado, or severe thunderstorm, and categorize the pictures based upon the different scales used to determine wind speed of these storms. (See Wind Scales in Reading 11: Scales in Meteorology.)

Connections

Hurricane hunters of the Air Force Reserve fly their Lockheed-Martin WC-130J aircraft into the middle of hurricanes. The purposes of these flights range from determining the circulation of a system to measuring the barometric pressure and wind speed inside the eye of hurricanes. Go to *www. hurricanehunters.com*.

Differentiated Learning

- For ESL students, it is important that they can transfer the numbers from the data and plot them accurately on the map. They can also prepare a flowchart to show the formation of a hurricane, similar to the flowchart above.
- For students who complete the Activity early, have them locate newspapers in cities that have been hit by hurricanes. These newspapers will contain many pictures of the damage inflicted by the hurricanes. Encourage students to research the effects of the storm surge and winds. See if students can develop plans for how to build a house near the coast where a hurricane may hit. For example, what might the criteria be for building the house above ground or withstanding winds?

Answers to Student Questions

1. Hurricane Ike struck Cuba on two different coastlines. The buildings, roads, and infrastructure in Cuba are not well constructed, which means that a hurricane will cause extensive destruction.

2. Ike kept a fairly straight track along the mid-Caribbean Sea, and then veered slightly northwest once it entered the Gulf of Mexico.

3. Once Ike made landfall, the storm continued up through the Midwest and into the Ohio valley, causing flooding in many areas. A hurricane's effect is far-reaching and causes torrential rain, tornadoes, and flooding inland from where the hurricane made landfall.

Resources

www.weather.com/outlook/
wxready/articles/id-36

www.nhc.noaa.gov/HAW2/
english/disaster_prevention.
shtml

www.hurricanesafety.org/
hurricanesafetychecklists.shtml.

www.nhc.noaa.gov/
archive/2005/KATRINA_
graphics.shtml

www.nhc.noaa.gov/pastall.
shtml

www.hurricanehunters.com

4. Once Ike made landfall, the storm continued over land through the central part of the United States. A hurricane usually continues inland for a while and then changes into a tropical depression, then an extratropical depression, and finally a storm front. Rain continues to fall and winds continue to blow, but the severity of these depends on many factors. (Strong winds and heavy rains caused the most damage inland. Near the coast, flood waters from the storm surge caused the most damage.)

5. Ike downgraded to a tropical storm between 12:00 and 6:00 p.m. on September 13.

6. The relationship between wind speed and surge is directly proportional. If the wind speed is greater, this causes higher waves and a greater storm surge. Louisiana cities received less of a storm surge since it was farther away from the eye of the storm. Another reason is the actual location of the instrument. Storm surges are recorded by instruments, and the placement of these devices can affect the readings obtained. If a bay or barrier island is protecting the instrument, less of a storm surge will occur. In addition, if the location is further inland, the storm surge is less.

Assessment

• At the beginning of the Activity, make sure the family units each have a list of items to take for the evacuation and a list of things to do to prepare their homes. Determine if students understand what items might be important. For example, middle school students may not think of financial and mortgage papers, family albums, medicine, and extended family and friend contact information. You can assess these lists based upon the number of items and the importance of each item to a family who is forced to evacuate. For example, give one point for each item contained in the American Red Cross Preparedness Document (move outdoor furniture indoors, close all windows, turn refrigerator to lowest setting, turn off propane or gas tanks and line, fill the car with gas, and collect the following supplies: a three-day supply of food and water for each family member, flashlight with extra batteries, first-aid kit, medications, simple tools, sanitation and personal hygiene items, personal documents, a three-day supply of clothes, cell phones and chargers, contact information, cash, maps, baby supplies, pet supplies, and a blanket).

• During the Activity, monitor students to make sure they are plotting the latitude and longitude coordinates of Hurricane Ike so that it follows the correct path.

• At the end of the Activity, you can assess the Answers to Student Questions, the completion of **BLM 19.1**, and students' answers on **BLM 19.2**.

Answer to BLM 19.1: Hurricane Ike—Tracking Map

Date_____   Activity 19: Riding the Wave of a Hurricane

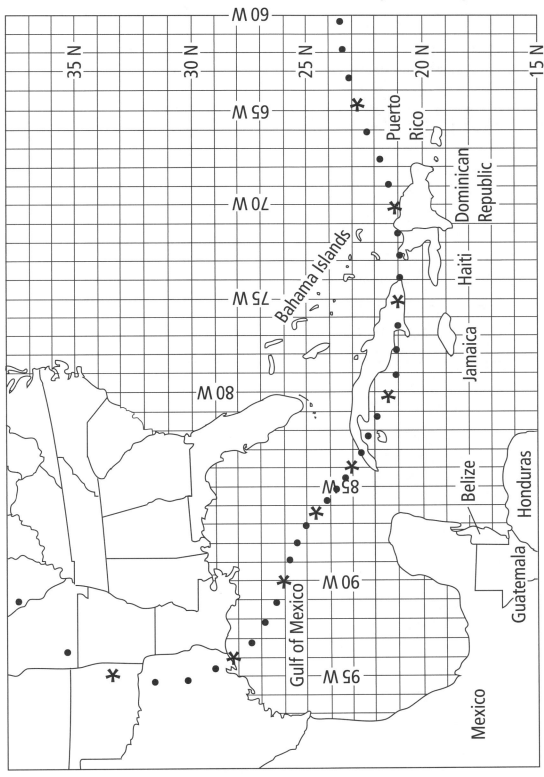

Teachers' Guide 19

Answers to BLM 19.2: Hurricane Watches and Warnings

Date _____   Activity 19: Riding the Wave of a Hurricane

For each of the dates and times below, for which locations would you issue hurricane watches and warnings? Base your decisions on how far and in which direction the storm traveled in the previous 24 hours.

Date / Time	Where Is the Hurricane Watch?	Where Is the Hurricane Warning?
07 / 1800	Bahamas and Haiti	Cuba
09 / 0000	Florida Keys	Cuba
12 / 1800	Port Aransas, Texas	Morgan City, Texas
13 / 0900	New Orleans, Louisiana	Morgan City, Texas

Readings

Introduction

The following Readings provide background information on the underlying concepts in the Activities included in this book. The Readings go beyond what is found in the background information in the Activities. They can be used as supplementary information for the teacher, or to enhance classroom discussions.

Earth's Atmosphere

Meteor is a Greek term that refers to anything in the air. *Meteorology* is the study of atmospheric phenomena and their interactions with and effects on land surfaces, oceans, and life in general. Earth's atmosphere plays a crucial role in shaping the planet's weather, climate, and life-supporting characteristics. Ninety-six to 99% of what is in the air is the same, no matter where you are in the atmosphere (up to about 100 km). It is the remaining 1–4%, the fraction that varies in composition from place to place and from time to time, that has the biggest impact on us in terms of precipitation, pollutants, and global warming. Practically all of that small percentage is water vapor. The other variable gases in this tiny fraction include carbon dioxide, ozone, and pollutants such as sulfur dioxide, nitrogen oxide, and carbon monoxide. Not counting these variable gases, the rest of the air is a fairly homogeneous mixture of gases—mostly nitrogen (about 78%) and oxygen (about 21%). The air also includes suspended particles. The particles in the atmosphere come from different sources such as volcanoes, wind-borne pollen and dust, vehicle exhaust, industrial plants, and combustion processes.

The atmosphere is vitally important to Earth, but its size, relative to Earth itself, is minuscule. Compared with the radius of Earth (6,370 km), the depth of the atmosphere is quite shallow (120 km). It amounts to a thickness of just 2% of the radius of Earth. Even more startling, over 99% of the mass of the atmosphere is restricted to a layer that is only 40 km thick. That is less than 1% of the radius of Earth.

Atmospheric Levels

Atmospheric characteristics, such as temperature, pressure, moisture content, and particle type and concentration, can vary from place to place and from time to time. These variations are responsible for the ever-changing weather patterns we experience. Although temperature varies, there is a general pattern in how it varies with height. These variations can be used to identify four major layers of the atmosphere. (See **Figure R1.1**.)

The lowest layer of the atmosphere is the troposphere. In this layer, temperatures typically decrease with increasing altitude. We live in this layer where all weather phenomena (e.g., rain, snow, hurricanes, and thunderstorms) occur. Most of the mass of the atmosphere (well over 50%) is contained in the troposphere. The storms and clouds that make up the visible sky are concentrated in the lower seven or so miles of the troposphere. Most of the gases from volcanic eruptions settle in the troposphere.

The stratosphere lies above the troposphere. The temperature of the lowest portion of the stratosphere is nearly constant, while the upper portion warms quickly with

Reading 1

Topic: atmosphere
Go to: *www.scilinks.org*
Code: PSCM 014

Figure R1.1
Earth's atmosphere has four main layers distinguished by how the temperature varies with height.

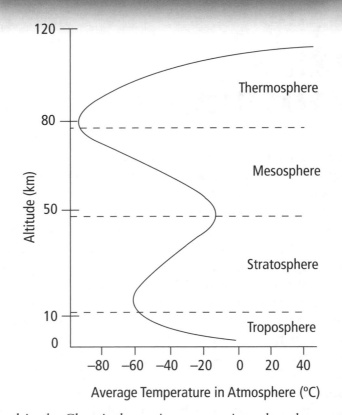

increasing altitude. Chemical reactions are activated as the upper part of this layer absorbs ultraviolet radiation from the Sun. These chemical reactions create and maintain a layer of ozone (O_3) within the upper stratosphere. The ozone layer absorbs most of the Sun's ultraviolet (UV) radiation, which results in increased temperatures in this region of the stratosphere. Since the ozone layer absorbs most of the Sun's UV radiation, it shields Earth's surface from receiving too much of this radiation. Overexposure to UV radiation has been shown to promote the onset of melanoma (skin cancer). Human activities introduce various substances into the atmosphere that pose a threat to the ozone layer because of their chemical reactions with ozone. Chlorinated fluorocarbons (CFCs), which were found in some aerosol sprays and refrigerants, are no longer used (except in rare cases) because of their destructive effects on the ozone layer (see Reading 3: The Facts About Ozone).

At even higher levels of the atmosphere, we find the two outer layers of the atmosphere—the mesosphere and the thermosphere. These layers are made up of relatively small concentrations of gaseous atoms and molecules. Temperatures within the mesosphere generally decrease with increasing altitude, while the opposite is true for the thermosphere. In the thermosphere, high-energy radiation from the Sun is absorbed by certain gases, heating them up. This creates a very warm region. The high temperature also makes the molecules separate into a region of charged particles called the ionosphere, which is located primarily within the thermosphere. Some long-distance radio communication systems depend upon the ionosphere for their transmissions. The charged particles within this region reflect the radio signals and extend their effective transmission range. (See **Figure R1.2.**)

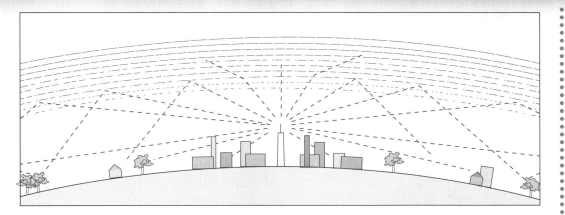

Figure R1.2
Earth's ionosphere reflects radio transmissions, extending their range.

At the uppermost reaches of the atmosphere, Earth's magnetic field guides high-speed particles from the Sun toward Earth's polar regions. These particles collide with and ionize molecules of gas, which causes visible light to be emitted. The resulting brilliant displays are called the aurora borealis in the Northern Hemisphere and the aurora australis in the Southern Hemisphere.

Atmospheric Pressure

The Earth's atmosphere is a thin layer of trillions and trillions of gas atoms and molecules. All of these air atoms and molecules have mass, and they exert pressure on Earth and other objects within the atmosphere. Atmospheric pressure is the weight exerted by the column of air that extends to the top of the atmosphere above a specific area. Air pressure is at its maximum at Earth's surface. It decreases with increasing altitude because the mass of the air above decreases. At sea level, atmospheric pressure averages about 1,013 millibars (equal to the pressure exerted by a 1.03 kg object on an area equal to 1 cm^2). The force due to atmospheric pressure at any point is the same in all directions—up, down, and sideways. This force is also the same on every part of our bodies. Since our bodies exert an equal force from within, atmospheric pressure is not felt as weight.

Atmospheric pressure can be measured by an instrument called a barometer. One type of barometer is a J-shaped glass tube containing liquid mercury with a vacuum space at the top of the tube. (See **Figure R1.3**.) The height to which the mercury rises in the tube due to the weight of the atmosphere is a measure of the atmospheric pressure. We can express atmospheric pressure in inches or millimeters of mercury (in. Hg or mm Hg), although meteorologists typically use millibars (mb) or pascals (Pa).

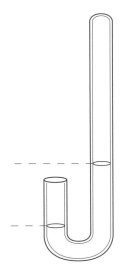

Figure R1.3
A mercury barometer measures atmospheric pressure.

Composition and Evolution

Like Earth's ecological and biological systems, the atmosphere has evolved over time. As it evolved, it changed in properties and composition. Earth's atmosphere was created mainly from gases that came from inside Earth. It is believed that dissolved gases escaped from Earth's interior as the planet cooled and the crust solidified. The gravitational pull of the planet trapped the gases close to Earth.

Outgassing from Earth's interior continues today in active volcanoes and provides clues to the composition of the early atmosphere. Volcanic emissions include nitrogen (N_2), water vapor (H_2O), sulphur dioxide (SO_2), carbon dioxide (CO_2), and trace gases such as argon (Ar). Oxygen (O_2), the life-sustaining gas required by many living things, makes up over 20% of our present atmosphere. Yet, it is absent from the list of volcanic gases. Was oxygen present in Earth's original atmosphere? The answer may be found in the analysis of rocks that were exposed to the atmosphere very early in Earth's evolution—4 billion years ago. Oxygen is chemically active and combines readily (through oxidation) with other elements to form oxides. Thus, rust on iron and iron-containing minerals give evidence of the presence of oxygen. The early rocks show no evidence of oxidation, which suggests that oxygen was not present in the early atmosphere.

Examination of these early rocks and other clues provide evidence of changes in the atmosphere over time. Scientists have studied ancient air bubbles trapped in amber (hardened tree resin) that is 85 million years old. These tiny bits of the ancient atmosphere have shown concentrations of oxygen 50% higher than we find in today's atmosphere. This suggests that the amount of oxygen in the atmosphere varied at least over the past 100 million years. What accounts for the introduction of oxygen and the differing levels of oxygen in the atmosphere from its beginning to our present atmosphere? Some scientists theorize that very intense solar radiation in the early atmosphere split the oxygen from the hydrogen in water (H_2O). Others believe that the first atmospheric oxygen came from plant life. Through photosynthesis, plants consume carbon dioxide and produce oxygen. Evidence of the rapid expansion of plant life over Earth's surface is linked in the geologic record with evidence of the appearance of oxygen in the atmosphere. This suggests that the addition of oxygen to the atmosphere occurred with the establishment of plant life. The reasons for the changes in oxygen level are not completely understood.

Our Impact on the Atmosphere

The concentrations of other important gases, such as carbon dioxide, have also changed as Earth's atmosphere has evolved, and the atmosphere continues to change today. A very important factor in current atmospheric evolution is that humans can now drastically alter the atmosphere's composition. Emissions from power plants, automobiles, and other human sources have an important impact on the level of pollutants in the atmosphere. Increasing amounts of certain particles and gases that trap long-wave radiation emitted by Earth may be contributing to an overall pattern of global warming (see Reading 6: Global Warming and the Greenhouse Effect). In addition, pollutants in the atmosphere react with one another and with naturally occurring components of the atmosphere to form potentially hazardous compounds such as acid rain (see Reading 7: Environmental Effects of Acid Rain). Our effect on the balance of atmospheric components translates to an impact on the entire global environment—ecology, climatic systems, and weather.

El Niño Southern Oscillation (ENSO)

A striking example of the close relationship between the ocean and the atmosphere is seen in the phenomena known as El Niño and La Niña (from the Spanish terms meaning "little boy" and "little girl"). Collectively, scientists refer to these events as the El Niño Southern Oscillation, or ENSO. This name was used for the tendency of the phenomenon to arrive around Christmas. The ENSO cycle refers to the year-to-year variations in sea surface temperatures, rainfall, surface air pressure, and atmospheric circulation that occur across the equatorial Pacific Ocean. El Niño and La Niña represent opposite extremes in the ENSO cycle. El Niño (warm phase) refers to the above-average sea surface temperatures that periodically develop across the east-central equatorial Pacific; La Niña (cold phase) refers to the periodic cooling of sea surface temperatures across the east-central equatorial Pacific.

In 1997–98, the world witnessed a major ENSO event. The eastern equatorial Pacific Ocean warmed 5°C to 9°C above normal, resulting in atmospheric disruptions to the jet streams in both hemispheres of the globe. The end results were floods or droughts throughout much of the world's midlatitudes. California experienced increased precipitation, which led to localized flooding, mudslides, and damage to lives and property throughout much of the central and southern coasts. In contrast, the northern tier states from the Rockies to the Great Lakes enjoyed a very mild winter—golf was played all year in Minnesota!

Weather Events

In normal years, the winds tend to blow from east to west across the waters of the tropical Pacific. The easterly winds push the surface waters westward across the ocean. In turn, this causes deeper, colder waters to rise to the surface. This "upwelling" of deep ocean waters brings with it the nutrients that otherwise would remain near the bottom. The fish populations living in the upper waters are dependent on these nutrients for survival. During El Niño years, however, the winds weaken, stopping the upwelling of the colder deep water. As the ocean warms, the warmer water shifts eastward and so do the clouds and thunderstorms that produce heavy rainfall along the equator. El Niño events occur on average every three to five years.

In essence, ENSO events happen because the relationship between the ocean and the atmosphere is disturbed. Sea surface temperatures only have to increase by 1°C for jet streams to bring storm activity to normally dry regions, and vice versa. During an

Topic: El Niño
Go to: *www.scilinks.org*
Code: PSCM 015

El Niño or La Niña, the changes in ocean surface temperatures affect the patterns of tropical rainfall from Indonesia to the west coast of South America. These changes in tropical rainfall affect weather patterns throughout the world.

El Niño's Effects

The 1982–83 El Niño was unusually strong. In Ecuador and northern Peru, up to 250 cm of rain fell during a six-month period, transforming the coastal desert into grassland dotted with lakes. Abnormal wind patterns also caused the monsoon rains to fall over the central Pacific instead of on its western edge, which led to droughts and disastrous forest fires in Indonesia and Australia.

Overall, the loss to the global economy as a result of El Niño amounted to more than $8 billion. Likewise, the record-breaking El Niño winter of 1997–98 resulted in unusual weather in many parts of the world. In the United States, severe weather events included flooding in the Southeast, major storms in the Northeast, and flooding in California.

More recently, there have been two occurrences of El Niño, one ending in 2010. While the effects of El Niño have diminished in 2011, La Niña also has decreased. This most recent occurrence caused 2010 to tie with 2005 as the warmest global ocean surface temperature on record. ENSO influenced global temperature and precipitation patterns when it shifted to La Niña conditions.

La Niña

By May 1998, the El Niño event was essentially over, but rapid cooling in the Eastern Tropical Pacific led to a La Niña event. La Niña is characterized by below-normal sea surface temperatures in the eastern equatorial Pacific; therefore, its effects tend to be nearly opposite those of El Niño. For example, whereas El Niño led to massive flooding in California, La Niña led to below-normal precipitation in California and the Southeast.

In the past 15 years, there have been three minor La Niña events and a stronger one (the strongest since 1988) that occurred from 2007 to 2008. Most recently, La Niña returned in May 2010 and began to diminish in April 2011. This La Niña combined with record high ocean temperatures in the Indian Ocean and resulted in floods and snowstorms in the United States, including the December 2010 North American blizzard. La Niña will continue to have global impacts even as the episode weakens through the Northern Hemisphere. Expected La Niña impacts during April to June 2011 in the United States include an enhanced chance for below-average precipitation across much of the South, while above-average precipitation is favored for the northern plains. An increased chance of below-average temperatures is predicted across the northern tier of the country (excluding New England). A higher possibility of above-average temperatures is favored for much of the southern half of the contiguous United States. (Teachers and students can compare these predictions with actual weather data.)

Consider the dimensions of this climate event: a body of open ocean some 1,240 km wide and 300 km from north to south across the equator, cooling by up to 10°C in the space of 30 days! Ocean–atmosphere interactions demonstrated an enormous ability to adjust the temperature and weather of Earth.

ENSO and Global Warming

Some scientists now think that these constant natural adjustments may in part be caused by the increase in the greenhouse gases that have led to increased heat energy in the global system. The El Niño and La Niña events are, in fact, linked with massive heat (and cooling) transfers. Advanced computer models, new ocean/atmosphere data buoys in the Atlantic and the Indian Oceans, a system of buoys in the Pacific Ocean known as the Tropical Atmospheric Ocean Array, and more scientists trained in both oceanography and meteorology (called climatologists) will shed new light and insights on ENSO in the future. Next to the seasons, ENSO is the strongest element affecting climate on this planet.

The current research and computer modeling suggest that there is much debate as to the exact relationship between ENSO and global warming. A large number and complexity of variables are needed to study the relationship. The two large ENSO events of 1982–83 and 1997–98 cannot conclusively be linked to the increase in global warming. If global warming is directly impacting ENSO and the intensity of its effects, then the El Niño phenomenon could become more and more intense and destructive.

The Facts About Ozone

Earth's ozone layer protects all life from the Sun's harmful radiation, but human activities have damaged this natural shield. Less protection from ultraviolet light will, over time, lead to higher skin cancer and cataract rates, and crop damage. The United States is cooperating with over 140 countries to phase out the production of ozone-depleting substances in an effort to safeguard the ozone layer.

The Ozone Layer

Earth's atmosphere is divided into several layers. The lowest region, the troposphere, extends from Earth's surface up to about 10 km in altitude. Virtually all human activities occur in the troposphere. Mount Everest, the tallest mountain on the planet, is only about 9 km high. The next layer, the stratosphere, continues from 10 km to about 50 km. Most commercial airline traffic occurs in the lower part of the stratosphere.

Most atmospheric ozone is concentrated in a layer of the stratosphere about 15–30 km above Earth's surface. Normal oxygen, which we breathe, has two oxygen atoms and is colorless and odorless. Ozone is a molecule containing three oxygen atoms. Ozone forms naturally when ultraviolet light from the Sun causes some of the molecular oxygen (O_2) to break down to atomic oxygen (O). The highly reactive atomic oxygen then combines with molecular oxygen (O_2) to form ozone (O_3). Ozone is blue in color and has a strong odor. Ozone is much less common than normal oxygen. Although it forms mostly in the stratosphere above 25 km, it gradually drifts downward by mixing with other gases and because it is slightly more dense than other gases. About 2 million out of every 10 million air molecules are normal oxygen, but only three molecules out of every 10 million are ozone.

However, even the small amount of ozone plays a key role in the atmosphere. The ozone layer absorbs a portion of the radiation from the Sun, preventing it from reaching Earth's surface. Most importantly, ozone absorbs the portion of ultraviolet light called UVB (ultraviolet radiation with wavelengths roughly between 280 and 320 nm). UVB has been linked to many harmful effects, including various types of skin cancer and cataracts.

Ozone molecules are continually formed and destroyed in the stratosphere. The total amount, however, remains relatively stable. Think of the concentration of the ozone layer like a river's depth at one location. Although water is constantly flowing in and out, the depth remains constant at that location.

Although ozone concentrations vary naturally with sunspots, the seasons, and latitude, these processes are well understood and predictable. Scientists have kept records for several decades that detail normal ozone levels during these natural cycles. Each natural reduction

Topic: ozone
Go to: *www.scilinks.org*
Code: PSCM 016

in ozone levels has been followed by a recovery. Recently, however, convincing scientific evidence has shown that the ozone shield is being depleted well beyond changes due to natural processes.

Ozone Depletion

Ozone is depleted by natural causes. Ultraviolet radiation also breaks down ozone resulting in molecular oxygen (O_2), thus depleting the amount of ozone. Two natural gases that destroy ozone are nitric oxide (NO) and nitrogen dioxide (NO_2). These gases react with ozone to break it down to form oxygen. Bacteria produce these oxides of nitrogen at Earth's surface. The oxides of nitrogen eventually find their way to the stratosphere and react with ozone and break it down. The net result of the natural decay of ozone has varied, but gases and processes developed by humans have increased the speed of ozone depletion.

For more than 50 years, chlorofluorocarbons (CFCs) were thought of as miracle substances because they are stable, nonflammable, low in toxicity, and inexpensive to produce. CFCs were used as refrigerants, solvents, foam-blowing agents, and in other smaller applications. Chlorine or bromine are known ozone-depleting substances. Other chlorine-containing compounds include methyl chloroform (a solvent) and carbon tetrachloride (an industrial chemical). Halons and methyl bromide contain bromine. Halon is an extremely effective fire extinguishing agent. Methyl bromide is an effective produce and soil fumigant.

All of these compounds have atmospheric lifetimes long enough to allow them to be transported by winds into the stratosphere. Because they release chlorine or bromine when they break down, they damage the protective ozone layer. The discussion below of the ozone-depletion process focuses on the long-term depletion caused by CFCs, but the basic concepts apply to all of the ozone-depleting substances, including short-term depletion from volcanic eruption aerosols.

In the early 1970s, researchers began to investigate the effects of various chemicals on the ozone layer, particularly CFCs, which contain chlorine. They also examined the potential impacts of other chlorine sources. Chlorine from swimming pools, industrial plants, sea salt, and volcanoes does not reach the stratosphere. Chlorine compounds from these sources readily combine with water. Repeated measurements show that they rain out of the troposphere very quickly. In contrast, CFCs are very stable and do not dissolve in rain. Thus, there are no natural processes that remove the CFCs from the lower atmosphere. Over time, winds drive the CFCs into the stratosphere.

The CFCs are so stable that only exposure to strong ultraviolet radiation breaks them down. When that happens, the CFC molecule releases atomic chlorine. One chlorine atom can destroy more than 100,000 ozone molecules. The net effect is the destruction of ozone faster than it is naturally created. To return to the analogy comparing ozone levels to a river's depth, CFCs act as a siphon, removing water faster than normal and reducing the depth of the river. Large fires and certain types of marine life produce one stable form of chlorine that does reach the stratosphere. However, numerous experiments have shown that CFCs and other widely used chemicals produce roughly 85% of the chlorine in the stratosphere, while natural sources contribute only 15%.

Large volcanic eruptions can have an indirect effect on ozone levels. Although Mount Pinatubo's 1991 eruption did not increase stratospheric chlorine concentrations, it did produce large amounts of tiny particles called aerosols (different from consumer products also known as aerosols). These aerosols increase chlorine's effectiveness at destroying ozone. The aerosols only increased depletion because of the presence of CFC-based chlorine. In effect, the aerosols increased the efficiency of the CFC siphon, lowering ozone levels more than would have occurred otherwise. Unlike long-term ozone depletion, however, this effect is short-lived. The aerosols from Mount Pinatubo have already disappeared, but satellite, ground-based, and balloon data still show ozone depletion occurring closer to the historic trend.

One example of ozone depletion is the annual ozone "hole" over Antarctica that has occurred during the Antarctic Spring since the early 1980s. Rather than being a literal hole through the layer, the ozone hole is a large area of the stratosphere with extremely low amounts of ozone. Ozone levels fall by over 60% during the worst years.

In addition, research has shown that ozone depletion occurs over the latitudes that include North America, Europe, Asia, and much of Africa, Australia, and South America. Over the United States, ozone levels have fallen 5–10%, depending on the season. Thus, ozone depletion is a global issue and not just a problem at the South Pole. Average total ozone values in 2006–2009 remain at the same level as the previous assessment in 1998, at roughly 3.5% and 2.5% below the 1964–1980 averages respectively for 90°S–90°N and 60°S–60°N latitude. The ozone loss in the Arctic winter and spring between 2007 and 2010 has been variable, but the loss has remained in a range comparable to the values prevailing since the early 1990s.

Reductions in ozone levels will lead to higher levels of UVB reaching Earth's surface. The Sun's output of UVB does not change; rather, less ozone means less protection, and hence more UVB reaches Earth. Studies have shown that in the Antarctic, the amount of UVB measured at the surface can double during the annual ozone hole. Another study confirmed the relationship between reduced ozone and increased UVB levels in Canada during the past several years. Laboratory and epidemiological studies demonstrate that UVB causes nonmelanoma skin cancer, plays a major role in malignant melanoma development, and is linked to cataracts.

Even with normal ozone levels, all sunlight contains some UVB. Thus, it is always important to limit exposure to the Sun. However, all life forms, not just humans, are affected by increased UVB radiation. Some crops and certain types of marine life are particularly sensitive to UVB radiation; plastics and other materials also undergo UVB degradation.

The World's Reaction

The initial concern about the ozone layer in the 1970s led to a ban on the use of CFCs as aerosol propellants in several countries, including the United States. However, production of CFCs and other ozone-depleting substances grew rapidly afterward as new uses were discovered.

Through the 1980s, other CFC uses expanded and the world's nations became increasingly concerned that these chemicals would further harm the ozone layer. In 1985, the Vienna Convention was adopted to formalize international cooperation on this issue. Additional efforts resulted in the signing of the Montreal Protocol in 1987. The original protocol would have reduced the production of CFCs by half by 1998. As of 2011, the Montreal Protocol is working, but it will take several decades for ozone to return to 1980 levels. The concentrations of ozone-depleting substances have been decreasing after reaching a peak in the 1990s, and ozone column amounts are no longer decreasing. (The ozone column is a measure of how much ozone is contained in a vertical column of air.) Midlatitude ozone is expected to return to 1980 levels before 2050, which is earlier than predicted previously. However, the recovery rate will be slower at high latitudes. Springtime ozone depletion is expected to continue to occur at polar latitudes, especially in Antarctica, in the next few decades.

After the original Protocol was signed, new measurements showed worse damage to the ozone layer than was originally expected. In 1992, reacting to the latest scientific assessment of the ozone layer, the parties decided to completely end production of halons by the beginning of 1994 and of CFCs by the beginning of 1996 in developed countries.

On April 29, 2010, the United States, Mexico, and Canada submitted a proposed amendment under the *Montreal Protocol on Substances That Deplete the Ozone Layer* to phase down hydrofluorocarbon (HFC) consumption and production. The North American–proposed amendment updates the HFC phasedown schedule for both developing and developed countries and provides clearer direction on addressing HFC by-product emissions from hydrofluorocarbon production.

The Stratospheric Protection Program

In addition to regulating the end of production of the ozone-depleting substances, the Environmental Protection Agency (EPA) implements several other programs to protect the ozone layer under Title VI of the Clean Air Act. These programs include refrigerant recycling, product labeling, banning nonessential uses of certain compounds, and reviewing substitutes.

The EPA also implemented the Significant New Alternatives Policy (SNAP) Program to evaluate and regulate substitutes for the ozone-depleting chemicals that are being phased out under the stratospheric ozone protection provisions of the Clean Air Act (CAA). Section 612(c) of the CAA requires the EPA to publish a list of acceptable and unacceptable substitutes for ozone-depleting substances. The SNAP program does not require that substitutes be risk free to be found acceptable. The Agency interprets Section 612 as a mandate to identify substitutes that reduce risks.

Countries around the world are phasing out the production and use of chemicals that destroy ozone in Earth's upper atmosphere. The United States has already phased out production of those substances that have the greatest potential to deplete the ozone layer. At the same time, we have ensured that businesses and consumers have alternatives that are safer for the ozone layer than the chemicals they replace. These vital measures are helping to protect human health and the global environment.

Air Pollution and Environmental Equity

A National Decision to Make Our Air Cleaner

The Clean Air Act, passed in 1963 and amended in 1970 and again in 1990, is a decision Americans made to achieve better air quality through public policies. Based on scientific information, the Clean Air Act has built on the strengths of the scientific, environmental, and policy lessons we have learned as a nation over several generations. The Clean Air Act defines the responsibilities of the Environmental Protective Agency (EPA) for protecting and improving the nation's air quality, which includes the ozone layer in the stratosphere. Other aspects of the law include emission limitations, ozone protection, motor vehicle emission and fuel standards, aircraft emission standards, clean fuel vehicles, and acid deposition control. Legislation passed since 1990 has made several changes, all minor.

The Act's overall goal is to reduce airborne air pollution in the United States. It achieves this by defining standards for regulating the impact of human activity on air quality. It establishes programs for monitoring human impact, for educating us about human impact, and for cleanup. It also establishes mechanisms for making sure standards are met.

In 1990, Congress dramatically revised and expanded the Clean Air Act, providing EPA even broader authority to implement and enforce regulations reducing air pollutant emissions. The 1990 Amendments also placed an increased emphasis on more cost-effective approaches to reduce air pollution. Even though the Clean Air Act is a federal law, states, local governments, and Native American tribes actually implement the law's requirements. For example, representatives from these agencies work with companies to review and approve permit applications for things such as industrial chemical processes. In March 2011, EPA issued the Second Prospective Report that looked at the impacts of the Clean Air Act from 1990 to 2020. This study estimated that the direct benefits from the Act Amendments would reach almost $2 trillion for the year 2020. That figure dwarfs the direct costs of implementation ($65 billion).

Types of Pollutants

Airborne pollutants are regulated under the Clean Air Act. One group, called "criteria" pollutants, includes six pollutants: ozone, particulate matter, carbon monoxide, nitrogen oxides, sulfur dioxide, and lead. These criteria pollutants are discharged in relatively large quantities by a variety of sources, and they threaten human health and welfare across

the country. The EPA sets national standards for each criteria pollutant, and each state must ensure the national standards are met. Failure to do so is called "non-attainment." Unfortunately, concentrations of human activity often lead to concentrations of pollution. Many urban areas are classified as "non-attainment areas" for at least one criteria air pollutant.

Another group of pollutants includes those that are immediately hazardous to human health. Most are associated with specific sources. Some cause cancer, and some produce other health and environmental problems. This group of toxic substances is large and contains some familiar names. Benzene, for example, is a potent cancer-causing substance released chiefly through burning gasoline. Another hazardous pollutant is mercury. Trace amounts of it are released when coal is burned. Mercury is also released by incinerators burning garbage and by weathering paint. Until 1990, mercury was used in latex paints to prevent mildew.

Areas of non-attainment for criteria pollutants are classified according to extent of pollution. Generally speaking, the five classes range from "easy to clean up quickly" to "will take a lot of work and a long time to clean up." The Clean Air Act uses these classifications to tailor cleanup requirements to the severity of the pollution and to set realistic deadlines for achieving cleanup goals. If deadlines are missed, the Act allows polluters more time to comply. However, a missed deadline in a non-attainment area usually means stricter requirements must then be met, such as those set for even more polluted areas.

States do most of the planning for cleaning up criteria air pollutants, using a system of permits to make sure power plants, factories, automobiles, and other pollution sources meet cleanup goals. Cleaner fuels, cleaner vehicles, better maintenance programs for vehicles already on the road, and other systems are also used. If pollution should get worse, pollution control systems could be required for smaller sources of pollution.

Setting the Standards

According to the Clean Air Act, the EPA must identify categories of the major sources of these chemical pollutants and then develop "maximum achievable control technology" standards for each category over the next 10 years. The law says these standards are to be based on the best control technologies that have been demonstrated in these industrial categories. Under the Clean Air Act Amendments of 1990, EPA is required to regulate large or "major" industrial facilities that emit one or more of 188 listed hazardous air pollutants (air toxics). Air toxics are those pollutants that are known to cause or are suspected of causing cancer or other serious health effects, such as birth defects or developmental disabilities. On July 16, 1992, EPA published a list of industrial source categories that emit one or more of these hazardous air pollutants.

The Clean Air Act favors setting standards that industry must achieve, rather than dictating equipment that industry must install. This flexibility allows industry to develop its own cost-effective means of reducing emissions of air toxics and still meet the goals of the act. The act includes unique incentives for industries to reduce their emissions early, rather than waiting for federal standards. Sources that reduce emissions by 90% or more before the standards go into effect will get six additional years to comply with the act.

One of the major initiatives Congress added to the Clean Air Act in 1990 is an operating permit program for larger industrial and commercial sources that release pollutants into the air. Operating permits include information on which pollutants are being released, how much may be released, and what kinds of steps the source's owner or operator is required to take to reduce the pollution. Permits must include plans to measure and report the air pollution emitted.

The Clean Air Act also establishes a program for preventing accidental releases of air toxics from industrial plants, and for creating a Chemical Safety Board to investigate accidental releases that occur. Between 1982 and 1986, accidental releases of toxic chemicals in the United States caused 309 deaths, 11,341 injuries, and the evacuation of 464,677 people from homes and jobs.

The Clean Air Act establishes "enforcement" methods that can be used to make polluters obey laws and regulations. Enforcement methods include citations (like traffic tickets), fines, and even jail terms. The knowing violation of almost every requirement is now a felony offense. EPA and state and local governments are responsible for enforcing the Clean Air Act, but if they don't, members of the public can also sue EPA or the states or local governments to get action. Apart from these actions, citizens can also sue violators directly. The 1990 amendments strengthened EPA's power to enforce the act by increasing the range of civil and criminal sanctions available to it. In general, when EPA finds that a violation has occurred, the agency has three possible recourses: (1) it can issue an order requiring the violator to comply; (2) it can issue an administrative penalty order (use EPA administrative authority to force payment of a penalty); or (3) it can sue the violator in civil court. The actual enforcement of these amendments has rested on the desire of the president of the United States to interpret the enforcement.

In 2007, 12 states and several cities sued the EPA for not regulating carbon dioxide and greenhouse gases as air pollutants. In *Massachusetts v. EPA*, 549 U.S. 497, the Supreme Court decided that the EPA did have the authority to regulate CO_2 and greenhouse gases. Later that year, the EPA signed an Endangerment Finding under the Clean Air Act that stated that "the current and projected concentrations of the six key well-mixed greenhouse gases—carbon dioxide (CO_2), methane (CH_4), nitrous oxide (N_2O), hydrofluorocarbons (HFCs), perfluorocarbons (PFCs), and sulfur hexafluoride (SF_6)—in the atmosphere threaten the public health and welfare of current and future generations."

Environmental Equity

EPA is required by law to take environmental equity into account in all of its policy decisions. Environmental equity, also called environmental justice, describes the perception of fairness in how environmental quality is distributed across groups of people who have different characteristics. The environmental impact of a human activity, for example, is evaluated by EPA to determine how benefits, risks, and harm are distributed among people categorized according to gender, age, ethnicity, place of residence, occupation, income, and so on. Currently, environmental equity refers more specifically to how health risks are distributed across such groups. In the context of air quality, this generally refers to how exposed certain groups of people are to airborne toxic substances.

Early Beginnings

The first studies documenting the relationship between the geographic distribution of pollution and minority populations were published in the early 1970s. In its 1971 *Report to the President of the United States*, the Council on Environmental Quality acknowledged that racial discrimination adversely affects the ability of urban poor to control environmental quality where they live.

Environmental equity did not become a national issue, however, until 1982, when a predominantly African American community in North Carolina focused public attention on a government proposal to dump polychlorinated biphenyls (PCBs) in their community. Since then, it has become generally accepted that minorities are often disproportionately exposed to toxic substances in their residential environments. In 1983, the U.S. General Accounting Office found that three out of four commercial hazardous waste sites in the southeastern United States are located in predominantly nonwhite communities.

Another study was conducted in Detroit, Michigan, in the late 1980s. After comparing the influence of both income and ethnicity on waste facility distribution, investigators discovered that ethnic minorities were four times more likely to live within a mile of a commercial hazardous waste facility, and that ethnicity was a better predictor of resident proximity to such facilities than was income.

Future Goals

As a result of these and many other efforts, by the early 1990s, environmental equity had moved from grassroots social movement through formal academic research into federal environmental policy. In 1994, President Bill Clinton issued Executive Order 12898, requiring all federal agencies to make achieving environmental equity an integral part of their mission. The EPA has established outreach strategies, internal offices, task forces, grant programs, advisory councils, and oversight committees designed specifically to address equity issues in environmental policy. Executive Order 12898 also required the EPA to address environmental equity in all of its education materials.

The impact of the Clean Air Act will continue into the next several decades. For example, the Act has been projected to prevent over 230,000 early deaths. Most of the $2 trillion in benefits will be attributable to reductions in premature mortality associated with reductions in ambient particulate matter. The remaining benefits are roughly divided among three categories of human health and environmental improvement: preventing premature mortality associated with ozone exposure; preventing myocardial infarctions and chronic bronchitis; and improving the quality of ecological resources and other aspects of the environment, the largest component of which is improved visibility.

Weather and the Redistribution of Thermal Energy

When we describe weather, we typically speak in terms of temperature, humidity, wind, and the presence or absence of precipitation. Weather, however, is not a set of random acts of nature, but a response to the unequal heating of Earth's atmosphere. Imbalances in rates of heating and cooling from one place to another within the atmosphere create temperature gradients. In response to these gradients, the atmospheric air and energy circulate, and thermal energy is redistributed. While there are a number of complicating factors within the redistribution process, it is important to understand this basic premise of the various forms of energy and how energy is transferred from one form to another in the atmosphere.

Three things are essential to understand about energy. First, there are many different kinds of energy (e.g., kinetic energy, gravitational energy, sound energy, thermal energy, and light energy). Second, energy can be transformed from one type to another. And, third, the total amount of energy remains the same (so, if one type decreases, at least one other type must increase). In other words, energy is conserved.

For the atmosphere, four types of energy are relevant. Air molecules that are higher in elevation are associated with a greater gravitational or potential energy than air molecules lower in elevation. Air that is moving together, as in the wind, has kinetic energy. The molecules and atoms that make up the air also move and vibrate independently of each other. This is called thermal energy. Radiant energy is the energy associated with the radiation and light received from the Sun or emitted from Earth (in the form of infrared radiation).

Heat versus Temperature

It is important to note the distinction between *temperature* and *heat*. The most common descriptions of weather generally relate to temperature: "How cold is it outside?" or "Is it going to be hot today?" What is the difference between temperature and heat? Temperature is defined as the *average* kinetic energy, or energy of motion, per atom or molecule of a particular substance. The higher the average kinetic energy of the molecules, the higher the temperature will be. Heat, on the other hand, represents the *total* kinetic energy of all of the atoms or molecules composing a given amount of a substance. Heat can also be defined as the energy transferred from one object to another as a result of a difference in temperature

Topic: weather and energy
Go to: *www.scilinks.org*
Code: PSCM 003

between the objects. To avoid any ambiguity, it is usually better to use the term "thermal energy" instead of heat.

The distinction between thermal energy and temperature can be appreciated through the following example. Compare a pot of water at 90°C, close to the boiling point of water, with a bathtub filled with water at 40°C. The water in the pot has a higher *temperature* than the water in the tub—that is, the average kinetic energy of the water molecules in the pot is higher than that in the tub. However, the water in the tub has more *thermal energy* because the tub contains so many more molecules of water. Thermal energy, remember, is the *total amount* of kinetic energy of *all* of the atoms or molecules composing a substance.

Heating Earth

Earth's atmosphere is heated by solar radiation (radiation from the Sun) and by terrestrial radiation (radiation emitted by Earth). For all practical purposes, we can say that Earth receives nearly a constant rate of radiant energy from the Sun. This energy, however, is not uniformly distributed throughout the planet. The 23.5 degree tilt in Earth's axis causes maximum intensities of solar radiation to strike the northern hemisphere during the middle months of the year and the southern hemisphere during the beginning and ending of the year. (See **Figure R5.1**.)

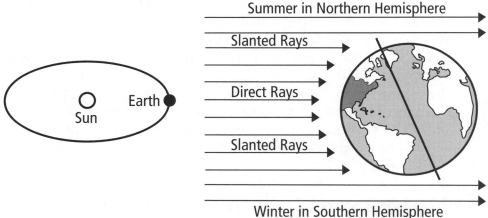

Figure R5.1
The amount of radiant energy absorbed on Earth depends on the number of daylight hours and on the incoming angle of solar rays. Compare the incoming angle of solar rays during winter and summer in the different hemispheres.

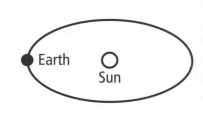

In addition, the curvature of Earth's surface affects the distribution of solar energy. At the equator, the Sun's rays fall most nearly perpendicular. This transmits the highest amount of solar radiation per area because those rays strike a smaller surface area than do rays striking near the poles. This concentrating effect means that the amount of energy per square unit of surface area is greater near the equator than near the poles. (See **Figure R5.2**; this is demonstrated in Activity 6.)

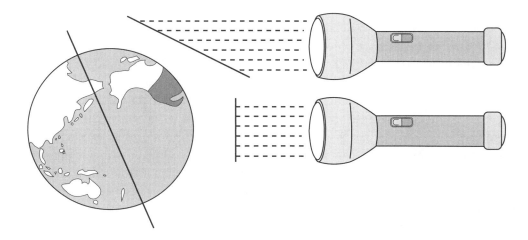

Figure R5.2
The angle at which radiant energy strikes Earth's surface affects how its surface heats. More energy is transferred per area where the Sun's rays strike Earth from directly overhead (near the equator) than where they strike Earth at a slanted angle (near the poles). Less energy per area transfers at an angle largely because the energy is dispersed over a much larger area than when the rays are perpendicular. This principle is demonstrated by measuring the area covered by a flashlight's beam on perpendicular and slanted surfaces.

The atmosphere is transparent to most incident solar radiation. However, some radiation is absorbed, scattered, or reflected by the atmosphere, depending on its wavelength. Radiation of some wavelengths is absorbed by water vapor, ozone, and dust particles; other wavelengths are scattered by air molecules; still others are reflected by clouds. A large portion of the total solar radiation reaching Earth passes through the atmosphere and reaches the ground, where either it is reflected or absorbed. Some land materials—for example, rocks, snow, and sand—readily reflect most of the Sun's radiation. In contrast, bodies of water absorb, rather than reflect, most of the radiant energy they receive.

Heat Transfer Within the Atmosphere

Overall, Earth's atmosphere transmits, scatters, and reflects more radiant energy from the Sun than it absorbs. Earth's surface, on the other hand, absorbs more radiant energy, on average, than it reflects. On knowing only these facts, you might expect the atmosphere to be cooling while Earth's surface heats. However, this is not the case because that imbalance is counteracted by the transfer of thermal energy from the surface back to the atmosphere.

Some of the energy transfer from the surface back to the atmosphere occurs via infrared radiation emitted by Earth. This infrared radiation is then absorbed by the atmosphere. The atmosphere also emits infrared radiation, some of which is absorbed by Earth and some of which is emitted to space. However, on the whole, Earth, being warmer, emits more than the atmosphere, and this imbalance results in some energy transfer from the surface to the atmosphere.

This remaining transfer of thermal energy occurs primarily through two different but interactive mechanisms: *sensible heating* and *latent heating*. *Sensible heat* refers to the thermal energy that we can feel, "sense," and measure with a thermometer. The transfer of sensible heat from Earth to the atmosphere involves the processes of conduction and convection. It accounts for about 23% of the remaining energy transferred into the atmosphere from Earth's surface. *Latent heating* involves the transfer of heat as a consequence of changes in phase of water. This kind of heating accounts for about 77% of the remaining energy transferred from Earth's surface to the atmosphere.

One mechanism of sensible heating—conduction—involves the transfer of energy from a warmer object to a cooler one through direct contact. Conduction is the principle underlying why the handle of a fireplace poker becomes hot when just the tip is left in a fire. Thermal energy is transferred from the fire to the tip of the poker, and the metal in the poker transfers (i.e., conducts) the thermal energy from one end to the other. Within the atmosphere, conduction is significant only in a very thin layer of air that is in immediate contact with Earth's surface.

Convection, on the other hand, is the process of heat distribution within a fluid (such as air), achieved through movement of the fluid itself. Convection is an important process in atmospheric heating. It results from density differences between parcels of air with differing temperatures. The process of atmospheric convection begins when a region of air near Earth's surface is warmed. Warmer air is less dense than cooler air (at the same pressure); thus, it rises from the surface (if both the warm air and cold air were at the surface). As it rises, it is replaced by the surrounding cooler air. That cooler air may, in turn, be warmed by the surface, become less dense and rise, repeating the process, as surrounding cool air continues to replace it. Convection currents or cells are established through this process, and the vertical exchange of energy results in the creation of thermals. (See **Figure R5.3**.) The principle of convection is used in home heating systems, with heaters or hot-air vents usually placed at floor level rather than near the ceiling.

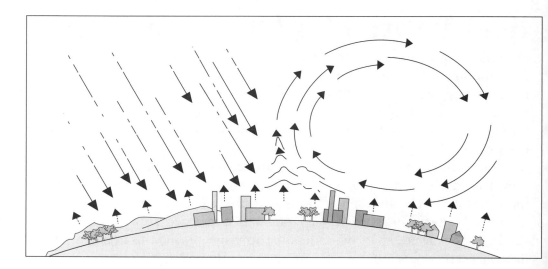

Figure R5.3
Heat transfer through convection

As previously mentioned, latent heating is a major mechanism for atmospheric heating, much more so than is sensible heating. Latent heat is the energy released or absorbed when a substance changes phase: from solid to liquid, liquid to gas, gas to liquid, and so on. The latent heat associated with changes in phase of water is revealed in **Figure R5.4**, which illustrates how the temperature changes as 1 g of ice at –10°C is transformed into 1 g of water vapor at 110°C. As energy is absorbed by the ice, its temperature increases until it reaches 0°C, the melting point of water. During this time, all of the absorbed energy goes into increasing the thermal energy of the ice. The ice must absorb an additional amount of energy to change its phase from solid to liquid (between points S and L on the graph in **Figure R5.4**). The amount of energy required for this transformation is the *latent heat of fusion*. During the phase change, all of the absorbed energy goes into weakening the bonds between the molecules. The temperature of the water remains constant until all of the solid ice is melted into liquid water.

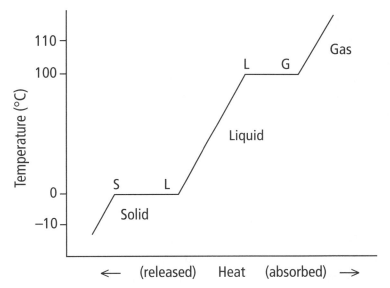

Figure R5.4
Changes of phase for water

As more energy is added to the gram of (now liquid) water, the water's temperature increases steadily until it reaches 100°C, water's boiling point. Just as with the transition from solid to liquid, an additional amount of energy must be absorbed by the water to change its phase from liquid to vapor. This amount of heat energy is the *latent heat of vaporization*. Just like the phase change associated with melting, the water's temperature remains constant until all the liquid is evaporated to water vapor, a gas. Unlike melting, however, the transition from liquid to vapor (and even solid to liquid) can occur at any temperature. The difference is that below 100°C only some of the absorbed energy goes toward evaporation, whereas at 100°C, all of the absorbed energy goes toward evaporation.

As more energy is added to the gram of water vapor, the temperature of the gas increases from 100°C to 110°C. If the process were reversed, the same amount of energy that was absorbed when the water was warmed would be released as the water cooled. Energy is released when the gas cools, when the gas condenses into liquid water, when the liquid cools, when the liquid freezes into a solid, and when the ice cools further.

The transfer of energy to the atmosphere via latent heating occurs as water on Earth's surface evaporates into the overlying air. When liquid water from the surface evaporates, energy is transferred from the surroundings (in the form of thermal energy on Earth) to the water (in the form of the latent heat in the water vapor). As air containing the water vapor is warmed by Earth's surface (through conduction and convection), it rises, carrying the water vapor with it. As the air rises, it expands and cools, and when the air becomes saturated, some of the water vapor condenses into water droplets. This change of phase releases the stored latent heat of vaporization into the atmosphere, where it warms the surrounding air further and causes it to rise more. As the rising air expands and cools, additional water vapor condenses, additional energy is released, and the process continues. It is important to note that the process of latent heating builds on the process of sensible heating and allows considerable energy to be transferred from Earth's surface into its atmosphere.

Local Effects of Heat Transfer

Since heating of Earth's surface is uneven, the transfer of heat energy to the atmosphere varies on a *local* as well as a *global* scale. Variations in atmospheric heating, in turn, result in the development of temperature gradients within the atmosphere. As is the case in other situations, there is a tendency toward evening out this heat distribution. Air moves and circulates (e.g., in convection cells) as a result. This motion causes winds. From the slightest breeze to a raging hurricane, temperature gradients are responsible for producing wind. It is important to remember, however, that winds can be created on a local as well as a global level.

An example of a local wind system caused by temperature gradients is the sea breeze/land breeze system that develops at a seashore or lakeshore. (See **Figure R5.5**.) Bodies of water change temperature more slowly than do land masses. Thus, a seashore or lakeshore heats faster than nearby water. During the day, the air over land tends to be warmer and has a lower density than does the air over the lake or ocean. The warm air above the land rises and the cooler air above the water moves in under the warm air to replace it; a sea breeze is established. At night, the land cools faster than the ocean, with the air above the land becoming cooler and more dense. The relatively warm air over the water rises and a land breeze results as the movement of cool air toward the water occurs.

Global patterns of air motion likewise develop from temperature gradients within the atmosphere. The distribution of heat from the warmer regions of Earth's surface throughout the rest of the globe is largely achieved by global winds in combination with deep ocean currents. Deepwater ocean currents slowly circulate cold water along the ocean bottom in a general direction from the poles toward the equator. Toward the surface, warm water moves from near the equator toward the poles to complete the convection cell. Likewise, warm and moist air from equatorial regions rises, while cool and dry air from the poles sinks and moves underneath the rising warm air. This produces a global wind pattern. The pattern is not strictly a circular cell because Earth's rotation deflects winds to the right of their direction of motion in the northern hemisphere and to the left of their direction of motion in the southern hemisphere. This deflection is called the Coriolis Effect (see Reading 9: The Inner Workings of Severe Weather).

Figure R5.5
Land and sea breezes result from differential heating and cooling of land and water.

Air Masses and Fronts

A region or body of air that has consistent temperature and moisture content throughout is called an air mass. When two or more air masses with significantly different properties meet, they do not readily mix. The two masses interact along a boundary called a frontal zone or front. There are several types of fronts, including the following:

Cold front: A cold air mass advances against a warm air mass, forcing the warm air upward. Clouds, precipitation, and sometimes severe weather result during the passage of a cold front. Cooler, dryer air moves into an area after the passage of a cold front.

Warm front: A warm air mass advances against a cooler air mass, riding up over the cooler air in front of it. Clouds and precipitation in the form of rain, snow, sleet, or freezing rain can result during the passage of a warm front. Warmer moist air moves into an area after the passage of a warm front.

Stationary front: A stationary front is a condition where neither the cold air mass nor the warm air mass can advance against the other. The interaction of warm and cool air along the front is responsible for rain, thunderstorms, and snow.

Occluded front: An occluded front is a condition created when a cold air mass advances against an equally cold or similar temperature air mass. Clouds and precipitation form in a wide band.

Frontal zones are responsible for the formation of much of the cloudiness, rain, and snow that occurs over the United States, especially in winter. At a frontal zone, the warmer moist air rises and cools, while cooler, dryer air sinks and warms. As the warm air mass rises, it expands into the lower pressure environment aloft and cools. As it cools, water vapor condenses, and condensation of water vapor releases latent heat, causing further lifting of the air mass. Winds develop as the warmer rising air results in lower air pressure near Earth's surface and cooler air moves into the low pressure area. A cloud begins to form when the air becomes saturated—that is, when the dew point is reached (see Reading 8: Weather's Central Actor: Water).

Although extremely complex, both global and local weather systems are based on relatively simple processes of heat transfer. Fronts, wind patterns, and convection cells each result from the unequal accumulation of thermal energy over Earth's surface and the mechanisms that exist for its redistribution. Understanding these basic processes forms the foundation for understanding the weather around us.

Global Warming and the Greenhouse Effect

The "greenhouse effect" has caught the imagination of the general population in the last two decades. What's more, the respected, generally conservative scientific establishment has become associated with dire predictions of future climate changes that the greenhouse effect may cause. But, how much do we actually know about the greenhouse effect? Can we really establish how much the climate will change, and when? The questions below will help outline what is currently believed about the greenhouse effect.

What Is the Greenhouse Effect, and Is It Affecting Our Climate?

The greenhouse effect is unquestionably real and is essential for life on Earth. It is the result of radiant energy absorption by certain gases in the atmosphere (called greenhouse gases because they become warmer in the process), and re-radiation downward of a part of that energy. Water vapor is the most important greenhouse gas, followed by carbon dioxide and other trace gases (e.g., methane and nitrous oxide). Without the greenhouse effect, the average temperature of Earth's surface would be about –18°C (0°F) instead of its present 14°C (57°F).

Are Greenhouse Gases Increasing?

Human activity has been increasing the concentration of greenhouse gases in the atmosphere (mostly carbon dioxide from combustion of coal, oil, and gas, plus a few other trace gases). There is no scientific debate on this point. At rates of increase observed over the past few decades, the concentration of carbon dioxide will double that of preindustrial levels in about 2070.

Carbon dioxide (CO_2) concentrations in the atmosphere increased from approximately 280 parts per million (ppm) in preindustrial times to 390 ppm in 2011 according to the National Oceanic and Atmospheric Administration's (NOAA) Earth Systems Research Laboratory, a 40% increase. Almost all of the increase is due to human activities. The current rate of increase in CO_2 concentrations is about 2.0 ppm/year. Present CO_2 concentrations are higher than at any time in at least the last 650,000 years.

Methane (CH_4) is also more abundant in the Earth's atmosphere now than at any time in at least the past 650,000 years. Methane concentrations increased sharply during most of the 20th century and are now 148% above preindustrial levels. As well, nitrous oxide

Reading 6

Topic: greenhouse effect
Go to: *www.scilinks.org*
Code: PSCM 018

(N_2O) has increased approximately 18% in the past 200 years and continues to increase. Many scientists attribute the increase in methane levels to agricultural activity.

Is the Climate Warming?

Global surface temperatures have increased approximately 0.8°C (1.4°F) since the late 19th century, and about 0.5° F over the past 40 years (the period with the most credible data). The slight increase is significant since this is a global average increase over many years, and it has increased the most in the last 40 years. The warming has not been globally uniform. Most of the warming has been since the 1970s, with stronger warming in the high northern latitudes than at the equator. Some areas (including parts of the southeastern United States) have cooled. The recent warmth has been greatest over North America and Eurasia between 40° and 70° north latitude. Warming, assisted by the effects of El Niño, has continued right up to the present.

An enhanced greenhouse effect is expected to cause cooling in higher parts of the atmosphere because the increased absorption of radiation energy from Earth in the lower atmosphere prevents the energy from reaching the lower stratosphere. Cooling of the lower stratosphere (at about 9,500 to 11,500 m or approximately 30,000 to 35,000 feet) since 1979 is shown by both satellite Microwave Sounding Unit and radiosonde data (a *radiosonde* is a balloon-borne package of instruments).

There has been a general, but not global, tendency toward reduced diurnal temperature range (the difference between high and low daily temperatures) over more than 40% of the global land mass since the middle of the 20th century. Cloud cover has increased in many of the areas with reduced diurnal temperature range. Even though brief periods of cooling have been observed, a general trend of warming remains. For example, a relatively cooler surface and tropospheric temperatures were observed following the 1991 eruption of Mount Pinatubo (along with a relatively warmer lower stratosphere), yet warming reappeared three years later.

Indirect indicators of warming such as borehole temperatures, snow cover, and glacier recession data are in substantial agreement with the more direct indicators of recent warmth.

Some long-term trends can be identified in global or hemispheric sea ice cover since the late 1970s when satellite measurements began. For example, Northern Hemisphere sea ice coverage has been generally below average since the early 1990s. Sea ice coverage has decreased in the past 30 years, and satellite images comparing the daily sea ice show that there is approximately 20% less ice covering the Arctic, indicating a continued warming trend.

A comprehensive review of key climate indicators confirms that the world is warming, and that the past decade was the warmest since humans started keeping detailed records. These indicators include ocean heat content, sea ice, sea surface temperature, sea level, snow cover, glaciers, humidity, temperature over land, and air temperature near Earth's surface (troposphere).

252

Are El Niños Related to Global Warming?

El Niños are not caused by global warming. Clear evidence exists from a variety of sources (including archaeological studies) that El Niños have been present for hundreds, and some indicators suggest perhaps for millions, of years. However, it has been hypothesized that warmer global sea surface temperatures can enhance the El Niño phenomenon. It is also true that El Niños have been more frequent and intense in recent decades. For example, there have recently been two minor El Niño events: 2008–09 and 2010.

Is the Atmospheric/Oceanic Circulation Changing?

A rather abrupt change in the El Niño Southern Oscillation (ENSO) behavior occurred around 1976–77, and the pattern has persisted. There have been relatively more frequent El Niño episodes, with only rare excursions into the other extreme (cold phase, or La Niña episodes) of the phenomenon. This behavior, and especially the recurring El Niño events since 1990, is highly unusual in the last 120 years (the period of instrumental record). Changes in precipitation over the tropical Pacific are related to this change in the ENSO, which has also affected the pattern and magnitude of surface temperatures.

Is the Climate Becoming More Variable or Extreme?

On a global scale, there is little evidence of sustained trends in climate variability or extremes. This, perhaps, reflects inadequate data and a dearth of analyses. However, on regional scales, there is clear evidence of changes in variability or extremes. For example, scientists have observed that many glaciers are receding. NOAA plotted the glacier mass balance and concluded that glaciers on average lost approximately 50% of their mass from 1940 to 2008. People living where there is constant permafrost have stated that the permafrost is no longer permanent. Many scientists warn that the thawing permafrost may release large amounts of carbon that has been trapped in plant material and frozen for roughly 12,000 years.

In areas where a drought usually accompanies an El Niño event, droughts have been more frequent in recent years. Other than these areas and the few areas with longer term trends to lower rainfall, little evidence is available of changes in drought frequency or intensity. In some areas, there is evidence of increases in the intensity of extreme rainfall events, but no clear global pattern has emerged. Despite the occurrence in recent years of several regional-scale extreme floods, there is no evidence of widespread changes in flood frequency. This may reflect the dearth of studies, definition problems, and/or difficulties in distinguishing the results of land use changes from meteorological effects.

There is some evidence of recent (since 1988) increases in extreme extratropical cyclones over the North Atlantic, while intense tropical cyclone activity in the South Atlantic appears to have decreased over the past few decades. What seems to be happening is a northerly trend of extratropical cyclone tracks. Scientists predict that more intense storms might occur with global warming. However, the current increase in activity appears to be of a cyclical nature, not global warming. Elsewhere, changes in observing systems confound the detection of trends in the intensity or frequency of extreme synoptic systems. There has been a clear trend toward fewer extremely low minimum temperatures in several widely separated areas in recent decades. Widespread significant changes in extreme high temperature events have not been observed. There is some indication of a decrease in day-to-day temperature variability in recent decades.

As far as temperature change is concerned, widespread significant changes in extreme high temperature events have not been observed, although there is some indication of a decrease in daily temperature. Areas that are commonly more dry or wet seem to have had more intense dry or wet spells in recent years. There has also been an increase of extreme precipitation. Over the last half of the 20th century, there has been an increase in extratropical cyclone activity in the northern hemisphere, while this has decreased in the southern hemisphere. Hurricane activity has also increased since 1980, peaking in 2005. Though data show changes and increased weather activity, it remains unclear whether these are spontaneous fluctuations or part of a long-term trend.

How Important Are These Changes in a Longer-Term Context?

For the Northern Hemisphere summer temperature, recent decades appear to be the warmest since at least about 1400 AD, and the warming since the late 19th century is unprecedented over the last 600 years. Older data are insufficient to provide reliable hemispheric temperature estimates. Ice core data suggest that the 20th century has been warm in many parts of the globe, but also that the significance of the warming varies geographically, when viewed in the context of climate variations of the last millennium.

Large and rapid climatic changes affecting the atmospheric and oceanic circulation and temperature and the hydrological cycle occurred during the last Ice Age and during the transition toward the present Holocene period (which began about 10,000 years ago). Based on the incomplete evidence available, the projected change of 1–3.5°C (2–7°F) over the next century would be unprecedented in comparison with the best available records from the last several thousand years.

Is Sea Level Rising?

Global mean sea level has been rising at an average rate of 1–2 mm/year over the past 100 years, which is significantly greater than the rate averaged over the last thousand years. The rate of sea level rise increased during the 1993–2003 period compared with the longer-term average (1961–2003), although it is unclear whether the faster rate reflects a short-term variation or an increase in the long-term trend. Recently (from 1994 to 2011), the rate of change for sea level rise has been 3.27 mm per year. For the past 15 years, sea level has been rising a little more than one-eighth of an inch per year. This is double the rate of sea-level rise during the past century, which followed 2,000 years of little change. During the next few decades, if sea level rise continues at current or greater rates, it will have serious effects on our coasts.

Can the Observed Changes Be Explained by Natural Variability, Including Changes in Solar Output?

Some changes, particularly during the early part of the 20th century, are well correlated with solar output, but the more recent warm era is not. Furthermore, it is not known precisely how much of the current warming trend is attributable to solar variability and other natural causes; however, comparing model experiments with and without various forcing mechanisms like solar variation reveal that a larger fraction of the warming observed over the past 50 years is due more to the increase in greenhouse gases than to natural variations. Consequently, while the variation in globally averaged temperature over the past century may be a consequence of both natural and anthropogenic influences, the observed changes cannot be entirely explained (or even mostly explained) by natural variability.

Carbon Exchange Policies

As a result of the Kyoto Protocol, initiatives were passed to give out incentives encouraging land management practices that result in a reduction of release of carbon dioxide to the atmosphere. Part of this initiative was to reduce the carbon footprint and have carbon traded as a commodity. Basically, emitters of carbon dioxide can trade or buy more commodities, allowing them to pollute more or less. The intent is to cap the current amount of carbon dioxide and slowly reduce the amount being released. Companies will have to begin to clean up their pollution output or pay more to pollute. The incentive is to slowly diminish the size of carbon footprint that an industry leaves on the environment.

Another effort to reduce the carbon footprint is to capture carbon dioxide so that it can be transported and used in other industries. In February 2010, President Obama established a task force on Carbon Capture and Storage (CCS) to speed the development of clean coal technologies. CCS is expected to decrease domestic greenhouse gas emissions and preserve the option of using abundant domestic fossil energy resources.

Environmental Effects of Acid Rain

Air Pollution Creates Acid Rain

Scientists have discovered that air pollution from the burning of fossil fuels is the major cause of acid rain. Acid rain occurs when emissions of sulfur dioxide (SO_2) and oxides of nitrogen (NO_X) react in the atmosphere with water, oxygen, and oxidants to form various acidic compounds. This mixture forms a mild solution of sulfuric acid and nitric acid. Sunlight increases the rate of most of these reactions.

These compounds then fall to Earth in either wet form (such as rain, snow, and fog) or dry form (such as gas and particles). About half of the acidity in the atmosphere falls back to Earth through dry deposition as gases and particles. The wind blows these acidic gases and particles onto buildings, cars, homes, and trees. In some instances, these gases and particles can eat away the things on which they settle. Dry deposited gases and particles are sometimes washed from trees and other surfaces by rainstorms. When that happens, the runoff water adds those acids to the acid rain, making the combination more acidic than the falling rain alone. The combination of acid rain plus dry deposited acid is called acid deposition. Prevailing winds transport the compounds, sometimes hundreds of miles, across state and national borders.

Electric utility plants account for about 70% of annual SO_2 emissions and 40% of NO_X emissions in the United States. Mobile sources (transportation) also contribute significantly to NO_X emissions, with 50% coming from cars, buses, trucks, and other forms of transportation. As a result of several laws and public awareness, 2005 emissions were 40% lower than 1980 levels. Overall, more than 20 million tons of SO_2 and NO_X are emitted into the atmosphere each year.

In 2003, the Environmental Protection Agency (EPA) designed State Implementation Programs under the Clean Air Act. Under this, the NO_2 Budget Trading Program was implemented to further reduce NO_2 (nitrogen dioxide) emissions from power plants and other large combustion sources. By limiting NO_2, the hope was to reduce ground-level ozone (smog) during summer months in the eastern United States.

Acid rain causes acidification of lakes and streams, and contributes to the damage of trees at high altitudes. In addition, acid rain accelerates the decay of building materials and paints, including irreplaceable buildings, statues, and sculptures that are part of our nation's cultural heritage. Before falling to the earth, SO_2 and NO_X gases—and their particulate matter derivatives, sulfates and nitrates—contribute to visibility degradation and impact public health.

Since the implementation of the EPA's Acid Rain Program (ARP) under the 1990 Clean Air Act Amendments, the United States has experienced significant benefits. The ARP required emission reductions of both SO_2 and NO_2 from the electric power industry by setting a cap on the total amount that could be emitted. The achievements of the ARP led to both public and environmental benefits, some of which include benefits to human health; reductions in acid deposition; the beginnings of recovery from acidification in freshwater lakes and streams; improvements in visibility; and reduced risk to forests, materials, and structures. By reducing SO_2 and NO_X, many acidified lakes and streams have been substantially improved so that they can once again support fish life. Visibility has improved, allowing for increased enjoyment of scenic vistas across our country, particularly in national parks. It was foreseen that stress to our forests along mountain ridges from Maine to Georgia would be reduced, and deterioration of our historic buildings and monuments would be slowed. These have been accomplished but to a lesser degree than anticipated. Finally, the Acid Rain Program has helped reduce the concentrations of SO_2 and NO_X in the air, which, in turn, has reduced sulfates, nitrates, and ground level ozone (smog), leading to improvements in public health.

In addition to the Acid Rain Program, the Clean Air Interstate Rule was implemented in 2005 to limit emissions by requiring states to limit seasonal NO_2 emissions that contribute to the formation of ozone. For example, Georgia and Texas instituted laws for controlling particulate matter. Massachusetts, Connecticut, and Oklahoma passed laws to control ozone-depleting aerosols. Several other eastern states have rules in place controlling both.

Surface Waters

Acid rain primarily affects sensitive bodies of water, that is, those that rest on top of soil with a limited ability to neutralize acidic compounds (called buffering capacity). Many lakes and streams examined in a National Surface Water Survey (NSWS) suffer from chronic acidity, a condition in which water has a constant low pH level. The survey investigated the effects of acidic deposition in more than 1,000 lakes larger than 10 acres and in thousands of miles of streams believed to be sensitive to acidification. Of the lakes and streams surveyed in the NSWS, acid rain has been determined to cause acidity in 75% of the acidic lakes and about 50% of the acidic streams. Several regions in the United States were identified as containing many of the surface waters sensitive to acidification. They include, but are not limited to, the Adirondacks, the mid-Appalachian highlands, the upper Midwest, and the high elevation West.

Acid rain control has produced significant benefits in terms of lowered surface water acidity. In 1995, it was predicted that if acidic deposition levels were to remain constant over the next 50 years (the time frame used for projection models), the acidification rate of lakes in the Adirondacks that are larger than 10 acres would rise by 50% or more. The decrease in SO_2 emissions required by the Acid Rain Program reduced acidification due to atmospheric sulfur to 40% of the 1980 levels by 2002 (which was eight years ahead of schedule). Without the reductions in SO_2 emissions, the proportions of acidic aquatic systems in sensitive ecosystems would remain high or dramatically worsen.

The impact of nitrogen on surface waters is also critical. Nitrogen plays a significant role in episodic acidification, and new research recognizes the importance of nitrogen in long-term chronic acidification as well. Furthermore, the adverse impact of atmospheric nitrogen deposition on estuaries and other large water bodies may be significant. For example, 34% of the nitrogen in the Chesapeake Bay comes from atmospheric deposition. Nitrogen is an important factor in causing eutrophication (oxygen depletion) of water bodies.

Forests

Acid rain has been implicated in contributing to forest degradation, especially in high-elevation spruce trees that populate the ridges of the Appalachian Mountains from Maine to Georgia, including national park areas such as the Shenandoah and Great Smoky Mountain national parks. There also is a concern about the impact of acid rain on forest soils. There is good reason to believe that long-term changes in the chemistry of some sensitive soils may have already occurred as a result of acid rain. As acid rain moves through the soils, it can strip away vital plant nutrients through chemical reactions, thus posing a potential threat to future forest productivity.

Visibility

Sulfur dioxide emissions lead to the formation of sulfate particles in the atmosphere. These particles have decreased substantially by 65% over the past 20 years. Sulfate particles account for 50–70% of the visibility reduction in the eastern part of the United States, affecting our enjoyment of national parks, such as the Shenandoah and the Great Smoky Mountains. The Acid Rain Program is expected to improve the visual range in the eastern United States by 30%. Based on a 2007 study of the value that national park visitors place on visibility, the visual range improvements expected at national parks of the eastern United States due to sulfur dioxide reductions would be worth $1 billion annually within three years.

Several regional haze rules were implemented in the 1990s and 2000s to enhance visibility and reduce haze. In 1999, one of these rules mandated that states must develop implementation plans to reduce visibility-impairing pollution. In 2000, the Western Regional Air Partnership (WRAP) annex was submitted, outlining recommended submissions for sulfur dioxide, as well as an emissions trading program to ensure emission milestones would be met in several western states. The WRAP annex was finalized in 2005. A Best Alternative Retrofit Technology (BART) program was passed in 2006 under another regional haze rule, with requirements to improve visibility in specially protected areas.

Materials

Acid rain and the dry deposition of acidic particles are known to contribute to the corrosion of metals and deterioration of stone and paint on buildings, cultural objects, and cars. The corrosion seriously depreciates the value to society of everything from cars to cultural objects. Dry deposition of acidic compounds can also make buildings and other structures appear dirty, leading to increased maintenance costs. To reduce damage to automotive paint caused by acid rain and acidic dry deposition, some manufacturers use acid-resistant paints. However, at an average cost of $5 for each new vehicle, the total additional cost is $61 million per year for all new cars and trucks sold in the United States. The Acid Rain Program will reduce damage to materials by limiting SO_2 emissions. The benefits of the Acid Rain Program are measured, in part, by the costs now paid to repair or prevent damage—the costs of repairing buildings and using acid-resistant paints on new vehicles—plus the value that society places on the details of a statue or grave marker lost forever to acid rain.

Health

Based on health concerns, SO_2 historically has been regulated under the Clean Air Act. Sulfur dioxide interacts with oxygen in the atmosphere to form sulfate aerosols, which may be transported long distances through the air. Most sulfate aerosols are particles that can be inhaled. In the eastern United States, sulfate aerosols make up about 25% of these particles. According to studies at Harvard and New York Universities, higher levels of sulfate aerosols are associated with increased sickness and death from lung disorders, such as asthma and bronchitis. The public health benefits of the Acid Rain Program have been significant by decreasing mortality, hospital admissions, and emergency room visits. This has been attributed to the decreased particulate matter in the air.

Decreases in nitrogen oxide emissions are also expected to have a beneficial impact on health effects by reducing the nitrate component of inhalable particulates and reducing the nitrogen oxides available to react with volatile organic compounds and form ozone. Ozone impacts on human health include a number of morbidity and mortality risks associated with lung disorders.

Clean Air for Better Life

By reducing SO_2 emissions by such a significant amount, the Clean Air Act promises to confer numerous benefits on the nation. Scientists project that the 10 million-ton reduction in SO_2 emissions should significantly decrease or slow down the acidification of water bodies and will reduce stress to forests. In addition, visibility will be significantly improved due to the reductions, and the lifespan of building materials and structures of cultural importance should lengthen. Finally, the reductions in emissions will help to protect public health.

In 1990, an updated Clean Air Act was issued to enforce regulations and reduce pollution and emission of hazardous gases. The suggested measures also included cost-effective ways to reduce these gases and particulates. In March 2011, the Second Prospective Report was released to look at the results of the Clean Air Act up to 2020. According to the report, the direct benefits are estimated to reach almost $2 trillion by 2020, completely eliminating public concern for the $65 billion spent.

Weather's Central Actor: Water

Water is a special substance, with properties very different from those of other compounds. It is the only substance on Earth that occurs naturally in all three states—solid, liquid, and gas. Liquid water covers nearly two-thirds of Earth's surface, and water in one form or another affects almost all living and nonliving things. As described in Reading 5: Weather and the Redistribution of Thermal Energy, water may change phase in response to changing conditions of temperature and pressure. Although the state and location of a molecule of water generally changes over time, the total quantity of water in all forms in Earth's hydrosphere is constant.

Hydrologic Cycle

The hydrologic, or water, cycle describes how this fixed amount of water moves through the environment. (See **Figure R8.1**.) Water is evaporated or transpired (released by plants) into the atmosphere, where it eventually condenses and returns to Earth's surface as precipitation. Here, it may be temporarily stored in glaciers, lakes, underground reservoirs,

Figure R8.1 The water cycle

Topic: water cycle
Go to: *www.scilinks.org*
Code: PSCM 006

or living things before returning to bodies of water (e.g., the ocean), or again being transpired or evaporated directly back into the atmosphere. At any one time, about 97% of Earth's water is in the ocean, 2.2% is frozen in ice caps and glaciers, and a mere 0.001% is in the atmosphere. The time that any given water molecule spends in one form or location may be fairly long, but the atmospheric part of the hydrologic cycle is especially dynamic.

The relatively small amount of water in the atmosphere is essential in creating Earth's weather systems and climate. Atmospheric heating, humidity, cloud formation, and precipitation are all directly related to the amount of water vapor (gaseous water) in the atmosphere.

The amount of water vapor in a given region of the atmosphere depends on the temperature and the extent to which water is available to enter the atmosphere as vapor. The amount of water vapor that can exist increases exponentially with the temperature. (See **Figure R8.2**.) A measure of moisture content is relative humidity. It is defined as the amount of water vapor present relative to the maximum amount of water vapor that can exist at that temperature. The amount is expressed as a percentage of the maximum amount that can exist. It is termed *relative humidity* because the same percentage for two different temperatures represents different actual amounts of moisture in the air. Relative humidity is generally spoken of in terms of perceived humidity or comfort level.

Figure R8.2

The amount of water vapor that can exist is a function of the temperature. More water vapor can exist when it is warmer than can exist when it is cooler.

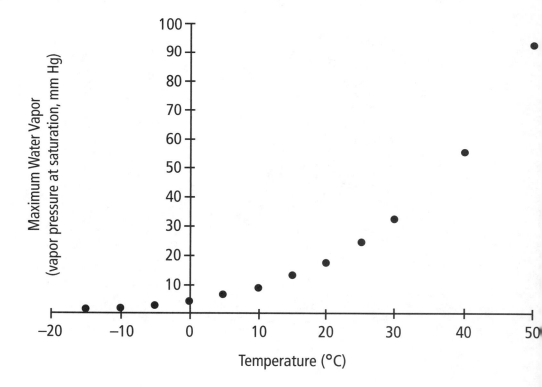

Air is saturated when the maximum amount of water vapor is present, and the relative humidity is reported as 100%. If warm, unsaturated air is cooled, it will eventually reach a temperature where the amount of water vapor already present will equal the total amount that can exist. At this temperature, called the dew point, the air becomes saturated and any further cooling will result in water vapor condensing to form water droplets, clouds, fog, or dew. The more water there is in unsaturated air, the less the air has to be cooled for condensation to occur. For this reason, the dew point can also be used as a measure of the actual amount of water vapor in the air. If the dew point is very close to the air temperature, then the air is said to be humid.

Water's Chemistry

The behavior of water in all states—solid, liquid, and gas—is largely attributable to its molecular structure. The water molecule is made up of one oxygen atom and two hydrogen atoms held together by covalent bonds. The arrangement of the atoms within a water molecule results in polarity, meaning that the water molecules have slightly positive and negative charges on opposite sides. The hydrogen side carries a slightly positive charge while the oxygen side carries a slightly negative charge. (See **Figure R8.3**.)

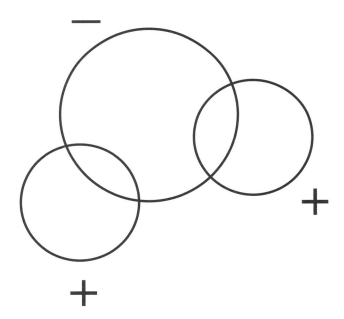

Figure R8.3
Schematic representation of a water molecule. Although neutral overall, the two hydrogen atoms each carry a slight positive charge while the one oxygen atom carries a slight negative charge.

While covalent bonds exist within water molecules, a cohesive force called hydrogen bonding acts between water molecules. Hydrogen bonding results from the attraction between the positively charged side of one molecule and the negatively charged side of another. Hydrogen bonds are largely responsible for properties of liquid water such as its dissolving power, surface tension, capillary action, and droplet formation.

Water must absorb or release a significantly greater amount of thermal energy to change its temperature a certain amount. This is also a result of the numerous hydrogen bonds that occur between water molecules. As the energy is absorbed, a large portion of the energy is used to bend or break the hydrogen bonds, meaning less is used to increase the temperature. This property is reflected in a measure called the specific heat. The specific heat of a material indicates the amount of energy required to change the temperature of the material. The greater the specific heat of a substance, the more energy absorption required for a given increase in temperature. Similarly, the greater the specific heat of a substance, the greater the amount of energy that will be released when its temperature is lowered.

Because of the large specific heat of liquid water and the transparency of water (which allows the oceans to absorb the radiant energy over a large depth), the ocean is able to absorb and store a large percentage of the radiant energy that Earth receives from the Sun while experiencing only slow, incremental changes in ocean temperatures throughout the year (as compared to the relatively quick temperature changes of the continents). The ocean is generally warmer than the continents in winter and cooler than the continents in summer. Since water absorbs and retains so much thermal energy, the ocean tends to moderate Earth's air temperature and climate, especially along coastal regions, where it buffers temperature fluctuations. In addition, the specific heat of water combined with the amount of water vapor in the atmosphere contribute to the warmest average temperatures in the Northern Hemisphere being in late July, rather than in late June when the Northern Hemisphere receives the most radiant energy from the Sun. Similarly, the coldest average temperatures in the Northern Hemisphere are in late January.

Water also has a large latent heat (the amount of energy associated with changes of state; latent heat is described in Reading 5: Weather and the Redistribution of Thermal Energy). This property of water also results from the hydrogen bonding between water molecules. In the solid (ice) state, water molecules are hydrogen bonded to each other in a regular crystal lattice. In liquid water, some of the bonds are stretched or broken, allowing molecules of water to line up in chainlike configurations that readily glide past one another. This gives water its fluid properties. In the vapor state (as found in the atmosphere), all of the hydrogen bonds between water molecules are broken and water exists as solitary molecules of gas. During the change of phase, all of the energy absorbed or released by the water is associated with the formation or breaking of the hydrogen bonds, rather than with a change in temperature.

Water, Precipitation, and Clouds

Water's chemistry makes it a special substance. However, when water falls from the sky in any of the many forms of precipitation, it is not acting alone. Atmospheric particles serve as condensation nuclei onto which water vapor condenses. Condensation nuclei are often microscopic in size and are introduced into the atmosphere from the soil, plants, ocean, and natural and human-made combustion processes. Condensation nuclei are necessary to decrease the rate of evaporation from the drop and allow water droplets to grow. As condensation continues, water molecules coalesce into cloud droplets, the precursors of raindrops and other forms of precipitation.

When the air in an air mass is below the freezing point of water and particles that serve as ice nuclei are present, ice crystals, rather than cloud droplets, may form. Ice crystals form via the deposition of water vapor directly to solid form; they result in a number of hexagonal (six-sided) shapes, which may develop into snowflakes (aggregates of snow crystals). Under slightly subfreezing conditions, cloud droplets often exist in a supercooled liquid form rather than freezing immediately. This is because freezing nuclei that help the liquid water freeze—many do this by having a shape similar to that of an ice crystal—are rare in the atmosphere.

When cloud droplets, supercooled cloud droplets, or ice crystals form in sufficient numbers, they become visible as clouds. The type, size, and shape of clouds depend on the nature of the cloud droplets or ice crystals and on existing atmospheric conditions. Clouds are most commonly classified according to their appearance, falling into one of three major subdivisions:

Cirrus (hairlike): high, feathery clouds composed of ice crystals

Stratus (layered): clouds composed of water droplets that form in layers

Cumulus (pile or heap): detached clouds composed of water droplets having the appearance of a mound, dome, or tower

Various prefixes and suffixes are added to these subdivision names to describe a particular cloud formation. For instance, when a cumulus cloud is producing rain or snow, the suffix "nimbus" is added, identifying the cloud as *cumulonimbus*.

Precipitation develops within nimbostratus, cumulonimbus, and some other types of clouds where sufficient numbers of cloud droplets, ice crystals, or supercooled cloud droplets have formed. When an ice crystal forms in a cloud of supercooled droplets, it rapidly grows at the expense of the surrounding droplets. (This is because, at any particular temperature, the evaporation rate from liquid water is greater than the sublimation rate from ice at that temperature.) Now the ice crystal begins to fall and collects more and more droplets by collision. When the ice crystal passes below the freezing level in the atmosphere, it melts to form a rain drop. Of all the rain that falls to Earth, 95% begins as snow in this way in the upper reaches of the cumulonimbus clouds.

If the raindrops then fall into air with a subfreezing temperature, they are supercooled and become freezing rain. When supercooled raindrops fall on cold surfaces, they freeze, producing a coating of ice. Sleet results when supercooled raindrops freeze in the air and reach the ground as small pellets of ice. Hailstones are ice pellets that are greater than 5 mm in diameter. They are formed in thunderstorms containing strong, persistent updrafts that carry the ice pellets up through colder air several times before they fall to Earth, giving the particles the opportunity to grow in size.

Precipitation and cloud formation, along with wind patterns and frontal zones, are extremely complex processes occurring within the atmosphere. Subtle variations in any number of conditions can turn a threatening or severe storm into a relatively harmless rain shower (see Reading 9: The Inner Working of Severe Weather). While varied and complex, weather phenomena—driven by the redistribution of energy in the atmosphere (see Reading 5: The Redistribution of Thermal Energy)—are all directly related to the unique properties of water.

The Inner Workings of Severe Weather

A vital function of weather forecasting is to provide timely warnings about the approach of dangerous weather. Accurately forecasting such events requires considerable information about developing weather systems. Much of this information is collected using observer networks, weather balloons, radars, and satellites. These data are compiled by the National Weather Service (NWS) and are made available to the public in numerous ways. However, predicting weather changes accurately also requires understanding the mechanisms that underlie complex weather systems. Knowing how severe weather works is crucial for anticipating when it will appear. Let's consider thunderstorms, tornadoes, and hurricanes.

Severe Thunderstorms and Tornadoes

A thunderstorm is a convective cloud that produces lightning and thunder. Both these phenomena are linked to the formation of strong up and down drafts within the cloud itself, although the exact mechanism is not completely understood. During a thunderstorm, positive charges accumulate near the cloud top while negative charges build up in the cloud base. If the electric potential across the cloud becomes large enough to overcome the insulating properties of the air within the cloud, a huge electrical spark—called an arc—occurs. (Most lightning occurs within the clouds; only 1 spark in 10 reaches the ground.) The arc results in a tremendous release of energy that superheats the surrounding air. This superheating, in turn, causes the air to expand explosively, resulting in a sonic boom: thunder. (For more on lightning and thunder, see Reading 10: Flash to Bang.)

Thunderstorms that occur in conjunction with a strong jet stream flow can produce tornadoes. In the United States, tornadoes occur most frequently in the late spring, although they can occur (and have occurred) in every region of the country and during every season of the year. Tornadoes appear as twisting gray funnels, cylinders, or ropes extending down from a cloud base. Two other identifying characteristics are an extremely loud, roaring noise—like a freight train—and an unusually intense period of lightning. Most tornadoes are fairly small—that is, a few hundred meters in diameter—and usually are short-lived, lasting only a minute or two in any one area. However, with wind speeds sometimes exceeding 190 kt (360 kph) and extremely low pressures, tornadoes can cause a great deal of damage as they pass. Cars, buildings, animals, and people may be thrown hundreds of meters. Water may be suctioned upward, leaving rivers, ponds, and small lakes dry. Many of the deaths that occur during tornadoes result from collisions with debris that is hurled through the air by the tornado's extremely strong winds.

Tropical Storms and Hurricanes

As devastating as tornadoes can be, historically they have been responsible for causing far less damage than hurricanes (called typhoons in the western Pacific). Hurricanes begin as atmospheric depressions—low pressure areas—over warm, tropical areas of the ocean. In these depressions, the air at the surface is heated and moistened by the warm ocean. As the warm air rises, it cools and loses its capacity to hold moisture. As a result, condensation and cloud formation begin, and latent heat is released into the atmosphere. A low pressure area develops beneath the rising warm air. This, in turn, causes an increase in the flow of air into the storm. Because of Earth's rotation, the incoming air is made to circulate counterclockwise around the center. (See **Figure R9.1**.) (Of course, this counter-clockwise rotation, known as the Coriolis Effect, occurs only in the Northern Hemisphere; converging air in a Southern Hemisphere depression circulates clockwise.) The direction of the rotation (counterclockwise in the Northern Hemisphere and clockwise in the Southern Hemisphere) is the same as the rotation of Earth (i.e., Earth rotates counterclockwise in the Northern Hemisphere and clockwise in the Southern Hemisphere). The difference is due to the way we view Earth (e.g., a clock would turn counterclockwise if you could view it from the opposite side).

The rotating winds converge within the low pressure area near the ocean's surface and are warmed. They also evaporate water from the ocean surface and carry it into the growing storm system. Once inside the low pressure area,

Figure R9.1
Converging winds are deflected into a circular pattern by the Coriolis Effect.

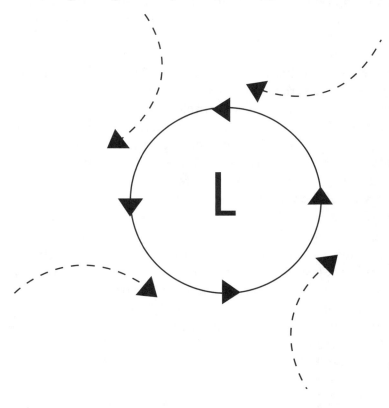

the moist air rises and the water vapor it contains begins to condense. The condensation process releases more latent heat, which warms the air further, and the cycle of storm development intensifies. As it continues, the pressure in the center of the depression further drops and the converging winds are drawn into the low pressure area at an increasingly faster rate. Precipitation begins in the region surrounding the central low pressure area. When maximum wind speeds within a tropical depression exceed 35 kt (66 kph), the storm is reclassified as a tropical storm and given an identifying name.

Most tropical storms (about 70%) continue to intensify while they remain over warm tropical waters, continuing the chain reaction described above. When maximum wind speeds within a tropical storm exceed 64 kt (119 kph), the storm is designated a hurricane. At these high speeds, the converging winds spin so rapidly that they are forced into a ring surrounding the central low pressure area. Within the central low—the eye of the hurricane—the winds are light, and there are few if any clouds. The eye is usually 20–40 km in diameter and is surrounded by a 20–50 km thick wall of intense thunderstorms, called the eye wall. The strongest winds of the storm—up to 150 kt (190–280 kph) in a mature hurricane—are found within the eye wall. Gusts there have been recorded in excess of 190 kt (360 kph)! Spiral cloud bands extend outward from the eye wall and rotate with the storm center. These bands consist of many individual thunderstorms.

As a hurricane and its associated thunderstorms move over the ocean, the winds create large waves, often the first actual warning sign of an approaching hurricane. When the storms approach a coastline, the winds and low pressure also cause a sharp increase in water level. This wind and pressure-induced abnormal rise in sea level is called a storm surge. Storm surges cause considerable flooding in low-lying coastal areas. In fact, storm surges are responsible for most of the death and devastation caused by hurricanes.

Hurricanes can last more than a week. As they move over land or colder water, hurricanes lose their sources of energy. The eye disintegrates and the storm's overall intensity is reduced. However, before dissipating, hurricanes that move inland generally bring heavy rains, strong winds, and flooding. Some hurricanes have produced their worst flooding long after coming ashore.

Since hurricanes are fueled by warm ocean waters, "hurricane season" occurs only when the water temperature is high enough (above 26°C) to sustain the development of tropical storms. Temperatures in tropical waters usually reach this level in late summer and early fall in the Northern Hemisphere.

Severe Weather Watch/Warning System

In an effort to keep people informed about occurrences of severe weather, the NWS has devised a watch/warning system. Forecasters issue a severe thunderstorm or tornado watch when the conditions during the following few hours will be right for the formation of a severe thunderstorm or tornado over a given region. People within a watch area are advised to be on the lookout for dangerous weather. When a severe thunderstorm or a tornado is sighted by ground observers or by radar, a warning is issued, advising people within the surrounding area to take protective measures immediately. In many tornado-prone areas, communities have emergency preparedness plans for coping with such severe weather.

Weather satellites effectively track tropical storms and hurricanes over the entire Earth. When these storms move to within a few hundred kilometers of land, airplanes equipped with special instruments and ground radars also are used to track their movement and determine their characteristics. When a possibility exists that a hurricane will come ashore within the next 48 hours, a hurricane watch is issued by the NWS. If landfall is likely within the next 36 hours, a hurricane warning is issued. When these are announced, quick evacuation of people in low-lying areas is essential.

Thunderstorms, tornadoes, and hurricanes are only three kinds of severe weather patterns. Similarly dangerous are events such as lightning, blizzards, severe heat waves, and flash floods. Over the last 20 years, in fact, flash floods have been the most deadly severe weather problem in the United States. Watches and warnings must be taken seriously to minimize the risks to life and property.

Flash to Bang Reading

- *October 16, 1992, Houston:* Thirty-five football players and coaches at practice were injured by lightning at 8:30 a.m. during light drizzle.
- *May 31, 2010, North Carolina:* One inmate was killed and five other prisoners were injured by lightning while leaving the recreation yard.
- *June 8, 2010, Ohio:* A 25-year-old female was killed by lightning while hiking up a mountain where her fiancé was about to propose.
- *June 15, 2010, Orlando:* A 34-year-old female letter carrier sheltering under a tree was critically injured by lightning.

Introduction

Lightning is the abrupt discharge of static electricity that reestablishes electrostatic equilibrium within a storm environment. It is one of nature's most spectacular displays, yet it remains far from being well understood. Each year across the United States, dozens of school children are killed or injured by lightning at outdoor extracurricular activities, during recess, or on the way to or from school. Lightning is the most frequent important weather threat to personal safety during the thunderstorm season. If people were better educated about the dangers of lightning, used common sense, and practiced safety techniques before, during, and after thunderstorms, fatalities and injuries from lightning strikes could be sharply reduced.

Deaths From Severe Weather

The threat of lightning sometimes receives less attention than other weather hazards such as hurricanes, tornadoes, and flash floods. In the last several decades, lightning has been one of the leading causes of weather-related deaths. For example, **Figure R10.1** shows that 41 people were killed by lightning on average each year from 2000 to 2009. Between 1959 and 2009, 3,919 people were killed by lightning in the United States, according to statistics from the National Oceanic and Atmospheric Administration (NOAA). Go to *www.weather.gov/os/lightning/stats/59-09_fatalities_rates.pdf*.

For the 30-year period beginning in 1966, lightning ranked just behind tornadoes and flash floods in weather-related deaths. (See **Figure R10.2**.) In addition, injuries are more than 2.5 times more numerous than deaths due to lightning, so the number of people affected by lightning every year is larger than generally perceived. Tornadoes, hurricanes, and flash floods are often spectacular, resulting in multiple deaths and massive destruction of property, so they make headlines. Lightning usually takes its victims one at a time, so it is not given the attention it requires as a common threat.

Project Earth Science: Meteorology, Revised 2nd Edition **271**

Topic: tornadoes
Go to: *www.scilinks.org*
Code: PSCM 021

Figure R10.1
Average yearly weather-related deaths in the United States between 2000 and 2009

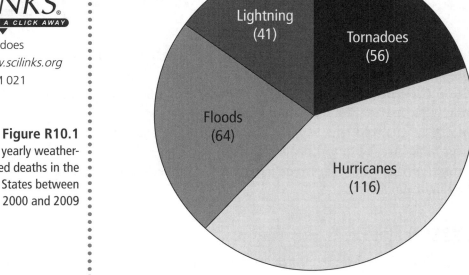

Source: National Oceanic and Atmospheric Administration (NOAA)
www.weather.gov/om/hazstats.shtml

Figure R10.2
Annual number of storm-related deaths in the United States from 1966–1995 (from Storm Data, National Climatic Data Center, NOAA, Asheville, NC)

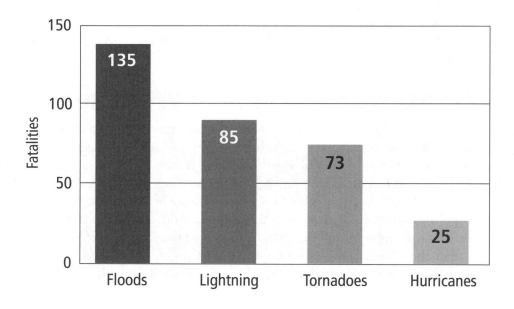

Lightning

To appreciate the scope of electrical activity and the threat from lightning, look at the over 15,000 lightning strikes to hit the ground in a six-hour period in the Midwest in **Figure R10.3**. This type of map is continuously produced by networks of electromagnetic sensors that chart cloud-to-ground lightning strikes for the continental United States and other countries. Such networks were developed for forest fire detection and utility company needs. However, uses have expanded into such applications as refueling and baggage handling at airports, crowd management at golf tournaments, thunderstorm monitoring and forecasting by weather services, and understanding the nature of lightning itself. The episode in **Figure R10.3** was related to an advancing cold front and associated thunderstorms. Two people were injured by lightning on this day at O'Hare Airport in Chicago.

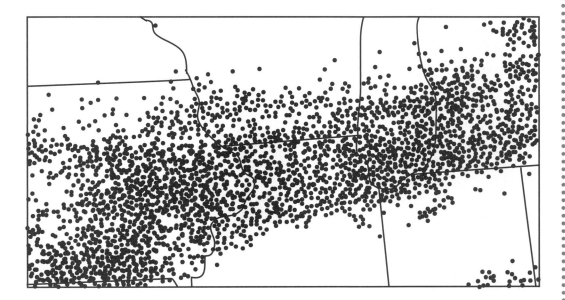

Figure R10.3
Map of more than 15,000 lightning strikes to ground in a six-hour period across the Midwest.

Lightning strikes can be quite spectacular, particularly when the bolt suddenly discharges electricity between charged regions of thunderclouds and the ground. However, only about 10% of lightning strikes are cloud-to-ground. The rest are either cloud-to-cloud or within a cloud (known as intracloud). Satellites are now equipped with sensors that can detect lightning flashes from above. The two detectors are the Optical Transient Detector (OTD) and the Lightning Imaging Sensor (LIS). These satellites were launched in 1995 and 1997 respectively, and the latter satellite is still collecting data. These optical sensors are basically high-speed cameras that can take visual pictures of the top of clouds in a certain wavelength. Soon, a newer instrument will be placed aboard a satellite that is in a geostationary orbit. The lightning Mapper Sensor (LMS) will detect all forms of lightning with a high spatial resolution.

Research findings determined from these satellite data are that lightning avoids the ocean, but it likes Florida. Lightning strikes are widely detected in the Himalayas and central Africa. Lightning almost never strikes the North Pole and the South Pole. Global patterns are probably not influenced by human activity. This means that buildings and metal communication towers do not increase the overall frequency of lightning.

Thunder

The distance to lightning from your location can be found using the fact that light travels enormously faster than sound. This difference leads to the "flash-to-bang" method:

- See the flash.
- Count the seconds to the bang of its thunder. Divide the number of seconds by 5 to give the approximate distance in miles from you to the lightning. For example, suppose it takes 15 seconds between the time when you see lightning and when you hear its thunder. Divide 15 by 5 to give a distance of about 3 miles from where lightning occurred to your location.

Thunder is produced when air immediately around the lightning channel is superheated, in less than a second, to 8,000–33,000°C. When air is heated this quickly, it explodes. When lightning strikes nearby, the sound may be a loud bang, crack, or snap. There often follows a rumbling or growling sound caused by sounds from different heights along the channel at farther distances than the nearby strike point. The sound reaches our ears at varying times and may last for several seconds.

Thunder often can be heard up to about 10 miles away (50 seconds from flash to bang) and rarely up to 15–25 miles away if one is in a very quiet location, especially at night. At those distances, however, thunder is heard as a very low rumbling. During heavy rain and wind, thunder will not be heard as far.

Several studies completed by NOAA have found that the average distance between successive ground strikes in the same storm was about 2–3 miles. Since this distance was an average, some flashes were within 2–3 miles, and the rest were beyond that distance. (Two to three miles corresponds to 10–15 seconds from flash to bang.) If you are within 2–3 miles of a flash, *the next flash can easily strike your location*. Also, remember that the 2–3 mile range is an *average*. Half of all subsequent lightning strikes fall beyond this range. (Subsequent ground strikes from the same storm have been reported to land up to 10 miles and farther away!) Knowing this makes it clear why precautions are needed even when the flash-to-bang exceeds 3 miles.

Lightning and People

National statistics show that most lightning fatalities occur between 10 a.m. and 7 p.m., which is when people are outdoors most often, but thunderstorms occur most often in the afternoon and evening. Lightning deaths are more frequent from late spring through early autumn, with July having the most fatalities. (See Figure **R10.4**.) The top 10 states for casualties and injuries in 2011 were, in order of casualties: Florida, Michigan, Pennsylvania, North Carolina, New York, Ohio, Texas, Tennessee, Georgia, and Colorado.

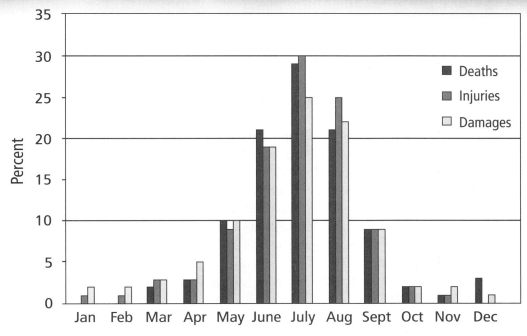

Figure R10.4
Monthly distribution of lightning deaths, injuries, and damage between 1959 and 1994 in the United States

Source: National Oceanic and Atmospheric Administration (NOAA), *www.nssl.noaa.gov/papers/techmemos/NWS-SR-193/techmemo-sr193-6.html*

In the last five years, Florida had the most lightning deaths and injuries. In a recent study for central Florida by scientists at Florida State University and Patrick Air Force Base, more lightning casualties occurred before or after the peak lightning activity. Such a pattern may occur because, at these times, the flash rate is lower and it is not raining as hard, so people may feel safer being outside.

The lightning statistics for central Florida have been the most commonly collected by scientists at NOAA due to the large number of lightning strikes annually. From 1959 to 2007, 84 people were killed by lightning in 10 counties, and 317 were injured. In central Florida, the most common lightning fatalities and injuries were, in order of occurrence:

1. near or in the water
2. near or under a tree
3. near a vehicle, home, or building
4. on a golf course, ball field, or similar situation

By contrast, lightning casualties in Colorado occur during climbing and hiking in the mountains more than any other single category; in Florida, casualties during water sports are the most frequent. Statistics show that agricultural lightning casualties are declining as people move to urban areas, and recreational lightning casualites are growing.

Lightning striking near a person, known as a side flash, can cause injury, blindness, deafness, or death. The side flash is a very important feature of the lightning hazard, because many casualties are not directly struck by the flash. The side flash hazard depends on many factors, especially the following:

- distance to the ground strike point
- soil conductivity (wet soil conducts better than dry soil)
- strength of the electric current

Side flash deaths are most common outdoors, but they also can happen indoors through telephones, electrical appliances, and water pipes connected to sinks, showers, or baths.

The risk of death or injury from a lightning strike may be greater than official data show. Recent research in Colorado indicates that deaths and injuries there are underreported by as much as 40%. In addition, some deaths and injuries are not reported when they are caused indirectly by lightning—from a lightning-caused fire for example—but not directly resulting from a lightning strike.

The underreporting of lightning-caused deaths and injuries may be 30% or more. About 20% of all people who are casualties of lightning are killed. It is estimated that the chances of any one person being a casualty of lightning is one in 600,000. Before his death due to other causes, Roy "Dooms" Sullivan, a park ranger from Virginia, was injured on seven different occasions by lightning.

Lightning and Property

Lightning strikes have damaged buildings, electrical transmitters, livestock, and aircraft electrical systems, and caused many forest and range fires. Any object has the potential to be struck by lightning, especially if it protrudes above the ground. Tall, metallic, isolated objects are especially vulnerable compared to other materials in the immediate surroundings.

When aircraft in flight are struck by lightning, the aircraft itself usually induces the flash. Typically, there is little or no damage to the flying aircraft. Commercial aircraft are struck by lightning once every 5,000 to 10,000 flight hours.

In 1967, *Apollo 12* flight and ground crews suffered anxious moments when the launch triggered two lightning strikes to the craft, causing minor damage. On March 26, 1987, an unmanned *Atlas-Centaur* rocket with a satellite was destroyed when lightning struck it shortly after liftoff.

Over $100 million damage by lightning is reported annually in the United States, but the amount is much larger for several reasons:

- *Uninsured* minor but frequent damage is caused by direct or indirect lightning strikes to houses, electronics, trees, and many other objects. A location in the United States with an average lightning frequency, such as the Midwest or East, is estimated to be struck once within every one-hundred-year period.
- *Protection* expenses are significant each year on such facilities as power lines and buildings.
- *Avoidance* costs are large (but hard to quantify) for construction crews who stop work in threatening weather, and recreation that is canceled or delayed.

The Lightning Flash

Electrical activity has been observed on Venus, Jupiter, Saturn, and Uranus, and may occur on other planets. On Earth, lightning originates in thunderstorms and occasionally in clouds during volcanic eruptions. There is a beneficial effect of lightning: It produces fixed nitrogen, which is necessary for fertilization of plants.

At any given moment, 2,000 thunderstorms are estimated to be underway around the world, and lightning strikes the ground about 100 times each second, or 8 million times a day. Data from the new networks of electromagnetic sensors (these sensors produced the data for **Figure R10.3**) indicate that about 25 million flashes strike the ground in the United States annually. The United States has at least 100 million lightning flashes every year. One ground lightning stroke can generate between 100 million and 1 billion volts of electricity. The air within a lightning strike can reach 50,000°F (or nearly 30,000°C).

Lightning is divided into two general types:

- cloud-to-ground lightning
- cloud discharge or in-cloud lightning

Cloud-to-ground lightning originates from the base of a thunderstorm. A path of ionized particles called step leaders forms, originating from the cloud. These particles are called step leaders because they lead the ionization process in a certain direction as the lightning forms. These step leaders surge downward about 50 m at a time, sometimes more in the horizontal than vertical, attempting to complete a channel with the ground. When the leader is close to the ground, one or more streamers of electricity reach upward from such objects as grass, tall trees, and buildings. The last surge of electricity or lightning within a step leader, before completing the channel with ground, is usually vertical. The entire process of recurrent electrical surges downward and streamers upward takes less than a second.

Once the channel is complete, a surge of electrical current from the ground moves upward along the channel, producing an upward-propagating bright luminosity. Negative charge, however, is being transferred to the ground. This discharge process is called a return stroke. After the first stroke, additional leaders can deposit negative charge down along the old channel and, as connection with the ground is established, another upward current surge occurs as the charge is brought to the ground. This process constitutes another return stroke. This can happen several times along the same channel.

The whole sequence of first and subsequent strokes is a flash. (See **Figure R10.5**.) A typical flash has two to four return strokes. However, one cloud-to-ground flash near Cape Canaveral produced 26 return strokes and lasted over two seconds!

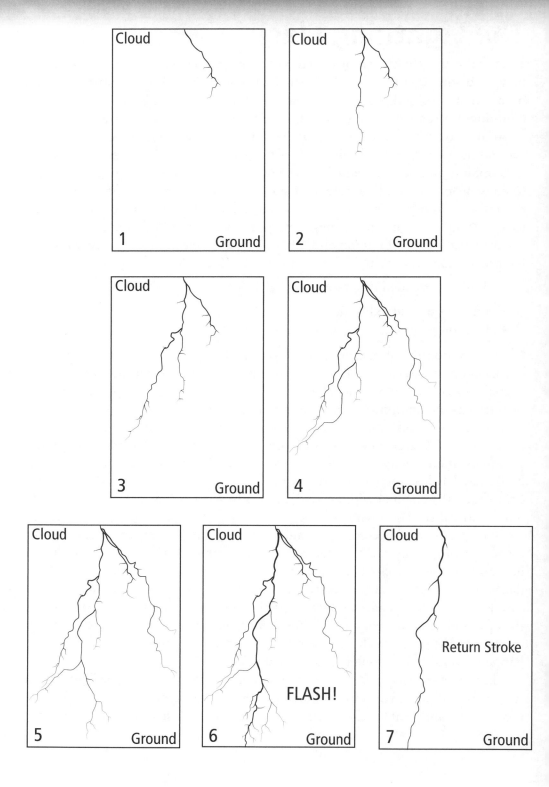

Figure R10.5
Diagram of cloud-to-ground lightning flash sequence

Since the leaders, streamers, and return strokes happen so fast, we cannot see luminosity propagate up the channel. However, we can see a flickering of the luminosity corresponding to different return strokes. The actual diameter of a lightning channel is 2–5 cm. Note the terminology here:

- A *flash* consists of one or more return strokes. Flickering indicates more than one return stroke.
- A *ground strike* is a flash that hits the ground.

We use only the terms *flash*, *return stroke*, and *ground strike* in this review—the word *bolt* has no clear definition for lightning.

A thunderstorm can produce several hundred megawatts of energy—comparable to the output of a small nuclear power plant. A flash has 1 billion volts of energy, with a peak current between 10,000 and 200,000 amperes. These amounts of energy account for the degree of damage to people and objects struck by lightning. The average flash could light a 100-watt bulb for more than three months. The brightness of a single flash is more than 10,000,000 light bulbs of 100 watts. It is no wonder that eye damage is common to people very near a strike. Unfortunately, harnessing this electrical power is not feasible. The flash would need to be where it is wanted, and it is so brief that no equipment could capture the tremendous surge without damage.

The Thunderstorm

Thunderstorms are usually like a dipole, where positive charges are found at the top, and negative charges are found at the base. The ground, normally negatively charged, reverses polarity under a thunderstorm and becomes positively charged. This reverse in polarity is caused by a strong negative charge at the base of the storm, inducing a positive charge below and around the storm on the ground. This positive charge follows the thunderstorm like a shadow until the storm dissipates. Charge separation in thunderstorms is produced in rapidly rising air interacting with precipitation (both ice particles and liquid drops) moving downward within the cloud. The stronger the convective activity, the stronger the electrical potential that is developed. Electrical charge in and around thunderstorms is very complicated and changes constantly on a scale of minutes.

The life cycle of lightning-producing storms can be as short as 30 minutes, although they often last for an hour (but they can continue for as long as 12 hours). Thunderstorms proceed through three stages:

- *Growth*: Towering cumulus clouds grow upward more rapidly than horizontally. A cumulus tower is visible as an isolated vertical column, or as a rounded bubble at the cloud top. A thunderstorm usually has several towers. Electrical activity in a cumulus tower usually starts when cloud-top temperatures reach –15°C to –20°C.
- *Mature*: Precipitation droplets form, and precipitation may be visible from the ground. The cloud is now a cumulonimbus, showing the smoother and streakier appearance of an icy top. It takes several minutes for precipitation from this

tower to reach the surface. On the ground, then, you may see the following: lightning may occur before any rain reaches the ground. First ground flashes in a cloud usually occur at this stage, but a few in-cloud flashes may happen earlier. Strong updrafts and weaker downdrafts are next to each other at up to 50 mph (80 kph) or more, and are several kilometers wide and high. The mature stage is the most intense, and has the most precipitation and electrical activity.

- *Dissipation*: With time, a downdraft spreads out after it reaches the ground. Typically, this cooler, outflowing air cuts off the inflow of moist, warm air feeding the updraft, and the thunderstorm weakens. There may be a few last ground flashes in the early dissipating stage; they are especially dangerous because the storm may appear to have died. Finally, precipitation and lightning stop; the storm dies.

Some thunderstorms produce a great deal of lightning and little rain on the ground, especially in the western United States, where such situations lead to forest and range fires. Storms in a moist subtropical environment may produce heavy rain and only a few flashes. Cloud-to-ground lightning can occur outside heavy precipitation, so taking shelter only when heavy rain is falling is not an adequate precaution from lightning.

Some Precautions

Procedures for avoiding lightning are summarized in safety pamphlets available from your nearest National Weather Service/NOAA and American Red Cross offices. Review them and *use common sense* before, during, and immediately after the strongest parts of thunderstorms. Even if no lightning has occurred, but conditions for lightning are favorable, take the proper precautions and practice lightning safety rules (see box below). Pay much more attention to the lightning threat than to the rain.

Once the storm has begun, remember the flash-to-bang method:

- See the flash.
- Count the seconds to the bang of its thunder, and divide by five.

Avoid Dangerous Lightning Situations!

1. Plan ahead!

- Be aware of other storms in your area. Check the forecast for thunderstorms. If today has active thunderstorms or if storms are predicted in your area, do not be caught where you cannot take shelter on short notice. Consider postponing activities to avoid being caught in a dangerous situation.

- Watch for signs of a developing thunderstorm, such as darkening skies, flashes of lightning, or increasing wind. Thunderstorms can grow quickly!

- Give yourself time to reach a safe place before lightning is an immediate threat. Storms can grow from the small towering cumulus stage into a lightning producer *in less than half an hour.*

- Designate a spotter to watch for the threat of lightning. Decide on rules for stopping whatever you and your group are doing, and decide in advance where to take shelter when it is necessary.

- Have a lightning safety plan. Know where you will go for safety and how much time it will take to get there. Make sure your plan allows enough time to reach safety.

2. Get to a safe place.

If you hear thunder, even a distant rumble, immediately move to a safe place. Fully enclosed buildings with wiring and plumbing provide the best protection. Sheds, picnic shelters, tents, or covered porches do NOT protect you from lightning. If a sturdy building is not nearby, get into a hard-topped metal vehicle and close all the windows. Stay inside until 30 minutes after the last rumble of thunder. If you hear thunder, do not use a corded phone except in an emergency. Cordless phones and cell phones are safe to use. Keep away from electrical equipment and wiring. Water pipes conduct electricity. Do not take a bath or shower or use other plumbing during a storm.

3. Do not be the highest object.

- Avoid standing in an open field or parking lot, riding a bicycle along an open road, standing on top of a mountain or rock outcrop, or riding in a boat in the open water.

- Do not be connected to or stand under anything taller than its surroundings: big trees, antennas, and towers. Do not touch anything connected to power lines, phone lines, cables, or plumbing coming into a building from the outside.

- Crouch on the balls of your feet, with your head down.

4. Always use common sense.

- Go inside a sturdy building or into a vehicle with a solid metal top. Do not contact any metal on the building or vehicle.

- Follow your safety plan, regardless of the stage of the game, the hike, or the fishing. You can always return to it *after* the storm has passed.

Source: National Oceanic and Atmospheric Administration (NOAA): Lightning Safety for You and Your Family at *www.weather.gov/os/lightning/resources/lightning-safety.pdf*.

Additional Resources

http://climate.virginia.edu/lightning/lightningsafety.html
www.fema.gov/areyouready/thunderstorms.shtm
www.georgiapower.com/storm/protect.asp
www.publicaffairs.noaa.gov/grounders/lightningsafety.html

Scales in Meteorology

What Is a Scale?

Scales are common in everyday life. Music, temperature, and fish have scales, although each of these is quite different. Of course, in science we are not talking about the series of musical notes or the plates that make the skin of fish or reptiles. The scales that concern us in meteorology are those that help us measure weight, distance, or temperature. Temperature is one of the most important functions of meteorology.

What purpose do scales have in science in general? Why do scientists develop scales? For example, geologists use a scale to measure the power and destruction of earthquakes. The magnitude or strength of an earthquake can be measured using the Richter scale, which measures the seismic vibrations of Earth.

For meteorology, temperature is key. Science has three major temperature scales—Fahrenheit, Celsius, and kelvin. (See Figure **R11.1**.) These are all measures of heat energy and molecular motion. There are many other temperature scales, but scientists worldwide have decided to standardize the use of temperature and have limited which scales are used in communicating scientific results. Fahrenheit is the historical English system of measuring temperature. It is based on water freezing at 32°F and boiling at 212°F—a range of 180°F. The Celsius scale is based on the freezing and boiling points of water and the range was arbitrarily set at 100°C. These measurements are based upon the average kinetic energy of molecules in an ideal gas, and they worked well for many situations until physicists and engineers started working with very cold temperatures. The kelvin temperature scale measures energy content and is based upon the random motion of molecules. The scale uses 0 Kelvin as the lowest temperature or absolute zero. In the kelvin scale, water freezes at 273.15K and boils at 373.15K. Thus, the kelvin and Celsius scales use the same degree unit—an increase of 1 kelvin is equal to an increase of 1° Celsius.

In meteorology, two main temperature scales are used—Celsius and Fahrenheit. In most of the world, weather temperatures are taken using the Celsius scale, but the United States continues to use the Fahrenheit scale. The conversion between temperature scales is relatively easy. Use the equations in **Figure R11.2** to change between Celsius and Fahrenheit, and vice versa.

Reading 11

Topic: temperature and scales

Go to: www.scilinks.org

Code: PSCM 022

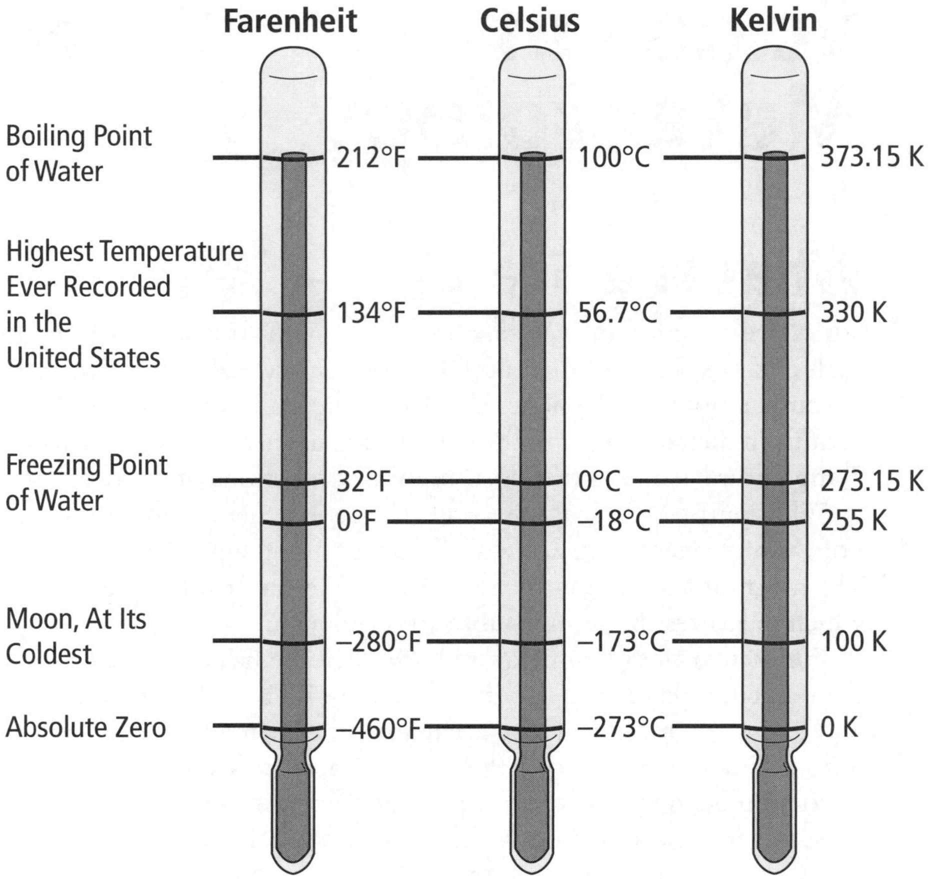

Farenheit   **Celsius**   **Kelvin**

	Farenheit	Celsius	Kelvin
Boiling Point of Water	212°F	100°C	373.15 K
Highest Temperature Ever Recorded in the United States	134°F	56.7°C	330 K
Freezing Point of Water	32°F	0°C	273.15 K
	0°F	–18°C	255 K
Moon, At Its Coldest	–280°F	–173°C	100 K
Absolute Zero	–460°F	–273°C	0 K

Figure R11.1

A comparison of the three temperature scales—Fahrenheit, Celsius, and kelvin

Figure R11.2

Formulas for Fahrenheit, Celsius, and kelvin scale conversion

Fahrenheit:	$°F = 32.0 + \frac{9}{5}\ °C$
Celsius:	$°C = \frac{5}{9}\ (°F - 32.0)$
Kelvin:	$K = °C + 273$

284

National Science Teachers Association

Wind

If an extraterrestrial spacecraft approached Planet Earth on an exploration mission, the first feature it would likely notice would be the ever-changing swirl of clouds across the face of this blue planet. From outer space, we can easily see interconnected weather patterns moving on a global scale. For meteorologists, this is the largest scale on which weather occurs, but it is not the only one. Circulations of all sizes occur on Earth and in the atmosphere. Meteorologists categorize air circulation according to size. General agreement exists on at least four spatial scales of atmospheric phenomena: *global, synoptic, mesoscale*, and *microscale*. The global and synoptic scales are often referred to in combination as the *macroscale*, the largest of scales. (See Figure R11.3.) Each of these weather scales influences one another and is, in turn, influenced by the others. For example, if a particular synoptic scale, such as a cold air mass, moves into a mountainous region, it will influence the microscale temperature in a particular valley. Often, weather on a particular scale is influenced by a nearby topographical feature of the same size. For example, mesoscale weather may be influenced by the proximity of a lake containing relatively cold water. This influence may produce onshore winds localized to the shoreline.

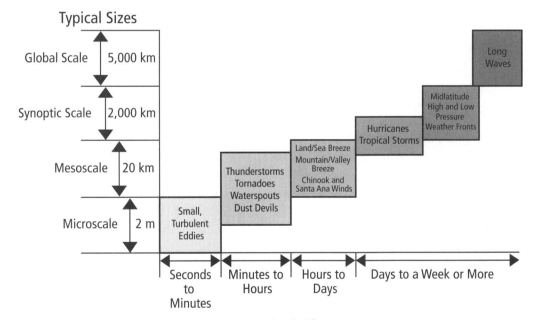

Figure R11.3
Time and space scale of atmospheric motion

The *global scale*, also known as the *planetary scale*, consists of the largest weather elements and patterns. Generally, elements thousands of kilometers and greater in dimension are considered global-scale elements. They include the general circulation features, such as the trade winds, prevailing westerlies, Rossby waves, and the jet streams, and regions of the atmosphere such as the tropics, the mid-latitudes, the polar regions, and the ozone layer.

Weather patterns that dominate a region are smaller than the global scale and are known as the *synoptic*, or *continental, scale*. This scale covers weather elements such as high and low pressure systems, air masses, and frontal boundaries. These items are commonly found on standard weather maps. The size range is usually the area of one continent, and may extend from the surface to the lower stratosphere.

The *mesoscale* covers weather or wind patterns in a smaller area. This scale, also known as the *local scale*, covers atmospheric elements from a few kilometers to 100 km in the horizontal dimension and from the surface to 1 km in height. Mesoscale circulations include squall lines, thunderstorms, tornadoes, and small tropical depressions. They also include local winds produced along shorelines and mountains. The mesoscale can be thought of as encompassing an area from the size of towns to that of metropolitan regions. Mesoscale weather is what you see on the weather maps and forecasts for a state or province.

The microscale includes all atmospheric processes smaller than a kilometer or so. Microscale circulations can be as large as individual clouds or as small as eddies caused by the wind interacting with buildings and trees. Such circulations can be seen in the movement of smoke from smokestacks, branches, dust, and paper, and last only a few minutes.

Wind Scales

The Beaufort Wind Scale, created by Britain's Admiral Sir Francis Beaufort (1774–1857), was one of the first scales based on wind speeds. As commander of the *HMS Woolwich*, a 44-gun man-of-war, Beaufort devised his wind force scale in the early 19th century to help sailors estimate the winds via visual observations. The numbers on the scale range between 0–12, and they measure wind speeds from calm (force 0) to hurricane strength (force 12). Each number represented a distinct measure of the behavior of wind on the sailing ship. The use of the scale depended upon someone looking at the ship, not the wind. For example, numbers 0–4 describe the wind in terms of the speed at which the boat is propelled. Numbers 5–9 represent how well the sails carry the wind. Numbers 10–12 were a reflection of the survival ability of the sails and ship due to high winds. The Royal Navy soon adopted the scale to be used on all ships. Initially, this scale did not incorporate wind speeds in mph or kph, but these have been added. The Beaufort Wind Scale continues to be used by weather spotters to estimate conditions in the absence of instrumentation during severe weather.

The Saffir-Simpson Hurricane Scale was developed in the United States in the 1970s. It is a scale with ratings of 1–5, based on the hurricane's intensity and estimates of the potential property damage and expected flooding. Wind speed is the determining factor in the scale, which ranges from Category 1 (74–95 mph) to Category 5 (greater than 155 mph). The scale provides examples of the type of damage and impacts associated with winds of the indicated intensity. In general, damage rises by about a factor of four for every category increase. The scale does not address the potential for storm surge, rainfall-induced floods, and tornadoes.

The descriptions of damage are dependent upon the local building codes in effect and how well and how long they have been enforced. For example, building codes enacted during the 2000s in Florida, North Carolina, and South Carolina are likely to reduce the damage to newer structures. Hurricane wind damage is also very dependent upon other factors, such as duration of high winds, change of wind direction, hurricane size (extent of hurricane-force winds), local bathymetry (depth of near-shore waters), topography, forward speed, and angle to the coast, which affect storm surge. For example, the very large Hurricane Ike (with hurricane force winds extending as much as 125 miles from the center) made landfall in Texas in 2008 as a Category 2 hurricane and had peak storm surge values of about 20 ft. The revised version of this scale is outlined below; it only incorporates peak winds:

Category 1: Sustained winds between 74–95 mph, 64–82 kt, or 119–153 km/hr.

- Some poorly constructed frame homes can experience major damage, involving loss of the roof covering and damage to gable ends, as well as the removal of porch coverings and awnings.
- Large branches of trees will snap, and shallowly rooted trees can be toppled.
- Extensive damage to power lines and poles will likely result in power outages that could last several days.

Category 2: Sustained winds between 96–110 mph, 83–95 kt, or 154–177 km/hr.

- Well-constructed frame homes could sustain major roof and siding damage.
- Many shallowly rooted trees will be snapped or uprooted, blocking numerous roads.
- Near-total power loss is expected with outages that could last from several days to weeks.

Category 3: Sustained winds between 111–130 mph, 96–113 kt, or 178–209 km/hr.

- Well-built frame homes can experience major damage involving the removal of roof decking and gable ends.
- Many trees will be snapped or uprooted, blocking numerous roads.
- Electricity and water will be unavailable for several days to a few weeks after the storm passes.

Category 4: Sustained winds between 131–155 mph, 114–135 kt, or 210–249 km/hr.

- Well-built homes also can sustain severe damage with loss of most of the roof structure and/or some exterior walls.
- Most trees will be snapped or uprooted, and power poles downed.
- Fallen trees and power poles will isolate residential areas. Power outages will last for weeks to possibly months.

Category 5: Sustained winds greater than 155 mph, 135 kt, or 249 km/hr.

- A high percentage of frame homes will be destroyed with total roof failure and wall collapse.
- Nearly all trees will be snapped or uprooted, and power poles downed.
- Fallen trees and power poles will isolate residential areas. Power outages will last for weeks to possibly months.

Also developed in the 1970s was the Fujita Tornado Scale (or F Scale), which categorizes tornadoes by intensity and area. The scale was divided into six categories: F0 (Gale), F1 (Weak), F2 (Strong), F3 (Severe), F4 (Devastating), and F5 (Incredible). This scale is also an estimate of wind speed associated with damage caused by the tornado to structures, flora such as trees, and fauna. This scale has been used to rate every tornado in the United States since 1950.

In 2007, scientists convened to update the scale, and as a result, the committee developed the Enhanced Fujita Scale (or EF Scale). The improvements were made to ensure continuity with past data and tornadoes. In addition, there is an enhanced description of damage, which includes multiple structures and vegetation, with examples and photos. The Enhanced Fujita Tornado Scale has 28 damage indicators with descriptions and an estimate of the wind speed.

All scales are used to measure some sort of phenomenon such as weight, distance, or temperature, using a system of defined marks set at fixed intervals. Scales are largely descriptive in nature and use both qualitative and quantitative data. The initial scale may be arbitrary, but the increments between measurements indicate a sequential method for describing observations and phenomena. Meteorologists use scales to help them describe weather conditions and predict weather.

Resources

This material was completely updated and revised by the authors for this new second edition. It is not meant to be a complete representation of resources in meteorology, but it should assist teachers in further exploration of this subject. The entries are subdivided into the following categories:
- General Resources
- DVD Resources
- Internet Resources by Activity

General Resources

Air, Water, and Weather
Elementary and Middle School, 2005
One of the titles in the *Stop Faking It! Finally Understanding Science So You Can Teach It* series, this book by William C. Robertson helps teachers develop a deep understanding of the properties of air and water, including pressure, the Coriolis force, the Bernoulli Effect, and density. The author uses these concepts as a foundation to explain weather patterns, including the jet stream, storm fronts, and the formation of tornadoes and hurricanes.

National Science Teachers Association
1840 Wilson Blvd.
Arlington, VA 22201
tel. 703-243-7100
www.nsta.org/store

The AMS Weather Book: The Ultimate Guide to America's Weather
General, 2009
Copublished with the American Meteorological Society, the author Jack Williams explains and illustrates the science behind America's varied and dynamic weather, from daily weather patterns to severe weather to air pollution and global warming.

University of Chicago Press
1427 E. 60th Street
Chicago, IL 60637
tel. 773-702-7700
www.press.uchicago.edu/index.html

DK Nature Activities: Weather Watcher
10–17 years, 2006
This book by John Woodward presents over 30 step-by-step activities and experiments through which students can explore aspects of weather, such as constructing a simple barometer to measure air pressure, making a wind vane to record wind direction, and making a rain gauge to measure rainfall.

DK Publishing
375 Hudson St.
New York, NY 10014
tel. 646-674-4000
http://us.dk.com

Dr. Fred's Weather Watch: Create and Run Your Own Weather Station
Ages 9–12; 2000
The authors Fred Bortz and J. Marshall Shepherd explain how weather is measured and why measurements of air pressure, temperature, and humidity, along with wind speed and direction are important to forecasting. The book provides illustrated instructions on how to make simple weather instruments.

Earth-Ocean-Atmosphere Explorer
Designed by EOA Scientific Systems Inc. in 2000, this CD-ROM is for grades 6–12. The main goal of the software is to allow students to experience science. It claims to increase students' engagement and test scores. The main topics covered are Astronomy, Life Sciences, Plate Tectonics, Oceanography, Meteorology, Weather Forecasting, and Earth as a System.

Environmental Protection Agency— EPA Student Center
The EPA's website links to water-related sites designed for students.

Erased by a Tornado
Ages 9–12, 2010
This book by Jessica Rudolph is one of eight titles in the *Disaster Survivors* series. The author tells the story of survivors who narrowly escaped death when tornadoes struck and educates readers about why tornadoes occur, where they occur, and how to stay safe in the event of a tornado warning. Other weather-related titles in this series include *Blitzed by a Blizzard*, *Hammered by a Heat Wave*, *Mangled by a Hurricane*, and *Struck by Lightning*.

McGraw-Hill
Available at *www.amazon.com*

www.amazon.com/Earth-Ocean-Atmosphere-Space-Explorer-Scientific-SystemsInc/dp/1552410102

Student Center
US EPA Region 5
77 W. Jackson Blvd.
Mail Code P-19J
Chicago, IL 60604
tel. 313-353-6353
www.epa.gov/students/water.html

Bearport Publishing Company, Inc.
45 West 21st Street, Suite 3B
New York, NY 10010
tel. 877-337-8577
www.bearportpublishing.com

Eyewitness: Weather
Grades 4–8, 2007
This title, from the series of DK Eyewitness Books, covers a range of topics related to weather, including weather signs and forecasting, the Sun, water in the air, clouds, rain, fronts and lows, lightning and thunder, snow, wind, tropical storms, frost and ice, and weather in the mountains, on the plains, and by the sea.

DK Publishing
375 Hudson St.
New York, NY 10014
tel. 646-674-4000
http://us.dk.com

Eyewitness: Weather
8–17 years, 2007
One of many books in the DK Eyewitness series, this title by Brian Cosgrove leads readers to discover the world's weather, from heat waves and droughts to blizzards and floods. A CD with clip-art and wall chart is included with this title.

DK Publishing
375 Hudson St.
New York, NY 10014
tel. 646-674-4000
http://us.dk.com

Full Option Science System for Middle School (FOSS/MS): Weather and Water
Grades 6–7; 2000–2003
Students conduct investigations and experiments, observe natural phenomena, make models, and create simulations. The unit contains a detailed teacher's guide, a materials kit, a resources book (containing images, data, and readings for each student), a lab notebook, and a multimedia CD-ROM.

Delta Education
80 Northwest Boulevard
Nashua, NH 03063
tel. 800-258-1302
www.deltaeducation.com

Global Warming?
Grades 6–9; 2005
Part of the *Event-Based Science Modules* by Russell G. Wright, this module about climate and climate change uses television news coverage of flooding in Savannah, Georgia, and other signs of climate change to establish the context for the study. Students are placed in the roles of participants in a UN-sponsored international conference as they analyze evidence of warming and make recommendations for reducing human contributions. Video components are available on YouTube. Links to websites with current and historic data

Event-Based Science Institute
www.ebsinstitute.com/index.html

about greenhouse gas concentration, temperature trends, and climate are available at the EBS Institute website.

Hurricane!
Grades 6–9; 2005
Part of the *Event-Based Science Modules* by Russell G. Wright, this updated book uses the devastation caused by an actual hurricane to provide the context for a task in which students form teams of experts who publish a newspaper account of a real hurricane that is approaching one of 11 American cities with a history of hurricane strikes and damage. Video components are available on YouTube. Links to websites with current information about hurricanes are available at the EBS Institute website.

The Invention of Clouds: How an Amateur Meteorologist Forged the Language of the Skies (Richard Hamblyn, Picador, 2002)
General; 2002
The author Richard Hamblyn tells the story of Luke Howard (1772–1864), the Quaker who created the classification of cloud types (*cirrus*, *cumulus*, and *stratus*) that is still used today.

Investigating Air
Investigating Air is an online interactive activity page that lets students place different objects in the air to see if they float, sink, or get pushed in the wind. Students can add fans to examine their effects.

Investigating Earth Systems: Module Investigating Climate and Weather
Grade 7, 2000
Students use inquiry-based investigations to explore how weather instruments work and how weather observations are made, and to learn about weather patterns, weather reports, and climate change.

Event-Based Science Institute
www.ebsinstitute.com/index.html

Picador Publishing
An imprint of Pan Macmillan
Pan Macmillan
20 New Wharf Road
London N1 9RR
tel. +44 (0)20 7014 6000
www.panmacmillan.com

www.learningbox.com/air/index.htm

It's About Time: Herff Jones Education Division
84 Business Park Drive, Suite 307
Armonk, NY 10504
tel. 888-698-TIME
www.agiweb.org/education/ies/cw/index.html

Isaac's Storm: A Man, A Time, and the Deadliest Hurricane in History
General; 2000
(Erik Larson, Vintage, 2000)
The author Erik Larson tells the story of the 1900 hurricane that hit Galveston, Texas, killing 8,000 people and destroying a third of the city, from the perspective of Isaac Cline, the senior U.S. Weather Bureau official in Galveston at the time.

Vintage Books
Available at *www.amazon.com*

Issues and Earth Science (IAES): Unit E: Weather and Atmosphere
Grades 6–8, 2003
In this fifth of seven units, students conduct experiments, collect and analyze data, create models, and read and analyze information. Included are a student book, a teacher's guide, and a kit containing the laboratory equipment and supplies required to conduct course activities. The kit provides supplies for use with up to five classes of 32 students each.

Science Education for Public Understanding (SEPUP)
Lawrence Hall of Science
University of California,
Berkeley, CA 94720-5200
tel. 510-642-8718
http://sepuplhs.org/index.html

Models in Technology and Science—Modules "Air and Water Movement," "Ice Cream Making and Cake Baking"
Grades 5–9, 2001
Students investigate patterns of fluid motion and heat transfer in these modules using readily available materials. Teacher guides are also available.

Pitsco
P.O. Box 1708
Pittsburg, KS 66762
tel. 1-800-835-0686
www.pitsco.com

NASA and NOAA—Sky Watcher Chart and Introduction to Clouds
This site shows a cloud chart that you can purchase from NOAA and display in your classroom.

www.nws.noaa.gov/os/brochures/cloudchart.pdf

NASA Earth Science Office—Interactive Global Geostationary Weather Satellite Images
Satellite data on oceans, atmosphere, energy, land, and life are displayed as interactive maps. The NASA GOES satellites have images for weather.

www.ghcc.msfc.nasa.gov/GOES

National Center for Atmospheric Research
The National Center for Atmospheric Research (NCAR) is a federally funded center devoted to service, research, and education in the atmospheric and related sciences. NCAR's mission is to understand the behavior of the atmosphere and related physical, biological, and social systems through research.

P.O. Box 3000
Boulder, CO 80307-3000
tel. 303-497-1000
ncar.ucar.edu/home

National Data Buoy Center
This website displays oceanographic and meteorological data from more than 1,000 buoys in the Pacific, Atlantic, and Indian oceans.

1007 Balch Blvd.
Stennis Space Center, MS 39529
tel. 228-688-2805
e-mail: webmaster.ndbc@noaa.gov
www.ndbc.noaa.gov

National Geographic—The Greenhouse Effect
National Geographic has an interactive slide-show about the greenhouse effect.

http://environment.nationalgeographic.com/environment/ global-warming/gw-overview-interactive.html

National Geographic Investigates: Extreme Weather
Ages 10 and up, 2008
In this title from the *National Geographic Investigates: Science* series, students can find out how weather scientists are using information about extremes of weather, and technology such as supercomputers and satellites, to predict climate changes.

National Geographic Store
777 South State Road 7
Margate, FL 33068
tel. 800-437-5521
http://shop.nationalgeographic.com/ngs

National Geographic Kids: Tornado!
Ages 10 and up, 2011
Authors Judy and Dennis Fradin use eyewitness stories and news reports to capture survivors' experiences in severe tornadoes.

National Geographic Store
777 South State Road 7
Margate, FL 33068
tel. 1-800-437-5521
http://shop.nationalgeographic.com/ngs

National Hurricane Center
The National Hurricane Center (NHC) provides detailed forecasting and locations of tropical storms and hurricanes.

www.nhc.noaa.gov

National Oceanic and Atmospheric Administration

The National Oceanic and Atmospheric Administration (NOAA) is the federal agency that provides daily weather forecasts, severe storm warnings, and climate monitoring. NOAA's National Weather Service is the sole official voice of the U.S. government for issuing warnings during life-threatening weather situations. The website for NOAA includes research, stewardship, and education components. Also included are listings of NOAA publications and products.

1401 Constitution Avenue, NW
Room 5128
Washington, DC 20230
tel. 202-482-6090
www.noaa.gov

NOAA Climate Services

This website provides resources and educational material about climate and climate change.

www.climate.gov/#education

NOAA—Greenhouse Effect

NOAA has a K–12 education resource page on the greenhouse effect.

www.oar.noaa.gov/k12/html/greenhouse2.html

NOAA—National Weather Service

The National Weather Service (NWS) "provides weather, hydrologic, and climate forecasts and warnings for the United States, its territories, adjacent waters and ocean areas, for the protection of life and property and the enhancement of the national economy."

U.S. Dept. of Commerce
National Oceanic and Atmospheric Administration
National Weather Service
1325 East West Highway
Silver Spring, MD 20910
www.weather.gov

Science Sampler: Clever With Weather

Middle School, 2011
In this article from *Science Scope*, the authors Rhonda Hoenigman and David Crowder share the modeling activity they developed to show their eighth-grade students how large-scale weather patterns are relevant to their local weather conditions.

National Science Teachers Association
1840 Wilson Blvd.
Arlington, VA 22201
tel. 703-243-7100
www.nsta.org/store

Science Sampler: Handmade Weather Instruments
Middle School, 2006
In this article from *Science Scope*, the authors Annette Ricks Leitze, Melissa A. Mitchell, Nancy A. Melser, and Margo J. Byerly provide activities using handmade devices to help students understand the science behind weather phenomena.

Science Sampler: Studying Storms to Understand Weather
Middle School, 2007
In this article from *Science Scope*, the author Shane Cavanaugh uses storms to present a five-week unit for students to learn about weather concepts using group discussions, online simulations, animations, and other resources.

Science Scope: Severe Weather
Middle School, 2004
In this poster insert from *Science Scope*, the author Evan B. Forde highlights safety issues related to hurricanes, flash floods, lightning, and tornadoes as part of the National Oceanic and Atmospheric Administration's (NOAA) mission to educate the public about hazardous weather conditions.

Storm of the Century: The Labor Day Hurricane of 1935
General; 2002
The author Willie Drye tells the story of this devastating hurricane, which hit the Florida Keys in 1935.

Tornado!
Grades 6–9; 2005
Part of the *Event-Based Science Modules* by Russell G. Wright, this updated book uses the devastation caused by an actual tornado to provide the context for a task in which students become forecasters in one of six

National Science Teachers Association
1840 Wilson Blvd.
Arlington, VA 22201
tel. 703-243-7100
www.nsta.org/store

National Science Teachers Association
1840 Wilson Blvd.
Arlington, VA 22201
tel. 703-243-7100
www.nsta.org/store

National Science Teachers Association
1840 Wilson Blvd.
Arlington, VA 22201
tel. 703-243-7100
www.nsta.org/store

National Geographic
Available at *www.amazon.com*

Event-Based Science Institute
www.ebsinstitute.com/index.html

different National Weather Service Forecast Offices. They track a developing severe weather situation and then, as it worsens, they broadcast an emergency warning to surrounding communities. Video components are available on YouTube. Links to websites with current information about tornadoes are available at the EBS Institute website.

United States Environmental Protection Agency—Acid Rain

The Environmental Protection Agency (EPA) website has links to information about the cause of acid rain, its effects, how acid rain is measured, and methods that are being used to reduce acid rain.

www.epa.gov/acidrain

Weather GeoKit

Grades 4–9

Activities allow students to measure and predict local weather, learn about forecasting, weather maps, layers of the atmosphere, global winds, warm and cold fronts, and pressure systems. The kit includes current weather websites, transparencies, maps, handouts, videos and *National Geographic* articles.

National Geographic School Publishing
Hampton-Brown
P.O. Box 4002865
Des Moines, IA 50340
tel. 888-915-3276
www.ngsp.com

The Weather Identification Handbook: The Ultimate Guide for Weather Watchers

General, 2003

The author Storm Dunlop provides a guide to the different types of weather phenomena that can be observed and the weather that may be expected. Topics include cloud types and formation, optical phenomena, precipitation, wind, severe weather, weather systems, satellite images, and weather maps.

The Lyons Press
Imprint of Globe Pequot Press
246 Goose Lane
P.O. Box 480
Guilford, CT 06437
tel. 888-249-7586
www.globepequot.com/index.php

DVD Resources

Eyewitness DVD: Weather
(60 minutes)
8–17 years, 2006
This DVD, published by Dorling Kindersley, takes the viewer on a tour of Earth's atmosphere and reveals the forces that make our weather, from hurricane to heat wave.

National Geographic: Tornado Intercept DVD
(60 minutes)
2005
Students can witness what happens inside a tornado as filmmakers use the Tornado Intercept Vehicle, the first vehicle ever to take a camera into a tornado's vortex, to shoot footage. *Into the Tornado* is also included as a bonus program.

NOVA Field Trips: Weather Gone Wild— Hunt for the Supertwister/Lightning!/ Hurricane!
(3 discs: 180 minutes)
General, 2004
This DVD set by NOVA includes three programs: *Hurricane!, Hunt for the Supertwister,* and *Lightning!*, as well as downloadable educational materials including program descriptions, viewing suggestions, discussion questions, and activities. Each of the three titles is also available as an individual DVD.

World Almanac Video's Guide to Extreme Weather
(148 minutes)
General, 2003
This DVD explores the effects of extreme weather and shows how meteorologists use technology to track severe storms and issue warnings to the public.

DK Publishing
375 Hudson St.
New York, NY 10014
tel. 646-674-4000
http://us.dk.com

National Geographic Store
777 South State Road 7
Margate, FL 33068
tel. 1-800-437-5521
http://shop.nationalgeographic.com/ngs

Shop PBS
www.shoppbs.org

www.amazon.com

Internet Resources by Activity

Activity 1: Weather Watch

Intellicast.com: Mixed Surface Analysis
Intellicast.com provides a surface map for the United States with clouds (infrared satellite) and precipitation (radar), along with fronts, isobars, and high and low sea-level pressure centers. (A one-day loop at three-hour intervals is also available, as well as links to 12-, 24-, 36-, and 48-hour forecast maps.)
www.intellicast.com/National/Surface/Mixed.aspx

NOAA National Weather Service Hydrometeorological Prediction Center: HPC's Surface Analysis Archive
HPC's Surface Analysis Archive contains surface maps with raw data from weather stations across the United States every three hours since 2006 (both United States and North America). The raw data include wind speed and direction, barometric pressure, temperature, and fronts.
www.hpc.ncep.noaa.gov/html/sfc_archive.shtml

NOAA National Weather Service— Hydrometeorological Prediction Center: North American Surface Analysis
HPC's surface map for North America contains observations about temperature, dew point, pressure, and wind at selected stations, along with fronts, isobars, and high and low sea-level pressure centers. Links are available for the corresponding map of the United States, with or without the surface observations indicated at the selected stations.
www.hpc.ncep.noaa.gov/html/sfc2.shtml

NOAA Hurricane Prediction Center— U.S. Radar Mosaic With HPC Surface Analysis
HPC's surface map for the United States contains observations about precipitation (radar), along with fronts, isobars, and high and low sea-level pressure.
www.hpc.ncep.noaa.gov/html/radar_mosaic.html

USA Today: National Weather Maps
USA Today provides a surface map for the United States with precipitation (radar), along with fronts, isobars, and high and low sea-level pressure centers. Links are available explaining the various symbols used on the map.
www.usatoday.com/weather/fronts/latest-fronts-systems.htm

Activity 3: The Pressure's On

NASA for Kids—It's a Breeze: How Air Pressure Affects You
This website was created by NASA for students to explore wind and breezes. The site contains easy-to-read content, easy-to-do experiments, discussion questions, and games.
kids.earth.nasa.gov/archive/air_pressure/index.html

NOAA National Weather Service— JetStream—Online School for Weather: Air Pressure
This website contains a content description and explanation of air pressure with "Learning Lessons" throughout for students to explore more about the content on their own. The lessons are easy to follow and connect directly to the topics in the reading.
www.srh.noaa.gov/jetstream/atmos/pressure.htm

University of Colorado—Interactive Simulations: Gas Properties
This online simulation allows students to visualize air as a bunch of moving particles

and to see how the particle motion and density is related to the air pressure.
phet.colorado.edu/en/simulation/gas-properties

Activity 4: The Percentage of Oxygen in the Atmosphere

CO_2Now.org: Earth's CO_2 Home Page
CO_2Now exists to track the carbon dioxide levels in Earth's atmosphere. This website has current and historic data, as well as future carbon dioxide concentration predictions. Other links at this site provide content information on topics related to carbon dioxide in the atmosphere.
http://co2now.org

CRC Handbook of Chemistry and Physics
This organization puts out a yearly handbook of standards, tables, and variables for all areas of science. In the section entitled "Properties of the solar system," the handbook lists the atmospheric composition of Earth and all the planets that have an atmosphere.
www.hbcpnetbase.com

Geology.com: Amber Yields Clues to the History of Oxygen in Earth's Atmosphere
The Geology.com website contains an article that explains how scientists have used amber and the insects found within it to determine Earth's atmosphere from 100,000 years ago.
http://geology.com/usgs/amber

The New York Times—Science: Breathing Room
The *New York Times'* science website contains a short article for children about Earth's atmosphere. This is a great way to introduce students to reading periodicals to ascertain information.
www.nytimes.com/2008/03/04/science/04qna.html

Activity 5: It's in the Air

Environmental Protection Agency
The Environmental Protection Agency's website is part of EPA's efforts to educate the public on particulate matter. It contains a short explanation of particulate matter and then provides additional links to understand related content such as particulate matter standards and designations, programs and requirements for reducing particulate matter, and additional publications.
www.epa.gov/pm

Environmental Protection Agency: Particulate Matter
The EPA's website provides a map of air quality, along with links about pollution and air quality standards and regulations.
www.epa.gov/pm

Environmental Protection Agency: Pollution Prevention (P2)—Where You Live
Pollution Prevention provides data on what individuals and cities can do to prevent pollution in local areas and cities.
www.epa.gov/p2/pubs/local.htm

Harvard University—GEOS Chem-Model
This site from Harvard University shows scientists and projects that use the GEOS satellite. This is an ideal site for extended learning for students who have an interest in learning more about how satellite data are being used.
acmg.seas.harvard.edu/geos/geos_people.html

NASA— MISR
This website from NASA provides information on the MISR satellite and the data it collects. This website provides a quiz archive of aerial images, world maps and animations, and a multimedia gallery for students.
www-misr.jpl.nasa.gov

NASA—MODIS

This website from NASA provides information on the MODIS satellite and the data it collects. Students can search for images and data related to the atmosphere, land, and ocean.
modis.gsfc.nasa.gov

NASA: New Map Offers a Global View of Health-Sapping Air Pollution

This website from NASA provides new images and interpretations from satellite data on air pollution. The resolution of this particular satellite allows it to estimate the concentration of fine particulate matter (diameters less than 2.5 micrometers) in the air, both for the United States and for the globe, which epidemiologists consider harmful to human health.
www.nasa.gov/topics/earth/features/health-sapping.html

Activity 6: Why Is It Hotter at the Equator Than at the Poles?

Naval Oceanography Portal: The Seasons and the Earth's Orbit

This website from the United States Navy explains the seasons and the Earth's orbit. It provides more detail than is found in the Activities in this book and explains perihelion, Milankovitch cycles, and changes in obliquity.
www.usno.navy.mil/USNO/astronomical-applications/astronomical-information-center/seasons-orbit

Newton Ask a Scientist

This government-sponsored website allows anyone to ask scientists questions related to science. In this particular question-and-answer session, the scientist explains the relation among the perihelion, aphelion, and seasons.
www.newton.dep.anl.gov/askasci/ast99/ast99578.htm

NOAA National Weather Service Forecast Office: Why Do We Have the Seasons?

This is an explanation for the seasons, put together by the National Weather Service Forecast Office in Flagstaff, Arizona, as part of their "Science Corner" series of questions and answers.
www.wrh.noaa.gov/fgz/science/season.php?wfo=fgz

Activity 7: Which Gets Hotter: Light or Dark Surfaces?

NASA—Satellites Pinpoint Drivers of Urban Heat Islands in the Northeast

This NASA website provides information on heat islands and supports the content with a video, satellite images, and graphics. The website also contains a list of links to specific cities and their information on heat islands.
www.nasa.gov/topics/earth/features/heat-island-sprawl.html

National Oceanic and Atmospheric Administration—National Climatic Data Center: Global Warming, Frequently Asked Questions

The National Climatic Data Center provides information, graphs, and other data in response to 11 frequently asked questions about global warming, including "Is the climate warming?" and "Is sea level rising?"
lwf.ncdc.noaa.gov/oa/climate/globalwarming.html

NOAA National Weather Service—JetStream—Online School for Weather: The Earth–Atmosphere Energy Balance

This NOAA website explains the energy balance created by the Sun's energy and where the energy goes once it strikes the atmosphere and Earth. This site also contains "Learning Lessons" as part of the topic "the atmosphere," which is part of the larger online "school for weather" (called "JetStream") from the National Weather Service for people interested in learning about the weather.
www.srh.noaa.gov/jetstream//atmos/energy.htm

National Oceanic and Atmospheric Administration—Ocean Service Education: Energy in the Ocean and Atmosphere
This website provides information from NOAA's National Ocean Service (which supports coastal and marine planning) on the relationship between oceans and climate, as part of its professional development websites for teachers. This particular site discusses the energy transfer between the atmosphere and the ocean. Subtopics of El Niño and Energy in the Atmosphere contain links for teachers and students.
http://oceanservice.noaa.gov/education/pd/oceans_weather_climate/energy_oceans_atmosphere.html

Activity 8: Up, Up, and Away!

NASA: Gas Density
This website provides information about gas density, from NASA's Glenn Research Center, as part of its "Beginner's Guide to Aerodynamics." It also provides links to activities for students in grades K–12.
www.grc.nasa.gov/WWW/K-12/airplane/fluden.html

Virtual ChemBook: Density Applications with Gases
This website from Elmhurst College contains information related to density and uses diagrams to explain the application of density to gases. The website also contains links to other sites for students to explore demonstrations related to the content.
www.elmhurst.edu/~chm/vchembook/123Adensitygas.html

Activity 9: Why Winds Whirl Worldwide

Catapult Design Blog: Testing Our Turbines in the NASA-Ames/AFDD Wind Tunnel
This website is from a company that develops wind turbines. This article discusses how one specific turbine was tested in NASA's wind tunnel.

http://catapultdesign.org/current-projects/testing-our-turbines-in-the-nasa-ames-wind-tunnel

How Stuff Works—How Wind Power Works
This website provides information on wind power and a video that demonstrates how wind power is captured.
http://science.howstuffworks.com/environmental/green-science/wind-power.htm

NASA: Wind Energy Research Reaps Rewards
This NASA news item from 2006 describes the U.S. Wind Energy Program led by NASA's Glenn Research Center. Information includes wind energy research and the history of how NASA has been an integral part in the development and research associated with wind energy.
www.nasa.gov/vision/earth/technologies/wind_turbines.html

The University of Texas at El Paso: Wind and Pressure Systems
This website from the University of Texas at El Paso describes pressure differences and how these create wind. There are maps to show air patterns and how they create wind.
http://research.utep.edu/Default.aspx?tabid=36037

Activity 10: Recycled Water: The Hydrologic Cycle

NOAA National Weather Service—JetStream—Online School for Weather: The Hydrologic Cycle
This NOAA website provides information about the hydrologic cycle, with lesson plans, as part of the topic "the atmosphere," which is part of the larger online "school for weather" (called "JetStream") from the National Weather Service for people interested in learning about the weather.
www.srh.noaa.gov/jetstream/atmos/hydro.htm

University of Illinois—A Summary of the Hydrologic Cycle

This website shows different representations of the hydrologic cycle by using an animated model.

ww2010.atmos.uiuc.edu/(Gh)/guides/mtr/hyd/smry.rxml

U.S. Geological Survey: The Water Cycle—Water Science for Schools

This website offers a brief description and illustration of the water cycle, along with tabular and graphical data on the distribution of water on Earth, as part of the U.S. Geological Survey's "Water Science for Schools." A more complete summary is also available.

http://ga.water.usgs.gov/edu/watercyclehi.html

Activity 11: Rainy Day Tales

Geography4Kids.com: Bio-Geo-Chemical Cycles: Water

This website discusses water, water conservation, the hydrosphere, and the water cycle in an easy-to-read format. This website also relates the water cycle to other types of cycles in the biosphere and geosphere.

www.geography4kids.com/files/cycles_water.html

NASA: Droplet and the Water Cycle

This website from NASA is designed for kids. This particular site tells a story of a water droplet and what it experiences in the water cycle. There is an interactive game in which students control the water droplet through its adventures in the water cycle.

http://kids.earth.nasa.gov/droplet.html

United States Department of Agriculture Natural Resource Conservation Service—Water Conservation

This website discusses the importance of water in your yard and what you can do to help conserve water. It provides helpful information for choosing appropriate plants and irrigation systems.

www.nrcs.usda.gov/feature/backyard/watercon.html

Activity 12: A Cloud in a Jar

NASA/NOAA Cloud Chart

This NOAA website shows two charts in PDF format that can be downloaded and printed. The first chart is an Introduction to Clouds, and the second one is a Sky Watcher Chart for clouds. (These can also be found in Spanish.) Related links are also available, including a cloud quiz and a cloud-type tutorial.

http://science-edu.larc.nasa.gov/cloud_chart

National Oceanic and Atmospheric Administration—Photo Library: Sky Scenes—The National Severe Storms Laboratory Album

This NOAA website contains photographs from the National Severe Storms Laboratory (NSSL), as part of the NOAA Photo Library. The photographs are free to use (as long as credit is given). Under the Collections tab, students and teachers will find a list of different collections of photos on different topics.

www.photolib.noaa.gov/nssl/clouds1.html

NOAA Satellite and Information Service—Cloud Products

This NOAA website shows the different instruments and views of water vapor and clouds that scientists use to study the weather and atmosphere. It includes different products that teachers can order related to clouds and satellite views.

www.osdpd.noaa.gov/ml/air/clouds.html

Science.Org—Cloud Identification Guide

This website contains a dichotomous key that students can use to classify clouds.

http://wvscience.org/clouds/Cloud_Key.pdf

Activity 13: Just Dew It!

Compressed Air Best Practices—The Importance of Dew Point for Medical Air Systems

This industry publication discusses the importance of dew point for medical air

systems, and describes how dew point can affect instrumentation.
www.airbestpractices.com/industries/medical/importance-dewpoint-medical-air-systems

NOAA National Weather Service—Graphical Forecasts: CONUS Area
This NOAA website shows a variety of maps related to dew point, temperature, precipitation, and hazards for the previous and future 12 hours.
www.weather.gov/forecasts/graphical/sectors/conus.php

NOAA National Weather Service Hydrometeorological Prediction Center—Relative Humidity Calculator
This NOAA website allows you to calculate the relative humidity without using a graph. If you know the temperature and dew point temperatures (in Fahrenheit or Celsius), the calculator will give you the relative humidity.
www.hpc.ncep.noaa.gov/html/dewrh.shtml

NOAA National Weather Service—JetStream—Online School for Weather: Learning Lesson: Drawing Conclusions—Dew Point Temperature Map
This is a dew point map derived from one of the activities for the online school. A link will take you back to the lesson plan.
www.srh.noaa.gov/jetstream/synoptic/ll_analyze_dp.htm

NOAA National Weather Service: Using Temperature–Dew Point Tables
This website is part of NOAA's national and regional information distribution network. This particular website contains a description of a method for converting wet-bulb and dry-bulb temperatures to relative humidity and dew point, and the tables for determining relative humidity and dew point (part of the "Fire Weather Training Modules" of the National Weather Service Forecast Office at Seattle, Washington).
www.wrh.noaa.gov/sew/fire/olm/temp_rh.htm

The Weather Channel: Current Dew Points
This website contains a map of the current dew points across the United States.
www.weather.com/maps/maptype/currentweatherusnational/uscurrentdewpoints_large.html

Weather Underground—U.S. Dew Point
This website contains multiple maps of the United States. Each map will display weather-related variables such as dew point, temperature, barometric pressure, and precipitation. In addition, you can click on a specific state and view various data stations and the weather data collected.
www.wunderground.com/US/Region/US/Dewpoint.html

Activity 14: Let's Make Frost

Cornell Cooperative Extension, Chemung County: Understanding Frost
This publication explains frost and freeze, and advises on how to prevent plants from freezing.
www.gardening.cornell.edu/weather/frost.pdf

Home and Garden Television
This website and television station have wonderful information on how to prepare a garden and yard for frost conditions.
www.hgtv.com

NOAA National Climatic Data Center—Climatic Data for Frost Protected Shallow Foundations (FPSF)
This website provides climatic data for builders so they can establish building policies and regulations related to permafrost conditions.
www.ncdc.noaa.gov/oa/fpsf

NOAA National Climatic Data Center—Freeze/Frost Maps
This NOAA website shows maps of the 90% and 10% probabilities for freeze and frost conditions.
www.ncdc.noaa.gov/oa/climate/freezefrost/frostfreemaps.html

The University of Arizona: Frost Protection
This website provides helpful information for residents in Arizona on how they can protect their plants against frost and freeze.
http://ag.arizona.edu/pubs/garden/az1002.pdf

Activity 15: It's All Relative!

HowStuffWorks: What is relative humidity and how does it affect how I feel outside?
This website explains meteorological terms, and provides answers for humidity and how it affects how we feel.
http://science.howstuffworks.com/dictionary/ meteorological-terms/question651.htm

Weather Underground: U.S. Relative Humidity
This website shows a map of the relative humidity of the United States, using color-coded areas.
www.wunderground.com/US/Region/US/Humidity.html

Activity 16: Moving Masses

European Center for Medium-Range Weather Forecasts—Analyzing and Forecasting the Weather of Early June 1944
This website describes the weather in early June of 1944. Students can read about the conditions and how meteorologists in the military were able to make a decision about invading France on D-Day.
www.ecmwf.int/research/era/dday

NOAA National Weather Service— Hydrometeorological Prediction Center: Top News of the Day
Home page for the Hydrometeorological Prediction Center, with links to the top news of the day, current weather maps, and forecast maps.
www.hpc.ncep.noaa.gov

NOAA National Weather Service: National Maps
This NOAA website contains weather forecast maps, in terms of precipitation, fronts, and high/low pressure centers, for the United States. Links are also provided to radar, river flooding, precipitation, air quality, and satellite maps.
www.weather.gov/outlook_tab.php

Activity 17: Interpreting Weather Maps

American Meteorological Society— Careers in Atmospheric Research and Applied Meteorology
This American Meteorological Society website discusses a booklet about careers in atmospheric research and applied meteorology. The website contains answers to questions such as these: What is meteorology? What do meteorologists do? Where do meteorologists work? Would meteorology be a good career for me?
www.ametsoc.org/pubs/careers.html

NOAA Center for Tsunami Research— Tsunami Forecasting
This NOAA website provides information on tsunami research, and uses video and graphics to explain how to predict a tsunami. The website also provides resources such as posters and publications.
http://nctr.pmel.noaa.gov/tsunami-forecast.html

NOAA National Severe Storms Laboratory: Forecasting Thunderstorms
This NOAA website describes how meteorologists forecast thunderstorms using models and satellite images (part of the "Severe Weather Primer" of NOAA's National Severe Storms Laboratory).
www.nssl.noaa.gov/primer/tstorm/tst_predicting.html

NOAA National Weather Service

This is the home page for the National Weather Service, with links to the top news of the day, forecast maps, and current weather maps (including radar, river flooding, precipitation, air quality, and satellite maps).
www.weather.gov

NOAA National Weather Service—Storm Prediction Center

This NOAA website provides animated maps of watches, mesoanalysis, conversion (severe thunderstorms), and fire potential for the United States.
www.spc.noaa.gov

Web Weather for Kids: Tips for Forecasting the Weather

This website for kids provides information on weather symbols and conditions so that students can make forecasts of the weather. Students can also input their zip code and find the forecast for their local area from four different sources.
http://eo.ucar.edu/webweather/forecasttips.html

Activity 18: Water Can Be Supercool!

The Aftermath Report—How to Prepare for a Hailstorm

This online blog allows individuals to comment on hailstorm activity and report damage and conditions. This particular website discusses how you can prepare for a hailstorm.
http://aftermathreport.com/2010/04/how-to-prepare-for-a-hail-storm

Agency Hail Suppression—Hail Formation

This European website explains the basis of hail formation using detailed pictures and drawings.
www.weathermod-bg.eu/pages/obr_en.php

Hail Formation

This website provides an image of how hail forms.
http://cdn.gotoknow.org/assets/media/files/000/315/320/original_diagram-Hail_Formation-1.jpg?1285631318

NOAA Hail.org

This website compiles data from NOAA to show the most recent hail events for the past 1–6 days, 2 weeks, and 3 weeks. Each mark on the map represents the hail size, ranging from less than 0.5 inches to more than 3.0 inches.
www.hail.org/map/NOAA.html

NOAA National Weather Service Forecast Office: Hail

This NOAA website shows images of hail and the damage that hail can produce. The website also illustrates how hail is formed and what you can do to prepare for hail (part of the "Severe Weather Awareness" series of the National Weather Service Forecast Office at Columbia, South Carolina).
www.erh.noaa.gov/cae/svrwx/hail.htm

NOAA National Weather Service Storm Prediction Center—Severe Weather Event Summaries

This NOAA website contains information on severe weather events. Students can search by day for past storm reports or find tornado-related fatality information. Students can also find trends, annual maps, and raw data on tornadoes.
www.spc.noaa.gov/climo/online

Activity 19: Riding the Wave of a Hurricane

Hurricane Hunters

This website provides information about hurricane hunters, a special squadron of the United States Air Force. You can view pictures of hurricanes from the inside and see the plane that flies into hurricanes.
www.hurricanehunters.com

NASA: Hurricane Structure

This NASA website has an interactive interface for showing the formation, structure, and movement of a hurricane. The site uses Flash to animate the content.
http://scifiles.larc.nasa.gov/kids/Problem_Board/problems/weather/hurricanebasics.swf

National Hurricane Survival Initiative—Hurricane Safety Checklists

This website provides information about hurricane safety and preparation. This site also provides checklists that you can use to prepare for a hurricane.
www.hurricanesafety.org/hurricanesafetychecklists.shtml

NOAA: Hurricane Basics

This book is a downloadable reference on hurricane basics. Everything a middle school student should know about a hurricane can be found in this book, which contains graphics and tables of information.
http://hurricanes.noaa.gov/pdf/hurricanebook.pdf

NOAA National Hurricane Center—Hurricane Preparedness

This NOAA website provides information on how you and your family can prepare for a hurricane. The information includes a disaster supply kit, how to secure your home, and what you can do with your pets.
www.nhc.noaa.gov/HAW2/english/disaster_prevention.shtml

NOAA National Weather Service—National Hurricane Center: 2008 Atlantic Hurricane Season Animation

High-resolution satellite animation of the 2008 Atlantic Hurricane, put together by NOAA's Environmental Visualization Laboratory. The animation on this website allows you to see high-resolution images of hurricanes.
www.nhc.noaa.gov/2008_season_animation.shtml

NOAA National Weather Service—National Hurricane Center: Katrina Graphics Archive

This website is an animated archive of the storm track of Hurricane Katrina. Different graphics can be isolated and viewed, such as three-day cone warnings, five-day cone warnings, strike probability, wind swaths and speed, and the wind table.
www.nhc.noaa.gov/archive/2005/KATRINA_graphics.shtml

NOAA National Weather Service—National Hurricane Center: NHC Archive of Hurricane Seasons

This NOAA website provides information for all past hurricanes. You can search by year for descriptions of hurricanes in the Atlantic or Pacific basins.
www.nhc.noaa.gov/pastall.shtml

NOAA National Weather Service—National Hurricane Center: National Hurricane Center GIS Data and Products

This NOAA website provides forecasts of Atlantic and Eastern Pacific Hurricanes (including tracks, cones of uncertainty, and watches/warnings). You also can click on the archive, which shows the names of all tropical depressions in previous years.
www.nhc.noaa.gov/gis

The Weather Channel—Hurricane Formation: Stages of Tropical Development

Learn how a hurricane develops from The Weather Channel. This website lists the five stages of hurricane development.
www.weather.com/outlook/wxready/articles/id-36

The Weather Channel: What to Do if a Hurricane Watch or Warning Is Issued

This website describes the difference between a hurricane watch and warning, and what to do if one of these is issued.
www.weather.com/outlook/wxready/articles/id-38

About the Authors

William R. Veal

William R. Veal is a science educator and chemist at the College of Charleston, South Carolina. He received a Bachelor's degree in chemistry from Trinity University in Texas, Master's degrees in chemistry and curriculum and instruction from the University of Utah, and a doctorate degree in science education from the University of Georgia. While at the University of Georgia, he worked as an educational consultant for The Weather Channel. He was the first to develop an online Earth science course for preservice and inservice teachers in North Carolina.

Veal currently works in the Departments of Teacher Education and Chemistry at the College of Charleston, South Carolina. His research interests involve reform-based science instruction in rural schools. This involves the understanding of how the local context and community impacts learning and instruction. He uses observational instruments and notes to study how and why teachers use place-based science examples in their instruction. Part of this research involves understanding how the local context influences students' feeling of self-efficacy.

Veal is also co-chair of the National Science Teachers Association/National Council for the Accreditation Teacher Education Audit Team. He has reviewed and audited secondary science programs for accreditation and compliance with national science preparation standards for over eight years. He currently serves as the Director of the Science and Mathematics for Teachers' Masters of Education Program at the College of Charleston, South Carolina.

Robert A. Cohen

Robert A. Cohen is a professor of physics at East Stroudsburg University of Pennsylvania in East Stroudsburg, Pennsylvania. He received his Bachelor's degree in meteorology from the Pennsylvania State University. He received his Master's and doctorate degrees in physics and atmospheric science from Drexel University. He also earned a Master's degree in Education from Temple University, through which he earned teaching credentials in secondary math and science.

Cohen's research in meteorology focuses on the structure of occluded extratropical cyclones, using numerical simulations to identify the evolution of airstream boundaries within the storm. He is also actively involved in science teacher preparation and physics education.

Index

A

absorptivity, 77, 79
acid rain, 36, 37, 93, 97–98, 99, 100, 109, 134, 141, 149, 153, 154, 156, 158, 180, 187, 222, 257–258, 259–260, 261, 262–263, 265–266
Acid Rain Program (ARP of EPA), 257–258, 259, 260
Activity Planners, xxiv, 14, 28, 38, 48, 58, 72, 82, 92, 102, 114, 126, 136, 148, 160, 174, 184, 196, 206
aerosols, 128, 129, 130, 131, 134, 135, 235, 258
air density, 74, 85, 90
    definition, 83
air freezing index (AFI), 157
air mass, definition, 175
air masses, 2, 83, 84, 85, 87–88, 180, 183, 249–250
air pollutants, 51, 239–242, 257–258
Air Pollution and Environmental Equity (Reading 4), **221, 239–242**
air pressure, 31, 33–37, 95-96, 186
    definition, 29
Alternative Preparation, 10, 25, 35–36, 45, 55, 68, 110–111, 133, 144–145, 155–156, 170, 181, 192, 203, 216
anemometer, 93, 98
angle of sunlight, 62, 65–71
    definition, 59
Answers to Student Questions, 11–13, 26–27, 37, 46, 56, 70, 80, 90, 100–101, 112, 124–125, 134–135, 146–147, 158, 171–172, 182–183, 194–195, 204, 217–218
aphelion, 69
Assessment, 13, 27, 37, 47, 57, 71, 81, 90–99, 101, 112, 125, 135, 147, 158, 173, 183, 195, 205, 218
atmosphere, Earth, 15, 21–24, 29, 39, 41, 49, 51, 53–57, 108, 113, 161, 221, 225–228, 245–248, 253
atmospheric pressure, 12, 93, 186, 227, 268–269
    definition, 2
axis of Earth, 65–66, 68, 69

B

Background, 1, 15, 29, 39, 49, 59, 73–74, 83, 93, 103, 115–116, 127, 137–138, 149, 160, 175, 185–188, 197, 207–208
barometer, 31, 33, 227
Beaufort Wind Scale, 98, 286
bonds, covalent, 263, 264
boundary between air masses (front), 175, 177
bromeliads, 138, 143

C

Calculating Dew Point (BLM 13.1), **140**
carbon, 17, 23, 39, 41, 43, 46, 255–256
Celsius temperature scale, 283–284
Changing the Variables (BLM 2.2), **20**
chemical reaction, definition, 39
chemistry of water, 263–264
chlorofluorocarbons (CFC), 234–235, 236
Clean Air Act (CAA), 237, 239, 257, 258, 260
climate changes, 229–231, 253–254, 255
climate versus weather, 7
cloud cover, 3, 11, 187, 189
cloud formation, 127–135
Cloud in a Jar, A (Activity 12), **127–135**
cloud types, 2, 11, 105, 127, 129, 134, 175, 182–183, 203, 265
cloud, definition, 127
clouds, 101, 103, 129, 134, 137, 201, 265–266
cold fronts, 179, 182, 183, 250
colligative properties, 156
color and heat flow, 73–81
Comparing Dew and Frost (BLM 14.1), **151, 159**
composition of the atmosphere, 15, 49, 227–228
computers and weather prediction, 7, 8, 213
conclusions. *See* Questions and Conclusions.
condensation, 103, 105, 108, 112, 113, 116, 121, 131–132, 135, 137, 138, 141, 149, 155, 161, 164, 263, 265, 269
    definition, 103
condensation nuclei, 131–132, 265
conduction, 246
Connections, 11, 37, 46, 56, 69, 80, 90, 100, 124, 134, 146, 157, 171, 182, 194, 203, 217
continental scale, 286
control, definition, 40
convection, 67, 90, 246
Coriolis Effect, 98, 99–100, 249, 268

covalent bonds, 263, 264
Creating Clouds in a Jar (BLM 12.1), **130**
crystals, frost and snowflakes, 149, 153, 154
cyclones, 97, 129, 207, 254

D

deaths from severe weather, 271–272, 274–276
density, 74, 77, 83, 84, 87–88, 90, 246
    definition, 89
density and temperature, 86
density, air, definition, 83
depletion of ozone, 234–235
deposition, 153, 257
    definition, 149
desalinization, 111
dew point, 139, 142, 143, 144, 145, 146, 147, 153, 164, 170, 187, 263
    definition, 137
differential heating, 67, 69
Differentiated Learning, 10–11, 26, 37, 46, 56, 69–70, 80, 90, 100, 111–112, 124, 134, 146, 157–158, 171, 182, 194, 204, 217
direct rays (sunlight), 66
distillation, 109
dry bulb temperature, 141, 163, 164, 171, 173

E

Earth's atmosphere, 15, 21–23, 29, 225
Earth's Atmosphere (Reading 1), **221, 225–228**
Earth's axis, 65–66, 68, 69
effervescent, definition, 16
El Niño Southern Oscillation (ENSO) (Reading 2), **221, 229–231**
El Niño's effects, 229, 230, 231, 252, 253
energy, 59, 77, 79, 93, 100, 207, 222, 243–250, 264, 266
    wind, 93, 100
Enhanced Fujita Scale (EF Scale), 288
ENSO. *See* El Niño Southern Oscillation.
Environmental Effects of Acid Rain (Reading 7), **222, 257–260**
environmental equity, 221, 239–242
Environmental Protection Agency (EPA), 51, 57, 80, 236, 239, 257, 258
equator and temperature, 59, 62, 65–71

National Science Teachers Association